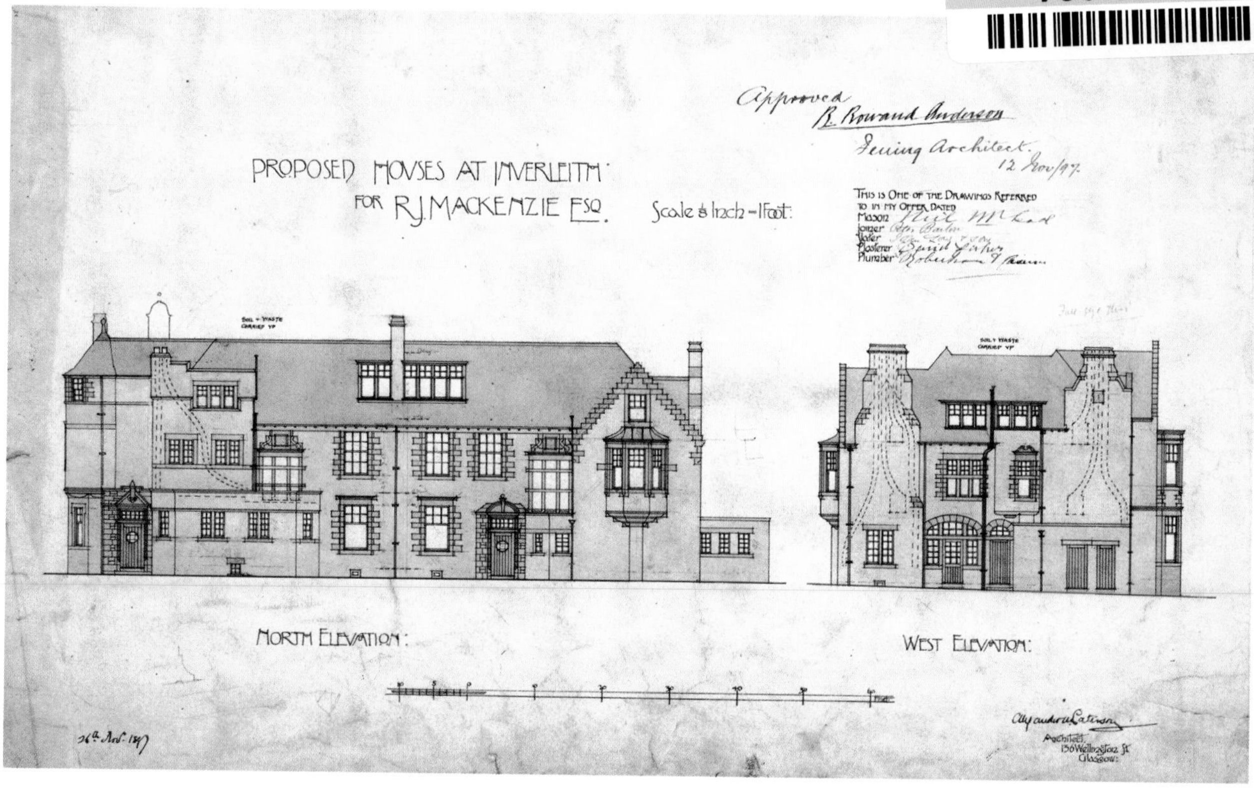

Creating a Future for the Past: the Scottish Architects' Papers Preservation Project

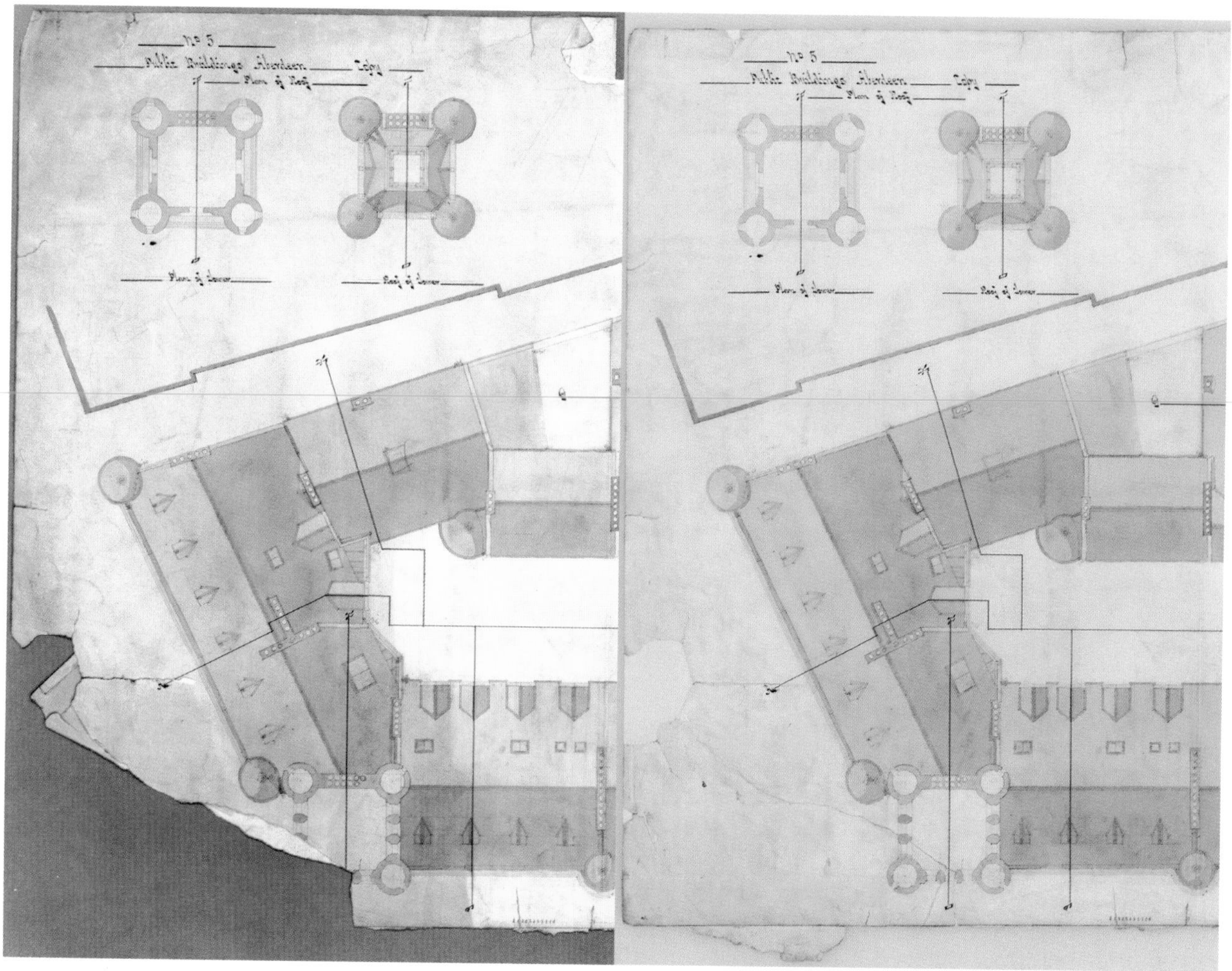

The **Royal Commission on the Ancient and Historical Monuments of Scotland** (RCAHMS) is responsible for recording, interpreting and collecting information about the built environment. This information is freely available to the public.

You can visit our public search room or contact us by telephone, letter, fax or email and staff will be pleased to assist with your enquiry.

We are open Monday – Friday, 9.30am – 4.30pm.

Our website gives information about the history, aims and work of RCAHMS, the services we provide and details of current projects, exhibitions and publications. You can also use the website to access the database using CANMORE and CANMAP.

RCAHMS
John Sinclair House
16 Bernard Terrace
Edinburgh
EH8 9NX

Tel: +44 (0) 131 662 1456
Fax: +44(0) 131 662 1477 / 1499

Email: nmrs@rcahms.gov.uk
Website: www.rcahms.gov.uk

Frontispiece
Top
North and West elevations of a house for R J Mackenzie, 9 Kinnear Road, Edinburgh by A N Paterson, c.1897, from the Cowie & Seaton Collection. [SC879002]

Bottom Left
Detail of roof plan of Municipal Buildings, Castle Street, Aberdeen, by Peddie & Kinnear, c.1865, from the Dick Peddie & McKay Collection (recto, pre-conservation). [SC879340]

Bottom Right
Detail of roof plan of Municipal Buildings, Castle Street, Aberdeen, by Peddie & Kinnear, c. 1865, from the Dick Peddie & McKay Collection (recto, post-conservation). [SC879343]

Front cover
Top
Perspective sketch of Well Court, Damside, Edinburgh by Sydney Mitchell, 1883-84, from the Sydney Mitchell & Wilson Collection. [SC684932]

Middle
Sketch details of interior design for the Radio Cinema, Bridgend, Kilbirnie by James Houston, c.1937, from the Houston & Dunlop Collection. [SC879098]

Bottom
Section and elevations of two storey houses, Clermiston, Edinburgh for the Edinburgh Housing Association Ltd by A H Mottram, 1934, from the Dunn & Findlay Collection. [SC879023]

Back cover
Top
Perspective elevation of Queenslie Primary School, Easterhouse, Glasgow by Alexander Buchanan Campbell, 1957, from the Buchanan Campbell Collection. [SC883730]

Middle
Castleson's Cafeteria, Largs by James Houston & Son, c.1965, from the Houston & Dunlop Collection. [SC 883760]

Bottom
Unexecuted design of proposed store for Marks & Spencer, 2-12 Argyle Street, Glasgow by Monro & Partners, c.1960-64, from the Monro & Partners Collection. [SC879283]

ISBN 1-902419-42-1

Contents

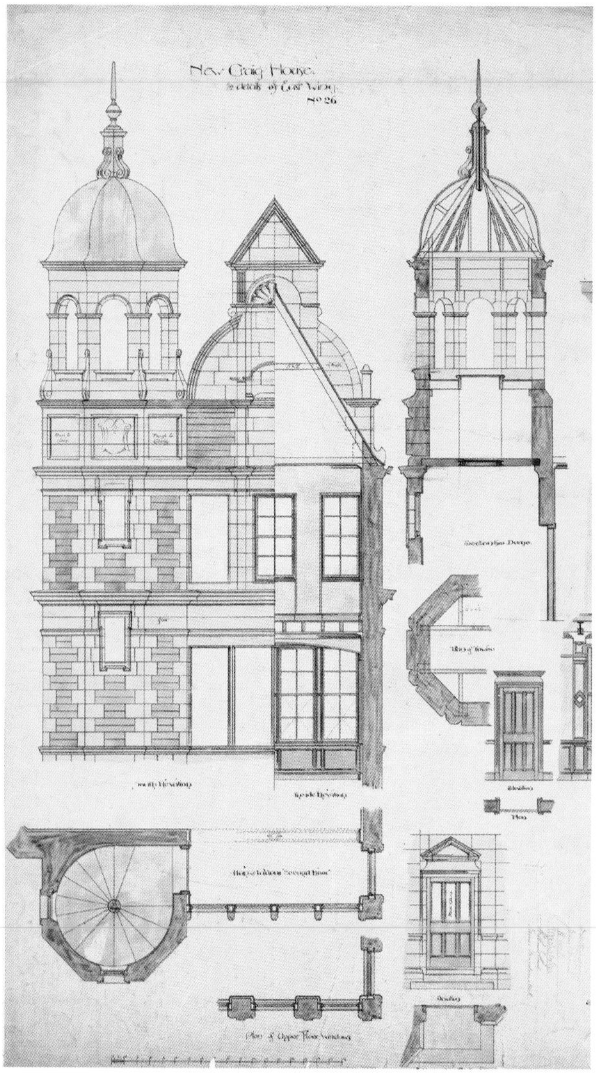

Foreword

It has been a great privilege to witness the Scottish Architects' Papers Preservation Project more or less from its inception through to its successful conclusion, both on time and within budget. Over a period of five years nearly 200,000 drawings, photographs and manuscripts, that had been deposited with the Royal Commission from 25 of Scotland's leading architectural practices, have been catalogued and conserved. Thus has this great treasure house of collections, that reflect the changing nature of the built environment over 120 years, been opened in an ordered and stablised state. It is now ready for use by scholars, students and specialists, and most of all by those who are keen to learn about their town, their house, their school or their workplace.

The process has seen the generation of a whole new range of skills, skills that are now much in demand both within the Royal Commission and by other projects and organisations. ICT developments throughout the project have led to the entire catalogue, and the digital images, being available online.

Online availability is of fundamental importance to the public who, from anywhere in the world, can establish precisely what exists before undertaking the commitment of a visit. Some collections are now held in the area of Scotland from which they originated, made possible by our colleagues at Aberdeen City Archives, the North Highland Archive and Glasgow City Archives.

Thus is the future of our past ensured. None of this would have been possible without the generous support of the Heritage Lottery Fund to which I must offer the Royal Commission's warmest thanks. To our steadfast partners in this project, the Royal Incorporation of Architects in Scotland, I offer salutations and thanks. Thanks also to the Gordon Fraser and Manifold Trusts.

What follows is an account of how the SAPP Project came into being, how it was conducted, and the lessons learnt thereby. There are also accounts of each of the collections made available by the project. Read on and enjoy!

Kathleen Dalyell
Chairman RCAHMS

Front façade of the Royal Commission on the Ancient and Historical Monuments of Scotland, 16 Bernard Terrace, Edinburgh. Drawings for the original building, a depository for the furniture specialists C & J Brown, by J R McKay, 1935, can be seen in the Dick Peddie & McKay Collection. Drawings showing the conversion to office premises for RCAHMS, c.1989-92, can be found in the J & F Johnston & Partners Collection. [SC674676]

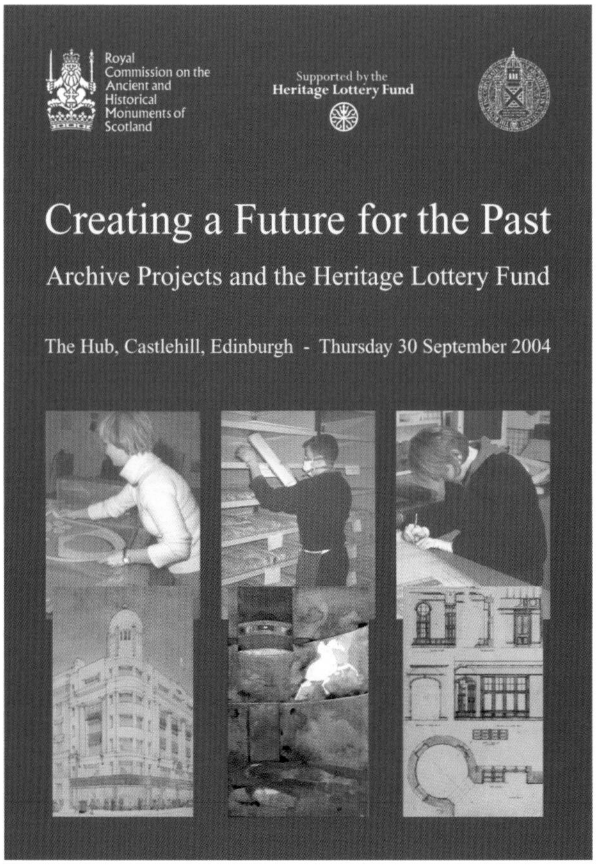
Royal Commission on the Ancient and Historical Monuments of Scotland
Supported by the Heritage Lottery Fund
Creating a Future for the Past
Archive Projects and the Heritage Lottery Fund
The Hub, Castlehill, Edinburgh - Thursday 30 September 2004

Programme for Creating a Future for the Past - Archive Projects and the Heritage Lottery Fund*, a colloquium to mark the conclusion of the projects, 30 September 2004.*

Introduction

The announcement by the Heritage Lottery Fund on 10 February 1999 that it had agreed to support the Scottish Architects' Papers Preservation Project (SAPPP) with a grant of £626,500 brought a welcome resolution to an application process that had been underway since 1996.

The development of SAPPP followed a decade of initiatives designed to identify architects' practice records held in private hands throughout Scotland. Spearheaded by the Royal Incorporation of Architects in Scotland (RIAS), these began with an investigation of surviving 1930s Scottish architectural drawings, undertaken as part of a research project. It became apparent that a high proportion of drawings from this period did not survive. In response to the concern thus generated, the Scottish Drawings Working Group was established to provide a forum for communication on the location of Scottish architectural drawings and to work, where possible, to prevent further loss. The Royal Commission on the Ancient and Historical Monuments of Scotland (RCAHMS) participated in these initiatives whilst pursuing the complementary Survey of Private Collections, a selective programme of photographic copying and listing that included, but was not restricted to, architectural practice records. Although it was evident that much had been destroyed as a result of the scaling down of architectural offices in the 1970s and 1980s, exactly what historical records survived within architects' practices was unknown.

In order to achieve an overview of the situation, the Scottish Survey of Architectural Practices (SSAP) was set up in 1992, through a collaboration between RIAS, RCAHMS, Historic Scotland and the Business Archives Council of Scotland at the University of Glasgow. Over a period of four years, SSAP surveyed 100 architectural practice archives and executed detailed listing of 17 key collections. In several cases this led to the deposit of material in the National Monuments Record of Scotland (NMRS), RIAS or local repositories across Scotland. Architects' papers held within public collections were also assessed.

Included in the practice papers identified by SSAP, were 24 collections that were either already in the ownership of RIAS and RCAHMS or were due to be transferred to public hands. These 24 collections contained what was estimated to be around 150,000 drawings, photographs and manuscripts dating from the mid-19th century to the late 20th century. Representing a range of practices, both large and small, with a wide geographical spread, all were considered to be of national, or outstanding local, significance. The SSAP, RIAS Council and RCAHMS worked together to construct a project to undertake cataloguing and conservation on these collections in order to make them available to the public for the first time. The SSAP was due to wind up, and neither RIAS nor RCAHMS had sufficient resources to fund such a substantial project, so an application to the Heritage Lottery Fund represented the best way forward to achieve the twin aims of preservation and accessibility. To be eligible for funding, RCAHMS was required to have ownership of all the collections. This issue was resolved with the gift to RCAHMS of seven collections owned by the RIAS (known collectively as the McKean Collection) and four collections that were still in practice or family hands.

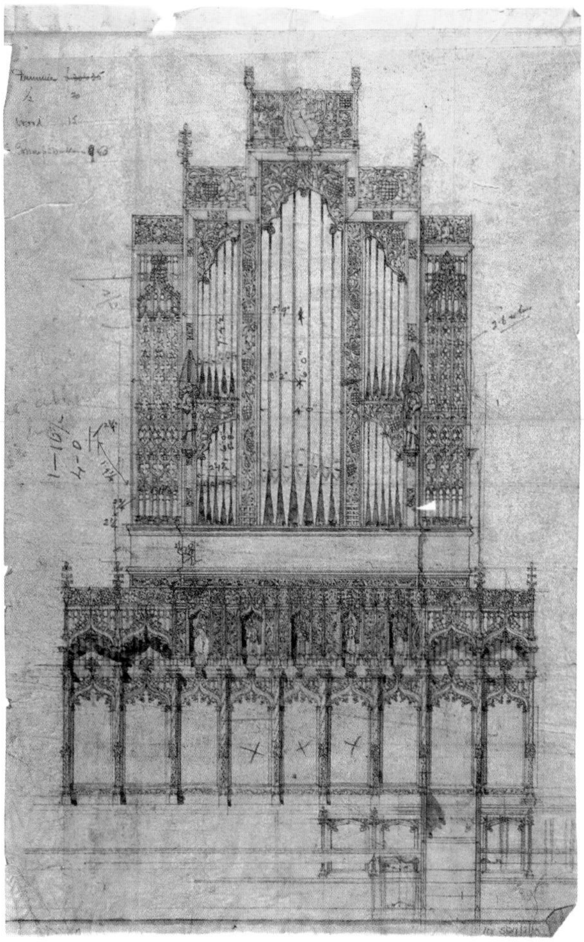

Design for an organ case for Martyr's Church, North Street, St Andrews by R S Lorimer, c.1913-14, from the Lorimer & Matthew Collection. [SC879214]

An outline programme of cataloguing was drawn up, based largely on the listing work undertaken in architects' offices by SSAP. This work involved two curatorial staff executing a basic sort of material, followed by one person calling out information and the other entering it into a computerised (Paradox) database.

An integral part of SAPPP as initially conceived was the extension of RCAHMS premises at 16 Bernard Terrace, Edinburgh, to accommodate the material once it had been conserved. It was estimated that the drawings, photographs and manuscripts would require as much as four times their original storage space once housed in appropriate archival packaging. Increased pressure on consultation space in the NMRS search room was also anticipated.

Unfortunately the proposed building work was judged to be ineligible, and had to be omitted in the final stage of the bid. This major change to the project prevented the flattening of a large proportion of the

View of main collection store at RCAHMS, 16 Bernard Terrace, Edinburgh showing installation of additional shelving, 2000. [SC891727]

View of additional shelving in main collection store at RCAHMS, 16 Bernard Terrace, Edinburgh, 2000. [SC891728]

Caledonian Insurance Company Head Office, 12-13 St Andrew Square, Edinburgh by Leslie Grahame Thomson, c.1937, a perspective by J Netherby Graham, from the Leslie Grahame Thomson (MacDougall) Collection. [SC465228]

rolled drawings, as space for additional plan chests was no longer available, and meant that accommodating re-packaged collections remained a challenge. A short-term solution was achieved with the re-fitting of RCAHMS collections storage areas in 2000. The cataloguing programme, however, remained as originally envisaged.

While the SAPPP application was being assessed, two nationally important collections of architects' papers were offered for sale to RCAHMS. Owing to the outstanding importance of these collections, RCAHMS submitted two further applications to the Heritage Lottery Fund, both of which were successful. In September 1998 a grant of £13,700 was awarded for the purchase of design material relating to Sir Robert Lorimer, which complemented material already held in the SAPPP Lorimer & Matthew Collection; and in January 1999 a grant of £100,200 was awarded to acquire the Dick Peddie & McKay Collection and to undertake a cataloguing and conservation programme in line with the SAPPP proposals. With this coincidence of timing it made clear sense to combine the management of the Dick Peddie & McKay Collection Project with that of SAPPP.

The primary aim was to preserve the collections and record the information contained within them, the selection criteria being that each group of papers chosen should have come from an architect's office. The collections themselves were not chosen as a coherent group since their survival, with very few exceptions, had primarily been fortuitous, no plans having been made for depositing them in the public domain. However, now that cataloguing has been completed, the collections can be used to trace themes and connections across them; they provide a valuable insight into the history of Scottish architectural practice. With a geographical spread covering virtually the whole of Scotland and material that ranges in date from the mid-19th to the late 20th century, a picture emerges of Scotland's architectural history reflected in the work of both large and small practices. The influence of social and economic trends, war and advances in building technology can be traced through the work of individual practices and their responses to particular circumstances can be compared. Methods of drawing production, whether in terms of draughtsmanship or use of materials, and the arrangement of office drawing stores have all been subjects of increasing interest as the body of material illustrating these issues has been catalogued.

As well as broad themes, particular connections may be made between collections. The movement of individual architects as they trained, practised and eventually ran their own firms can be traced. Design influences resulting from apprenticeships in particular practices can be understood and are further illustrated where architects are employed as perspectivists by other firms to prepare presentation drawings. Business history is illustrated with the growth and decline of practices

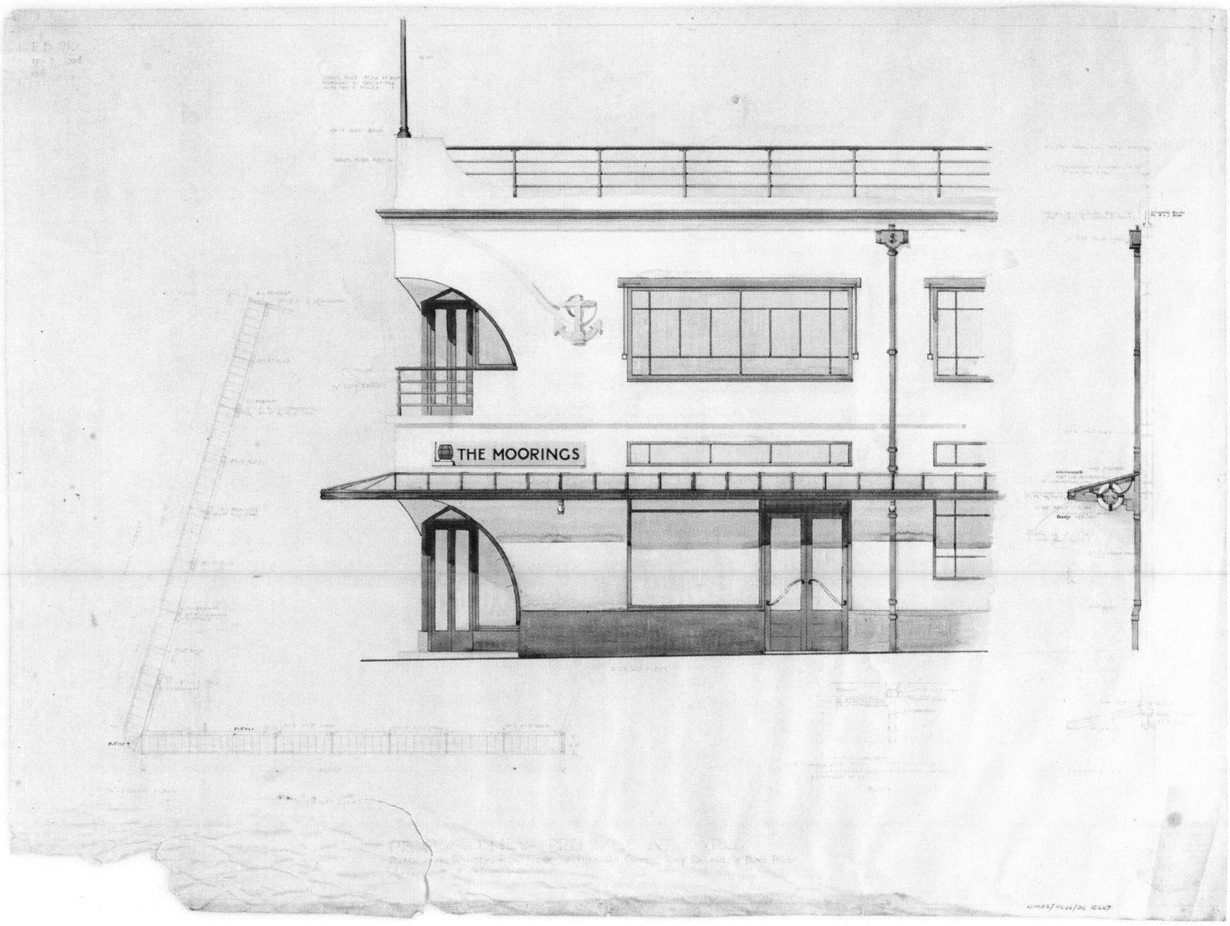

Elevation of The Moorings, Main Street, Largs by James Houston, c.1935, from the Houston & Dunlop Collection. [SC879099]

as they expand and merge with others, or shed staff and downsize their offices. Practice addresses inform an understanding of working practice. Drawings prepared in boarding houses evoke the early stages of fledgling practices, those choosing to live and work from the same address continuing an arrangement dating back to the early 19th century. Specific building histories are often illustrated by the connection of a practice from design through various alterations over time. In some cases, several practices can be seen to have worked on the same building. Key projects missing from a practice collection sometimes turn up in another when, in the course of carrying out building alterations, the original design drawings were acquired from the clients.

Some of these themes and connections are highlighted in the collection essays prepared for each of the collections catalogued as part of the projects. Many remain to be discovered by researchers for whom this invaluable resource is now available for the first time.

But what of the future? There are undoubtedly still practice collections of national importance in the private domain including those that have been created in the last 50 years. How will the digital age impact on what is, and should be, preserved? Current architectural practices rely increasingly on digital technology to create and store designs and detailed plans. The projects were planned around the secure foundation of a detailed survey of architects' office papers. It is now eight years since that survey was completed it will soon be time to continue this work in order to discover key collections for future preservation.

Project design and management

In addition to its main aim to make 25 collections of architects' papers from practices around Scotland accessible to a wide audience for enjoyment and study, the Scottish Architects' Papers Preservation Project and the Dick Peddie & McKay Project (hereafter 'the projects') aimed to facilitate the study of architectural practice by recording collections in their entirety; to enhance the profile of Scottish architects and architecture with a national and international audience; and to support the practice of collecting architectural material. The specific objectives of the projects were to provide an online catalogue to all the material; to stabilise and, where necessary, treat objects to allow them to be handled; to provide in-person and online access to a wide audience; and to make collections of local significance available within the relevant local community.

Staff at RCAHMS had long experience of cataloguing architectural material but the scale of this project and the new technology that it harnessed meant that methodologies and programmes had to be designed without substantial precedents. Several institutions in Scandinavia, Italy and North America had collected comparable material from architects' offices but few had been able to devote serious resources to their cataloguing and conservation. In the international archive community, as opposed to that of the architectural museum, research was being compiled on the preservation of 19th and 20th-century architects' collections but the findings were not available until well into the projects.

The collections had been acquired by RCAHMS in different ways; the majority were gifted by the architectural practice from which they originated. The collections were usually transported direct from the practice premises to RCAHMS, though in a few cases they were held by family members for some years after the closure of the practice. The storage of the drawings within the architectural practices varied from tightly rolled bundles wrapped in brown paper or plastic, usually housed in an attic or basement, to envelopes of folded drawings. A few were stored flat in portfolios or plan chests. Some collections were salvaged following the closure of a practice, and were retrieved in bin bags or from a skip on the pavement outside the practice office.

During the lengthy period of negotiation with the Heritage Lottery Fund, resources were not available (as they are now through the HLF Project Planning Grants scheme) to pilot the programme of work. It proved essential, therefore, to recruit the posts of project manager and project conservator one month in advance of the rest of the project team. In that month several preparatory tasks were undertaken. The content and condition of the collections were briefly assessed by surveying sample material from each collection. The local partner archives and those practices that still held their collections were visited, and a programme of work

View of Alexander Buchanan Campbell's office, 1 Royal Crescent, Glasgow, following the closure of his practice. The photograph was taken during the removal of the Collection by RCAHMS in 1994. [SC889167]

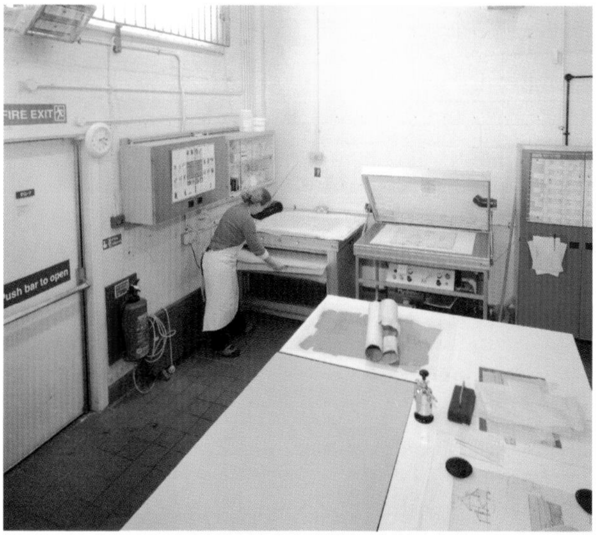

Paper conservator at work in the RCAHMS conservation studio, with the humidification dome to her right, 2003. [SC764909]

agreed. The project accommodation was set up and furniture, ICT and conservation equipment ordered. The accommodation comprised a cataloguing room with large tables; a conservation studio with a new heavy-duty guillotine, pneumatic vacuum table with humidification dome, and pneumatic paper press; and a sorting space in the store. Finally, the basic cataloguing methodologies (for both individual items and batches of items) and targets were devised.

The projects were the first substantial externally-funded cataloguing projects at RCAHMS to have their own discrete management structure and a dedicated project manager. It is testament to the success of this structure that it has subsequently been adopted for similar projects at RCAHMS. The team of staff working on the projects were directly managed by a dedicated project manager who had the day-to-day responsibility for the smooth running of the projects, as well as the immediate overview of programming and performance. This key post also acted as an advocate for the projects, both within RCAHMS and to external bodies, ensuring that the work not only complemented other projects and activities but could also lead the way in new developments in methodology and promotion. It was vital to the success of the projects to ensure that the focus always remained on delivering their objectives and project staff rarely strayed into other duties. The projects operated within the context of the Collections Section of the RCAHMS National Monuments Record of Scotland.

A two-tier system of committees was employed to oversee the projects. The first tier was a Management Group, which met quarterly and consisted of internal RCAHMS management staff and representatives of two key bodies – the Royal Incorporation of Architects in Scotland and the National Archives of Scotland. Chaired by the head of the National Monuments Record of Scotland, the Management Group dealt with issues of programme and methodology, and ensured a continuity of focus despite changes in the project staff. The second tier was an Advisory Group, which met bi-annually and was made up of experts in the fields of architectural history and archives. Chaired by the RCAHMS Chairman, the Advisory Group acted to steer major decisions on methodology and advise on details of individual collections. Neither the Management Group nor the Advisory Group were concerned directly with the projects' budgets.

The management of the projects' budgets, including all financial reporting to the Heritage Lottery Fund, was undertaken by the project manager in consultation with the chair of the Management Group. The unique nature of payment percentages, sunken costs and in-kind support that came with lottery funding meant that, while payment of invoices and payroll were operated centrally, the overall programme of expenditure was controlled by the curatorial staff involved in managing the project.

The monitoring of the project was undertaken both internally at RCAHMS and externally by the Heritage Lottery Fund. Internally, the project was reported on a quarterly basis to the Management Group, and to the National Monuments Record of Scotland Management and Programme Committees (the latter included Commissioner representatives). Externally, RCAHMS was fortunate to benefit throughout the projects from the experience of Heritage Lottery Fund case officer Caroline McIntyre and monitor Dr Michael Smethurst, who were instrumental in steering the projects to their successful conclusion. Staff timesheets and performance indicator figures were sent to the monitor monthly and both case officer and monitor visited the project quarterly to view progress first hand and to discuss any proposals for changes or new developments. These meetings, and the positive and open spirit in which they were conducted, played an important role in supporting and encouraging the project staff and ensuring the most efficient and effective use of the project resources. They also led directly to the extension of the Dick Peddie & McKay Project from two years to five and the SAPPP from three years to five.

Working to the project manager was a large team of conservation and curatorial staff. At its largest the team comprised 14 posts, at its smallest, six. In total, over the five-year life of the projects, there were four project managers (three of them promoted from within the project), 17 curatorial staff and ten conservators. This does not imply that it was an unhappy project, simply that it proved to be fertile ground for staff to gain valuable experience to enable, in many cases, career progression. This pattern of career development was an unforeseen benefit of the project, as graduates of history of art, history of architecture, and architecture itself, joined the projects, developed their skills, used them for the benefit of the projects, and then moved on to other projects or posts within RCAHMS or to similar organisations. The projects also saw staff return to higher education (both to study and to teach) as well as move into architectural practice. One member of staff completed a part-time MSc based on her work with the projects. Staff development was similar in the conservation studio where paper conservators gained valuable experience and moved on to other studios throughout the UK.

This level of staff turnover did require, however, regular recruitment, an effective training programme and good continuity in senior management. The project was fortunate to retain the same senior management team, of Collections Curator, Curator of Collections and Public Services, and Head of the National Monuments Record of Scotland, throughout. In addition the first project manager, who had previously undertaken the Scottish Survey of Architectural Practices, was promoted within RCAHMS and remained part of the management team.

The training undertaken by the project staff ranged from that provided in-house, on matters such as use of historical maps, geographic information systems, drawing scales, handling damaged material and the Oracle database; to externally provided ICT training and detailed conservation workshops. Curatorial staff also attended conferences organised by bodies including the Royal Incorporation of Architects in Scotland, the Architectural Heritage Society of Scotland and the Society of Architectural Historians of Great Britain. A series of three training days to encourage team building, while learning about specific buildings featured in the collections, took place in East Lothian, Edinburgh and Fife. The project staff also benefited from a programme of training organised for all RCAHMS staff on aspects of RCAHMS fieldwork and specific areas of the wider NMRS collections, as well as the collections of other archives in Scotland.

At the start of the projects, all posts were advertised in the national press but almost all subsequent recruitment used the more cost-effective route of web-advertising, using recruitment sites focused on the academic and museums sectors. This was effective for curatorial staff but additional measures were required to attract conservation staff, including use of email lists and direct targeting through presentations to the two UK institutions offering paper conservation courses.

A strong feature of the projects was the support and assistance they received from their team of volunteers, whose efforts were recognised by the Heritage Lottery Fund as an in-kind contribution to the projects' budgets. In the years preceding the projects, a small group of retired architects worked to list the contents of the practice collections that had been gifted to the Royal Incorporation of Architects in Scotland and that were held by RCAHMS. These lists provided a valuable starting point for the cataloguing process. During the projects, the volunteers fell into three main categories. First were the architects from the practices whose collections were being catalogued. Several of these architects had acted as curators of their practice collections over many years and had been instrumental in ensuring that their collections were transferred into public hands. They assisted the projects by providing information on their practice history and the organisation of their collection. In some cases they also provided hands-on help in organising and identifying material. Second were the experienced professionals and academics who had not worked within the practices but who had extensive knowledge of their buildings. They were invaluable in helping to interpret and contextualise complex collections and in identifying unmarked material. Third were the students of history of art, architectural history, and architecture from universities across Scotland and overseas. They assisted with a variety of tasks, and learnt new skills and gained work experience. Those on formal placements also undertook detailed research into an area of work represented in the collections. One of these students subsequently joined the staff of the projects upon graduating. Many of the volunteers were interviewed by the project staff about their knowledge and personal experience of the collections, at first informally but later using oral recording equipment.

One of the key objectives of SAPPP was to work with partner archives to make collections of local significance available to relevant local communities. Thus four collections, while remaining in the ownership of RCAHMS, were transferred to local authority archives to be held under Charge and Superintendence Agreements. They were George Bennett Mitchell & Son and Duncan & Munro, both held by Aberdeen City Archives; Sinclair Macdonald & Son, held by North Highland Archive in Wick; and Monro & Partners, held by Glasgow City Archives. The original intention was to undertake the cataloguing and most of the conservation work on these collections without re-locating them to RCAHMS offices in Edinburgh. The reasons were two-fold. First, to ensure best advantage could be made of local resources, particularly where the practice was still active. This took the form of interviews with surviving partners, and access to office libraries, business records and finding aids, as well as proximity to most of the buildings featured in the collections. The second reason was to ensure that lottery funding was in part spent in areas of Scotland outside the central belt. However, when all practical considerations of travelling time, subsistence expenses, availability of working space, and ease of staff management were taken into consideration, only a restricted amount of local working was possible.

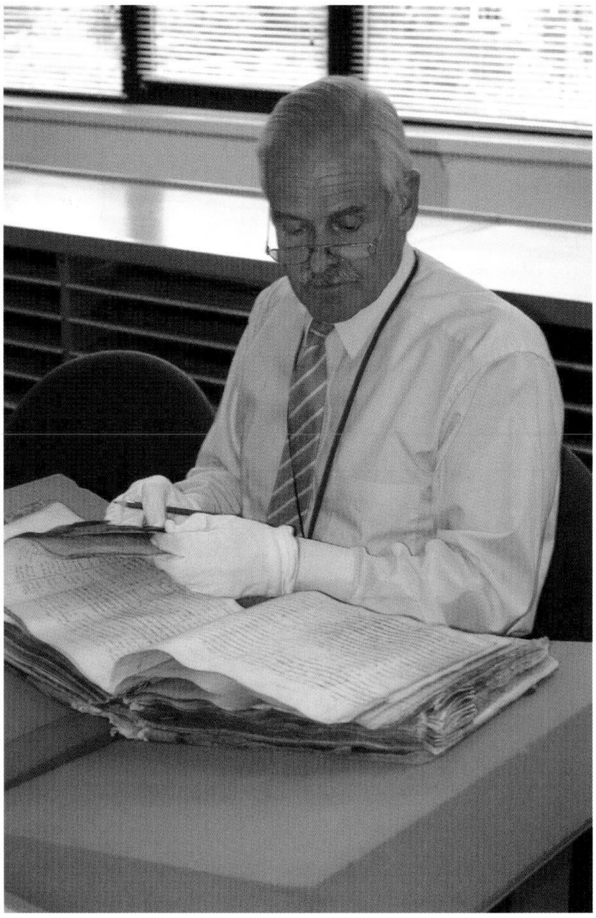

Volunteer John Knight working on the Scott Morton Collection, 2003. [DP001862]

Project development

The progress and methodology of both projects were reviewed at several key stages. The Dick Peddie & McKay Project was reviewed after one year, which led to the preparation of a grant increase application. SAPPP was reviewed three times – the first after 15 months; the second nine months later, which led to an application for a grant increase; and the third to consider how the project could be successfully concluded.

The Dick Peddie & McKay Project was reviewed half-way through its initial two year life-span, and it was immediately concluded that the original estimate of the size of the collection, which had been made under very difficult conditions prior to purchase, was short by a total of 13,500 drawings. It was also concluded that a programme of detailed conservation repair, not part of the original project, would allow a proportion of the very seriously damaged material to be made available to the public. After some negotiation, an application to the Heritage Lottery Fund to extend the project by three years, in order to catalogue the remaining 13,500 drawings and undertake detailed treatment on 550 drawings, was successful.

Decorative angel carved by Scott Morton & Co, for St Michael's Roman Catholic Church, Treeswoodhead Road, Kilmarnock, 1953, from the Scott Morton Collection. The drawing shows that the company at this time repaired drawings using pressure-sensitive tape; this has degraded over time. [SC879347]

The first project review of SAPPP was undertaken in January 2001 to evaluate whether the methodology developed was on track to successfully achieve the project targets. The first conclusion of the 45-page report prepared by the project manager was that in 42% of the time allocated to the project, only 23% of the cataloguing work had been completed. The cataloguing targets set for each of the two teams of two (600 items per week if catalogued individually or 1,500 if catalogued by batch) could be achieved but only on the most straightforward material. The report identified all the additional tasks – pre-sort hand-listing, condition assessment, handling, and research and drafting of collection essays – that were necessary and required greater provision of time than had been estimated. The lack of resources and opportunity to fully pilot the methodology in advance of the project was clearly a strong contributing factor in the underachievement of project targets. The other factors which adversely affected the achievement of targets in the first 15 months were staff changeover (a loss of nine man-weeks) and the redevelopment of the collections storage area which required staff to assemble 1,000 cube-tubes to temporarily re-house 80,000 drawings (a loss of three team-weeks). The pressure to re-configure the store came largely from the Heritage Lottery Fund's decision not to fund an extension to RCAHMS headquarters, as well as from the fact that when each of the collections was re-housed following cataloguing it required four times its original storage space.

By stream-lining the cataloguing methodology, cataloguing the majority collections by batch (rather than item-by-item), and devoting cost savings to the employment of additional cataloguing staff, the report proposed that 87% of the total project cataloguing target of 150,000 items would be completed in the three years available.

Nineteen of the collections would be catalogued in full by the projects. In five of the collections, however, material had to be prioritised for cataloguing. This was done, following a period of research into the provenance of the collection and the history of the practice, with the advice of the Advisory Group. The selection process sought to achieve a balance between what was important in terms of Scottish architectural history, what was significant within the context of the work of each practice, and what the public were most likely to want to study. In some cases a significant date in the practice history provided a cut-off point; for example, no projects that commenced after the death of James Shearer in 1961 were catalogued from the Shearer & Annand Collection. In the case of the George Bennett Mitchell & Son Collection, the practice's contract books were used to identify the most significant projects, in terms of cost, begun before the outbreak of the Second World War. For the Haxton & Watson Collection, material was selected by building type as the practice had stored its drawings for cinemas and social housing separately from the remainder of the collection. All items that were not prioritised for cataloguing were listed to provide basic access and were stabilised by being re-housed using archive-standard materials.

The second conclusion of the project review report was that, due to their poor condition, a substantial proportion of items could not be made available to the public without a further programme of conservation treatment. For the earlier collections this was due to severe mechanical damage (large tears) and for the later collections extensive use by the practices of pressure-sensitive tape, which had begun to degrade and stick the drawings together.

In September 2001, a year from the end of the SAPP Project, cataloguing progress was again reviewed and it was confirmed that the project was on track to complete 87% of the cataloguing target of 150,000 items in three years. At the request of the Heritage Lottery Fund, the cataloguing methodology was scrutinised to determine if it could be modified in order to achieve the original project target in full. It was concluded that to achieve this, the sorting of material into design or number order, and most of the description in the catalogue entry, would have to be omitted, reducing SAPPP to a basic listing exercise. The Advisory Group considered the issue and concluded that the project should deliver both access and excellence, and that the established methodology was the best way of achieving this. The Group concluded that it was better to provide a high standard of information for 87% of the original cataloguing target, than a lower standard in order to complete all 150,000 items. This argument was successfully presented to the Heritage Lottery Fund monitor and case officer who then supported a plan to apply for a grant increase.

The grant increase application for SAPPP was submitted in February 2002 and had two main objectives. First, to complete the cataloguing of the outstanding 13% of collection material that had been identified for cataloguing. Second, to begin a new programme of detailed conservation repair of 450 items from the Lorimer & Matthew and Sydney Mitchell & Wilson Collections. The priority and focus of the conservation programme in the first three years of the project had been to simply stabilise the material. In this second phase it was proposed to undertake detailed conservation treatment on drawings with severe mechanical damage (tears and losses and items in several pieces). Although around half of the SAPPP collections had material in this condition, resource constraints meant that only two could be prioritised for detailed repair. The application was successful and SAPPP was extended from its original three years to five.

In August 2003 a forward plan for the conclusion of both projects was prepared. Its starting point was to consider the 3,500 items that had not been prioritised for conservation treatment and that remained withdrawn from public use due to their poor condition. When the projects were conceived, digital technology and the digitisation of archive objects were in their infancy. By 2003 the technology was available to create a digital surrogate copy of a damaged drawing and to make that digital copy available to users online. A digital photographer was therefore employed for the final year of the projects to make 2,000 withdrawn objects available for study in digitised form. Restrictions on resources, and in some cases the extremely poor condition of the drawings, prevented all 3,500 items from being digitised. The second issue to be considered relating to the conclusion of the projects, was that despite the achievement of the full cataloguing target early in year five, several of the collections contained material in excess of what had been estimated; and that this material remained uncatalogued. The contracts of the cataloguing staff were extended by a few months and a further 11,800 items were catalogued. Thus by the end of year five a total of 195,800 items (159,700 from SAPPP and 36,100 from Dick Peddie & McKay) had been catalogued.

The SAPPP started with a total project cost of £835,344 including external funding of £626,500 from the Heritage Lottery Fund and £20,000 from the Royal Incorporation of Architects in Scotland. The Dick Peddie & McKay Project began with a total project cost of £152,275 with £102,200 funded by the Heritage Lottery Fund. Successful applications were made to the Heritage Lottery Fund to extend both projects, with further grants received of £209,000 for SAPPP and £85,500 for Dick Peddie & McKay. The total costs for both projects over five years were therefore £1,399,860, with a total grant from the Heritage Lottery Fund of £1,023,200.

At the start of the SAPP project, the projected division of the budget was 55% to be spent on salaries, 15% on general expenditure, 25% on conservation materials, and 5% on other. By the end of the project, 72% had been spent on salaries, 9% on general expenditure, 14% on conservation materials, and 5% on other. General expenditure was reduced largely due to less work taking place away from the office than anticipated, while the conservation budget was under-spent due to effective use of bulk ordering and the negotiations of discounts with key suppliers. With the agreement of the Heritage Lottery Fund, wherever money was saved under general expenditure or conservation materials, it was transferred to the salaries budget where it proved vital in increasing the size of the cataloguing team in order to achieve project targets.

All concerned with the projects were aware that the lessons learned throughout the five years would be of benefit to others in planning similar work. They also wanted the projects to have a clear and positive conclusion. The result was the publication of this report and the staging in September 2004 of the colloquium *Creating a future for the past – archive projects and the Heritage Lottery Fund.*

Cataloguing methodology

When the projects started in 1999, RCAHMS was already using an Oracle database to catalogue its collections, and the projects were able to make immediate use of the existing system with a few minor alterations. The cataloguing standard established by RCAHMS, and followed by the projects, was based on the method used by the Royal Institute of British Architects and was informed by the Architectural Drawings Advisory Group, an initiative of the Getty Art History Information Programme. It also draws on geographical standards established by the Ordnance Survey and thesaurus standards established by the Forum for Information Standards in Heritage (FISH). In addition, the catalogue is ISAD(G) compliant. The projects made a significant contribution to the development and implementation of consistent cataloguing standard methodology in RCAHMS.

In order to meet RCAHMS cataloguing requirements, it was necessary to accurately locate all identifiable buildings that were the subject of the material in the project collections. As a result, each catalogue record that describes material relating to an identifiable building is linked to information, including a National Grid Reference, on the geographic location of that building. GIS technology (Geographic Information Systems) is then used to plot the building on an interactive digital map. The creation of the location information for the projects was, after an initial period of using specialist staff, undertaken as part of the cataloguing process by the cataloguing staff.

The online public interface of the database, CANMORE, with the mapping facility CANMAP (www.rcahms.gov.uk/canmore) meant that as the collections were catalogued, the information became immediately available to the public and could be interrogated alongside all the other information contained in the RCAHMS database. This integration of the project collections with the full and varied collections of RCAHMS was a major strength of the projects. Users can now search the database by individual building, town, village or other geographical area using the interactive map. Searches can also be made by the same criteria and additionally by collection name and key words, by entering information in an online form. Thus the user can view catalogue records for all collection items that relate to the same building, or for all records by an architectural practice located throughout Scotland.

The first stage of the cataloguing process, which took no more than a few days, was termed the 'pre-sort'. The purpose of the pre-sort was two-fold: to record the existing order of the collection; and to bring all items for each building within the collection together. This not only made it straightforward for the user to see the complete range of material on an individual building, but it also minimised the number of boxes or folders that had to be retrieved in response to an enquiry. The complexity of the pre-sort was governed by the existing order of the material in the collection. In some collections the drawings had been carefully arranged and numbered by the practice prior to deposit, in others the material had been salvaged from a skip and had little order or identification.

From the inception of the projects, RCAHMS took the view that the records that had survived 150 years of Scottish architectural practice should be retained and catalogued in their entirety. This inclusive

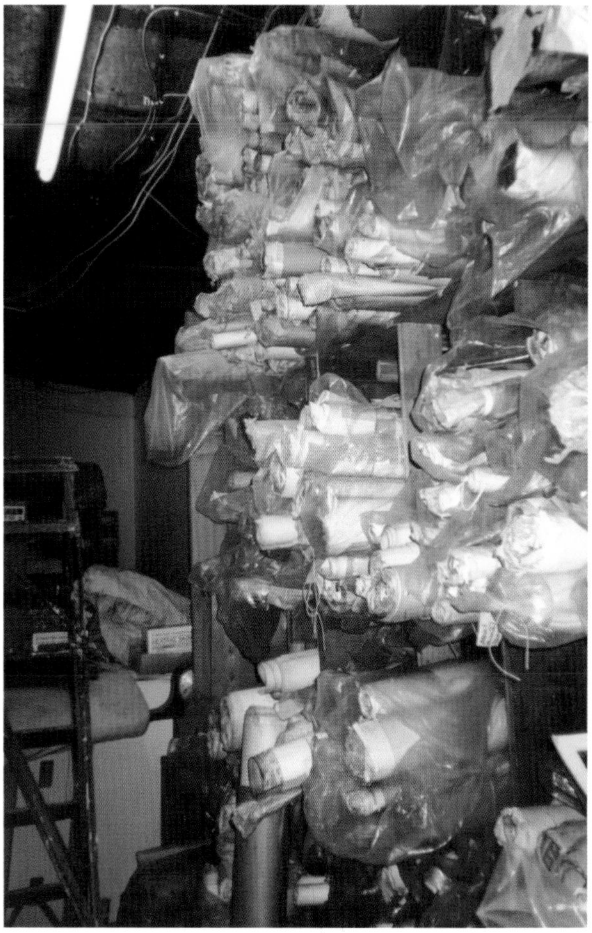

The Dick Peddie & McKay Collection at 99 Giles Street, Leith, Edinburgh, before its removal to RCAHMS, 1999. [SC889160]

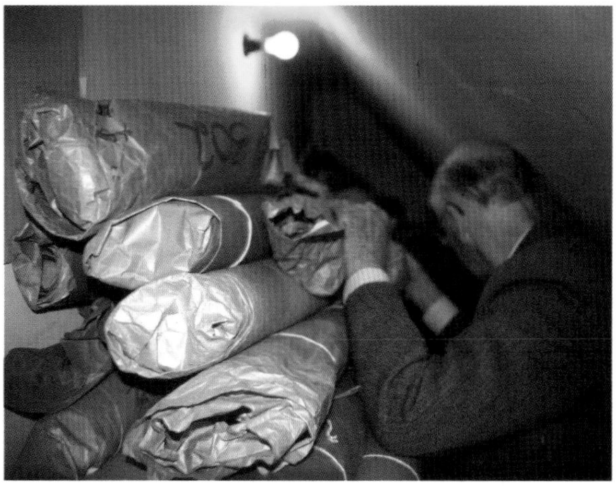

The Sinclair Macdonald & Son Collection as housed at 18 Princes Street, Thurso, before its removal to RCAHMS, 2000. [SC879392]

approach enabled designs to be followed from sketch to completion and for the character of a practice to be traced through its work over time. Thus the only weeding of material that took place at the pre-sort stage was the identification of un-annotated copies of surviving drawings, these were retained but not catalogued.

In the case of collections which had originally been gifted to the Royal Incorporation of Architects in Scotland and then transferred to RCAHMS to be part of SAPPP, the pre-sort process had been effectively completed earlier by the team of volunteers who had spent several years preparing lists detailing the contents of the collections. For other collections a list of projects created by the practice was a useful starting point.

The final task of the pre-sort was to box-up the material and prepare a list of the projects contained in each box.

The pre-sort was followed for each collection by a full sort of the drawings for each separate project within that collection, in preparation for cataloguing. Where possible, the order in which the practice had arranged the material was maintained. For example, with mid- to late-20th century collections, such as Buchanan Campbell or Shearer & Annand, it was possible to follow the drawing numbers assigned by the practice. For other collections, such as the early 20th century phase of the Lorimer & Matthew Collection, the chronological arrangement of material within projects was followed.

If a project contained distinct phases of work, these were brought together, even if the architect had allocated a different project number to each phase (the only exception to this was the Ian G Lindsay Collection whose existing arrangement worked well). For example, papers for a house that was built in 1910 and then extended in 1960, were brought together with the phases of work arranged sequentially. All original project numbers or references were recorded in a dedicated field of the catalogue record.

In cases where material was not identified, or where the material for a project was neither numbered nor dated, the cataloguer had to quickly assess and comprehend the design history of the project to ensure its careful ordering, numbering and presentation to the public. This was considered by staff to be the most intellectually challenging, and fulfilling, element of the cataloguing process. For projects involving alterations to an existing building, the 'plans as existing', if available, were a useful starting point for understanding the project. In general, the sorting process within projects followed the design process, starting with the overall design concept and leading through to the construction details, i.e. early presentation drawings or perspectives, then site plans, floor plans, sections, elevations, and finally details. Plans showing services and material from outside contractors were either ordered chronologically or numbered at the end of a project.

Three alternative methods were used to number the material in a collection. The first followed the original numbering of the collection by the practice, for example the Ian G Lindsay Collection had an numbering system created by the practice, with all projects prefixed with a 'W' followed by a running number. The second employed the original alphabetical arrangement of the collection as used by the practice. An example of an alphabetical systems was the Houston & Dunlop Collection, where papers had been stored alphabetically by client. The third option was created for collections without a clear existing arrangement or system. It involved grouping projects into decades, with all projects numbered by the earliest decade in which they appeared.

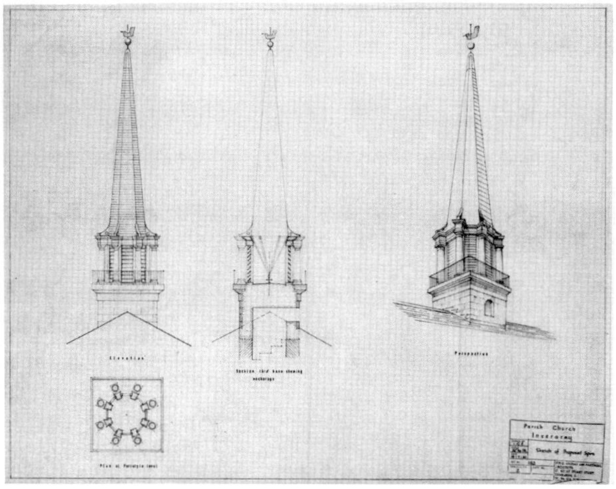

Sketch design for a spire for Inveraray Parish Church, Argyll by Ian G Lindsay & Partners, 1961, from the Ian G Lindsay Collection. The original spire, designed by Robert Mylne in 1802, had been removed in 1941 for safety reasons. [SC732542]

Methodology for numbering material within a collection

Adapting an existing numerical system
IGL W597/1/1
= collection name prefix/existing project number/batch number/item number

Adapting an existing alphabetical system
HD A/19/2/1
= collection name prefix/alphabetical group/project number/batch number/item number

Newly created decade system
CSE 1930/75/4/1
= collection name prefix/decade of earliest phase of project/project number/batch number/item number

NB The batch number refers to either a roll or folder of 7-14 drawings

The original project methodology required all material for every project within a collection to be fully sorted and numbered prior to cataloguing. This allowed the cataloguers to develop a complete overview of the collection before cataloguing it and ensured that all material for each project had been identified and brought together. The project review in January 2001 highlighted that cataloguing was falling seriously behind schedule. The methodology was thus adapted so that following the pre-sort, each project within a collection was sorted and then immediately catalogued. This speeded up the process since the material was handled only once and the knowledge gained in the sort process was immediately applied to the cataloguing. The drawback of this system was that the cataloguer did not have a good overview of the collection until all work on it was complete. In addition, when stray material was uncovered for a project that had been catalogued earlier, which happened regularly, it had to be added to the end of the project rather than appropriately integrated into the number or design process order.

Overall cataloguing methodology

Pre-sort whole collection
|
Box-up and create list of box contents by project
|
Sort the material within a single project
|
Number the material within a single project
|
Assess and record the condition of material within a single project
|
Catalogue the material within a single project
|
Re-house each batch of material within a single project

Cataloguing staff working in tandem. [DP001864]

The majority of material was catalogued in batches; a batch being a roll or folder of between seven and 14 drawings. This size range was determined by the optimum storage conditions. Each batch of material was described in a single catalogue record that gave the number of items in the batch, the date range of the material, and the information it contained. This system was particularly suited to large runs of working drawings that could be divided easily into groups of similar material (i.e. a batch of floor plans or service details). It was less suited, but could be made to work, with older collections where fewer drawings were prepared for each project and a batch of material might therefore include more than one project. Batch cataloguing was a new development for RCAHMS and evolved from discussions with members of the Advisory Group.

A minority of material, including photographs and small collections of presentation drawings, were catalogued item-by-item, which allowed a fuller level of description.

Most of the SAPPP collections were worked on by a team of at least two people. Each team had a designated lead cataloguer who was responsible for undertaking preliminary research, assembling information gathered from the cataloguing process and finally writing a collection essay. The collection essay, designed to be accessed online from any related catalogue record in the database, contains a practice history, provenance details, an account of how the collection was ordered and any changes introduced to that order, a discussion of the scope and content of the material in the collection, and a list of bibliographic or other collection references. This is accompanied by a report compiled by conservation staff outlining any treatments carried out on the collection and detailing how it was re-housed.

Cataloguing targets
Collections catalogued in batches
165 items per person per week

Collections catalogued item-by-item
120 items per person per week

NB These targets include sorting, numbering and cataloguing, as well as time for research, the creation of site location information, handling and re-housing.

Cataloguing achievement over five years
SAPPP: 159,700 items catalogued
Dick Peddie & McKay: 36,100 items catalogued

Conservation methodology

The principal aim of the conservation programme was to stabilise all the material in order to prevent it from further deterioration and to allow it to be handled. Prior to the projects starting, RCAHMS did not have a permanent conservator on the staff and the conservation studio required additional furnishings and equipment. While RCAHMS had experience of commissioning small programmes of conservation, there was no precedent for tackling very large volumes of material. In the first month of the project, before the full team started, rapid surveys were made of each of the collections, leading to a basic assessment of conservation needs.

When the collections first arrived at RCAHMS they suffered from a variety of problems. The provisional rapid surveys identified surface dirt, mould and water damage, tears and losses, folds, creases and crumpled edges, all with varying levels of severity. As each collection was assessed in detail, it became clear that the condition of some material was too poor to be made available to the public without the risk of further damage. In the first phase of the projects this material was catalogued, with a note on the catalogue record saying it could not be consulted due to its poor condition. This material was then stored apart from the main collection.

All collection items were re-housed in inert archival materials to stabilise their condition. Material was usually re-housed in the form in which it was received, i.e. rolled drawings remained rolled, flat drawings remained flat. The re-housing, which was undertaken by the cataloguers, often with the assistance of volunteers, started with the removal of the original wrapping papers, plastic bags or boxes. A sample of the original housing was kept for each collection. Immediately following cataloguing, the drawings were re-housed and provisionally labelled by the cataloguers.

Methodology for re-housing rolled drawings
Rolled drawings, in batches of 7-14 items, were supported by rolling them around an acid- and lignin-free tube. Each roll was then wrapped in acid-free archival paper (with folded-over ends for extra protection) and secured with unbleached cotton tape. Between four and six rolls were stored in an extendable archival box, known as a cube-tube, and placed on flat metal shelving.

Methodology for re-housing flat drawings
Flat drawings were stored individually, or in batches of up to four items, in 75 micron archival polyester pockets, sealed on two sides. Up to 12 drawings, usually in three polyester pockets, were stored in a single acid-free card folder, also sealed on two sides. Folders were then placed in a wooden plan chest. While it would have been desirable to replace the wooden plan chests with metal versions, it was not possible within the budget.

Paper conservator working on the Duncan & Munro Collection, 2000. [SC765080]

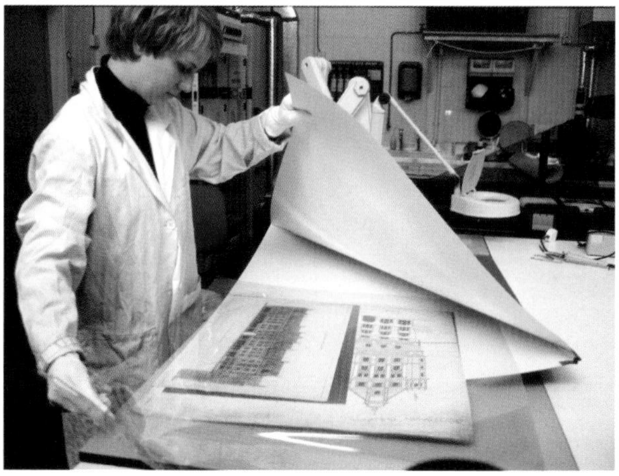

Rehousing drawings from the Dunn & Findlay Collection in 75 micron archival polyester pockets, 2000. [SC879395]

Re-housing also included the removal of elements that had become damaging to the collection material, including elastic bands that had become brittle and had adhered to the drawings, paper clips and pins that had rusted, and string which had worn through the paper and torn the drawings. The removal of these items benefited both the material and the public who would be handling the collections. It did not prove possible, with the available resources, to remove all damaging material. A compromise was reached where items that had not yet rusted were left, since correct environmental conditions would significantly slow down the rusting process.

When collections were sorted prior to cataloguing, their condition was assessed and recorded. Initially, an assessment team comprising project manager, conservator and lead cataloguer of the collection was used to select material for treatment. While effective in ensuring continuity of judgement across the collections, this method proved very time consuming and could not be sustained. Instead the cataloguers were carefully trained by the conservation staff in what to look for and record. The cataloguers could then combine a simple condition assessment with an informed judgement in the context of the project and/or collection on the significance of each item requiring treatment. This information was recorded in a spreadsheet, which proved useful in both tracking the progress of material being treated, and assessing requirements when preparing the grant increase applications.

Methodology for tracking conservation requirements
For each collection a workbook was created using a spreadsheet programme, with items recorded in worksheets according to the following assessments of condition:

- Requires preventative treatment
- Requires detailed repair
- Can be made available untreated if stored flat in a polyester pocket

Each worksheet listed the item number, then provided tick boxes for the following information:

- High curatorial priority
- Type of material – paper, tracing, manuscript, photograph or other
- Catalogued
- Treatment completed
- Item returned to collection

The spreadsheet could thus be used to provide information on the quantities of each type of material, the number of items in each condition category, and the number of items of high curatorial priority, as well as a combination of any of these.

Items identified as being affected by mould, or which had pressure sensitive tape used to repair earlier tears, were referred to the conservation team. If left, pressure sensitive tape causes further degradation to the object and can cause adhesion to an adjacent drawing in a roll, a significant problem for the many rolled collections. While all mould was prioritised for immediate treatment, not all drawings with pressure-sensitive tape could be treated within the project.

Methodology for treatment of mould
Mould was treated under a well ventilated fume hood using cotton wool and industrial methylated spirits or ethanol.

Detail of mould damage. [SC765084]

Plan of Dunrobin Castle, Sutherland by R S Lorimer, c.1915, from the Lorimer & Matthew Collection (pre-conservation). [SC765083]

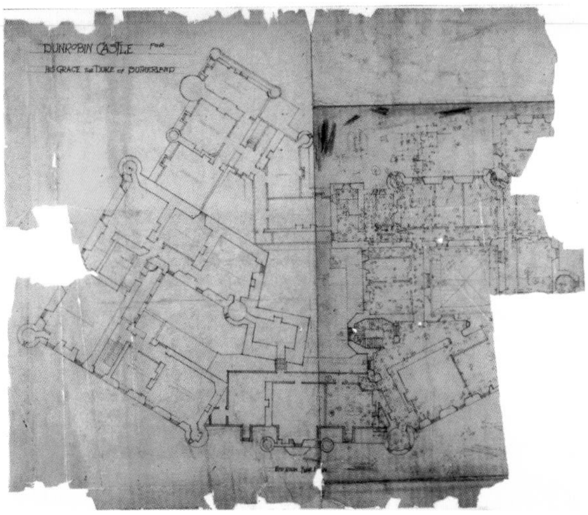

Plan of Dunrobin Castle, Sutherland by R S Lorimer, c.1915, from the Lorimer & Matthew Collection (post-conservation). [SC879381]

Methodology for removal of pressure sensitive tape
Pressure sensitive tape was removed using a heated spatula, then a rubber for moist residue, or a scalpel and sandpaper for dry residue. Small areas of tape were removed by the conservation assistant and the exposed minor tears were not repaired. This allowed a high volume of material to be returned to the roll and made available. Larger areas of tape were removed by the conservators and the exposed major tear repaired. Rolled drawings affected by tape that could not be prioritised for treatment were re-housed individually using a 50 micron polyester pocket, sealed only at one end to prevent buckling when re-integrated into the roll. The drawings could then be consulted but when the tape degrades the drawing will not adhere to other drawings, as it is contained in its dedicated polyester pocket.

In the first phases of both projects, all collection items that were catalogued were re-housed in appropriate archival materials and 2,000 items received treatment for mould damage or tape removal and tear repair.

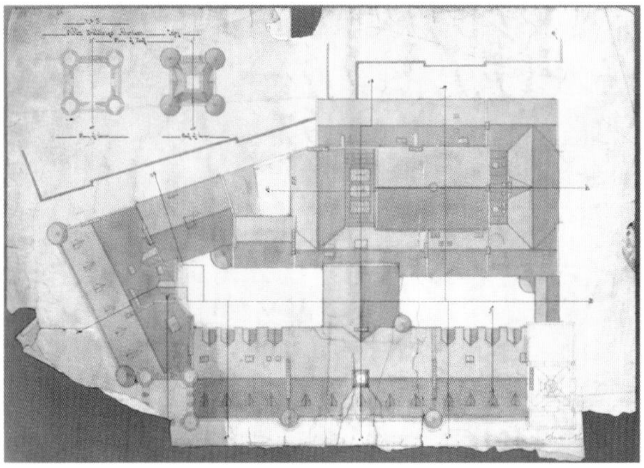

Roof plan of Municipal Buildings, Castle Street, Aberdeen, by Peddie & Kinnear, c.1865, from the Dick Peddie & McKay Collection (recto, pre-conservation). [SC879340]

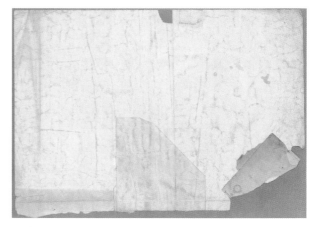

Roof plan of Municipal Buildings, Castle Street, Aberdeen by Peddie & Kinnear, c.1865, from the Dick Peddie & McKay Collection (verso, pre-conservation). [SC879356]

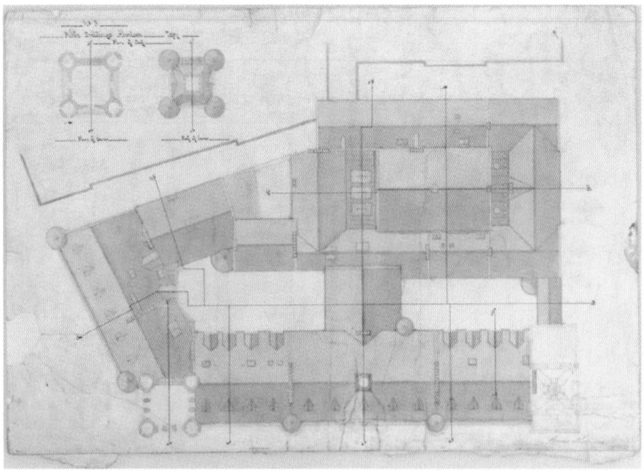

Roof plan of Municipal Buildings, Castle Street, Aberdeen by Peddie & Kinnear, c.1865, from the Dick Peddie & McKay Collection (recto, post-conservation). [SC879343]

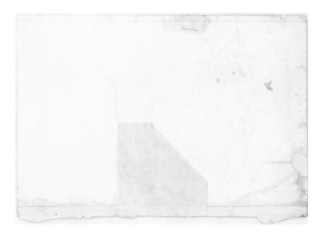

Roof plan of Municipal Buildings, Castle Street, Aberdeen by Peddie & Kinnear, c.1865, from the Dick Peddie & McKay Collection (verso, post-conservation). [SC879359]

Target for preventative treatment
7.5 items per person, per week.

The system of recording the treatment needs and curatorial priority of material in the conservation tracking spreadsheet allowed a clear assessment to be made of the volume and nature of material that was not treated in the first phase of the projects and which had been withdrawn from public use to prevent further damage. Around half of the collections had material in this category but due to resource constraints only three could be prioritised for detailed repair in the grant increase applications. Following discussion with the Advisory and Management Groups, as well as with the Heritage Lottery Fund monitor and case officer, the Dick Peddie & McKay, Lorimer & Matthew, and Sydney Mitchell & Wilson Collections were prioritised due both to the extent of the damage and the large number of buildings represented that were of international and outstanding national significance. The material for these buildings was well used by the public, particularly by those working on the conservation and re-use of historic buildings. Even within these three collections resource constraints prevented all withdrawn material being treated and a further stage of prioritisation was undertaken, this time on a purely curatorial basis. The principal aim of all treatments was to stabilise the drawing and allow it to be handled by the public. With the occasional exception of material prepared for exhibition, items were not conserved beyond what was required to achieve this aim.

Methodology for detailed repair
Material was prepared for treatment by being dry cleaned with a chemical sponge, eraser and soft brush. Tears were then repaired using either heat set tissue applied with a heated spatula, or Japanese tissue and wheat starch paste. Drawings were then flattened using a humidity chamber and then a pneumatic press. Other treatments included washing, infilling and lining.

Target for detailed repair
4 items per person, per week.

To complete the programme of detailed repair, a team of three paper conservators, supported by a conservation assistant, was required. Achieving successful recruitment and retention of conservation staff was challenging throughout the projects and occasionally resulted in a lack of consistency in approach. This appeared to be a common experience on similar, externally funded archive projects that could only offer fixed term appointments. SAPPP in particular suffered from serious recruitment and retention difficulties that meant that some work had to be outsourced to a private conservator. In addition, a partnership with the University of Edinburgh facilitated the employment by the University of a conservator for one year with the projects funding the equivalent of six months of work dedicated to its material. Both initiatives were funded from within the projects' budgets.

After the first phase of the projects, a total of 4,500 items (2.4% of the total) were withdrawn from use due to their poor condition. Using the grant increases, 1,000 of these items received detailed treatment, leaving a balance of 3,500 withdrawn items. The end-of-project review concluded that the most cost- and time-efficient way of making this material available for public study was to create surrogate digital copies that could be viewed online alongside the catalogue entry. The originals of all material that was digitised were retained and can be made available in the future should funds be provided to undertake detailed repair. A total of 2,000 items were digitised by a single photographer working full time for a year.

Digital photographer at work, 2004. [DP001863]

Methodology for digitisation of damaged drawings
The digitisation process was achieved by using the flat copy system within the RCAHMS photographic department. This system of placing the drawings between two panes of glass visually fused tears and temporarily flattened crumpled edges. The effect was that the drawing appeared less damaged and a comparatively good image of it was obtained. The drawing was then photographed using either traditional methods and scanning the negative, or by the use of a digital back to the camera. Both methods created a file size that allowed close viewing on screen and a print to be produced at photographic quality if required.

Digitisation target
45 drawings per photographer, per week

Conservation achievements over five years
Assessed, re-housed and stabilised: 195,800 items
Preventative treatment: 2,000 items
Detailed repair: 1,000 items
Digitised to facilitate access: 2,000 items

Promotion and use

The active promotion of the collections was not specifically required by the Heritage Lottery Fund when initial funding was granted in 1999. However, it was desirable from the outset to promote the collections in order to attract a broad range of users. In the execution of this promotion, the projects benefited from being part of an organisation with photography, graphic design, and web design skills all available in-house.

Display panels showing images and text were created to tour venues throughout Scotland, including libraries, museums, universities, and a selection of conferences. Some of the panels related to the projects as a whole whilst others related to specific collections, either highlighting their national importance (Dick Peddie & McKay) or targeting potential users in the areas where collections were stored locally (Sinclair Macdonald & Son, Duncan & Munro, George Bennett Mitchell & Son). A modular system allowed the selection of panels to be tailored to each venue or event. On several occasions they were transported from one institution to another within an area by a local authority van service.

Small exhibitions of original material were mounted in display cases in the NMRS public search room, including drawings from the Dick Peddie & McKay, Houston & Dunlop and Cowie & Seaton Collections. Four exhibitions of original material and photographic copies of material were staged at the Royal Incorporation of Architects in Scotland Gallery in Edinburgh. *Career Building – Drawings from the Scottish Architects' Papers Preservation Project* (2000) focused on significant early commissions from five collections worked on during the first year of the project. *What didn't they build? One hundred years of the Dick Peddie & McKay Collection* (2001) comprised 12 original drawings from the Dick Peddie & McKay Collection, along with photographs of country houses, churches, banks, offices and hotels built by the practice throughout Scotland. *Changing Buildings: Changing Times* (2002) featured original drawings from four collections, chosen to reflect the individual responses to change employed by architects over time. The final exhibition *From Sketch to Sculpture* (2003) used examples of designs for architectural ornamentation and sculpture from five collections. All exhibitions, of original and secondary material, were also mounted on the RCAHMS website. Additional web-only exhibitions were prepared on a variety of subjects, including the conservation and digitisation programmes and detailed aspects of the collections.

Between 2001 and 2003 the projects' staff undertook lecture tours of Scottish universities, to audiences that included students of history, history of art, architectural history and architecture. In some cases, such as at the Scott Sutherland School of Architecture in Aberdeen, the lecture formed part of a series organised by the students; on other occasions, such as at St Andrews and Strathclyde Universities respectively, the scheduling of lectures was planned to coincide with related honours courses or times in the academic year when students were considering dissertation topics. In 2003 the project manager and conservation staff gave presentations to paper conservation students at Camberwell College, London and the University of Northumbria, Newcastle. These were primarily to aid staff recruitment but also served as publicity for the projects.

Regular articles and information updates appeared throughout the course of the projects in both local and national newspapers, as well as in more specialist publications including the *Chartered Architect* and the Architectural Heritage Society of Scotland (AHSS) *Magazine*. In 2003, volume XIV of the annual AHSS journal *Architectural Heritage* was devoted to

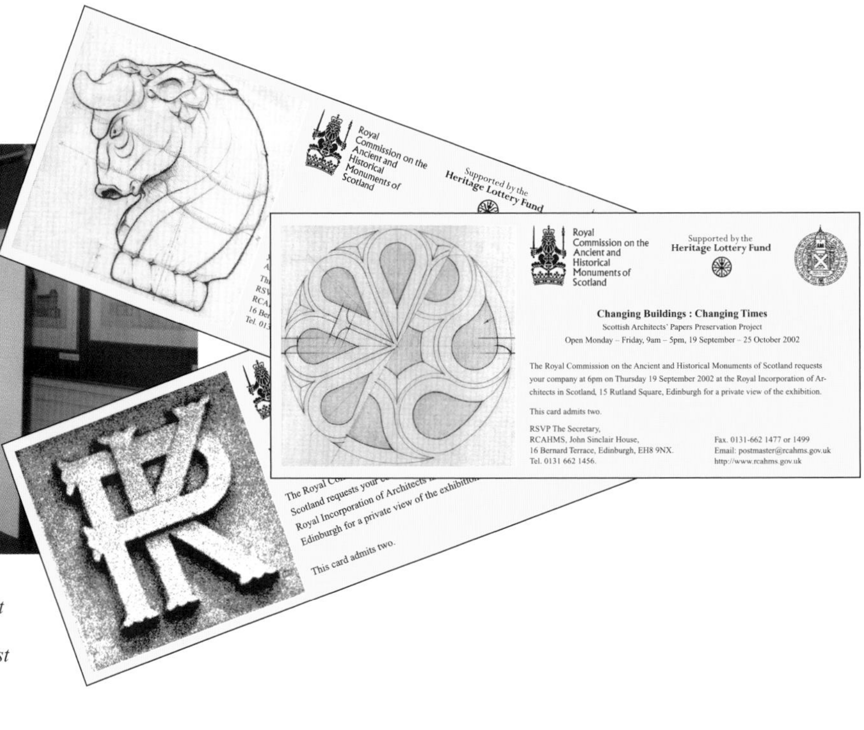

What didn't they build? 100 years of the Dick Peddie & McKay Collection*, exhibition held at Royal Incorporation of Architects in Scotland, Rutland Square, Edinburgh, 30 July - 31 August 2001.*

Elevation of the principal entrance front, Castle of Mey, Caithness by William Burn, 1819, from the Sinclair Macdonald & Son Collection. [SC637881]

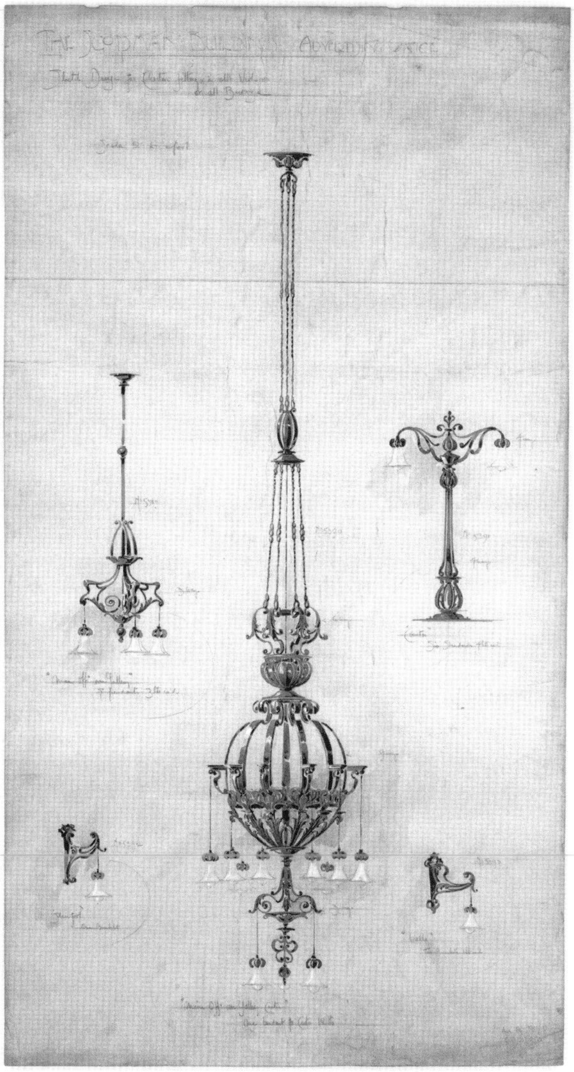

Light fittings for the advertising office, Scotsman Buildings, 20-26 North Bridge, Edinburgh by Dunn & Findlay, c.1900, from the Dunn & Findlay Collection. [SC587777]

essays inspired by the collections. This included an introduction to the projects and an illustrated summary of each of the collections. The progress of the projects was also reported in the RCAHMS *Annual Review*.

The aims, objectives and methodologies of the projects were presented to international peer

Dormers and chimney stacks, South West façade, Morgan Academy, Forfar Road, Dundee photographed by RCAHMS after fire damage, 22 March 2001. [SC642811]

organisations at the Tenth Congress of the International Confederation of Architectural Museums in Rio de Janeiro, Brazil, in 2000 and the First International Congress for Architectural Archives in Alcala de Henares, Spain, in 2004.

The steady promotion of the collections, coupled with the growing quantity of material made available to the public through cataloguing and conservation work, resulted in an increasing number of people using the collections in both a professional and personal capacity. The scope of interest included broad subjects such as architectural, art and social history, as well as more specific interests such as local and family history and research of individuals.

Architects working on the conservation and re-use of historic buildings regularly consulted the collections, sometimes for major projects such as the renovation work on Lympne Castle, Kent (restored by Robert Lorimer in 1905, and included in the Lorimer & Matthew Collection) and Castle of Mey, Caithness (restored by Sinclair Macdonald & Son during the 1950s and held in that Collection).

In 2001 the Scotsman Building, North Bridge, Edinburgh, was being converted from newspaper offices into a five-star hotel. The architects consulted the original drawings in the Dunn & Findlay Collection, and were particularly interested in the original interior fittings. Reproductions of the drawings were used in panels around the hotel.

A high-profile case where the collections were used was after the fire in 2001 at the Morgan Academy, Dundee. Inspectors from Historic Scotland, insurance loss adjusters and the appointed conservation architects all visited RCAHMS to consult the original Peddie & Kinnear drawings in the Dick Peddie & McKay Collection. The school has since been reconstructed. Similarly, A H Mottram papers for alterations to commercial premises on North Bridge, from the Dunn & Findlay Collection, were consulted to assist the analysis process in the aftermath of the devastating blaze in the Cowgate area of Edinburgh in 2002.

Other professionals who have used the collections

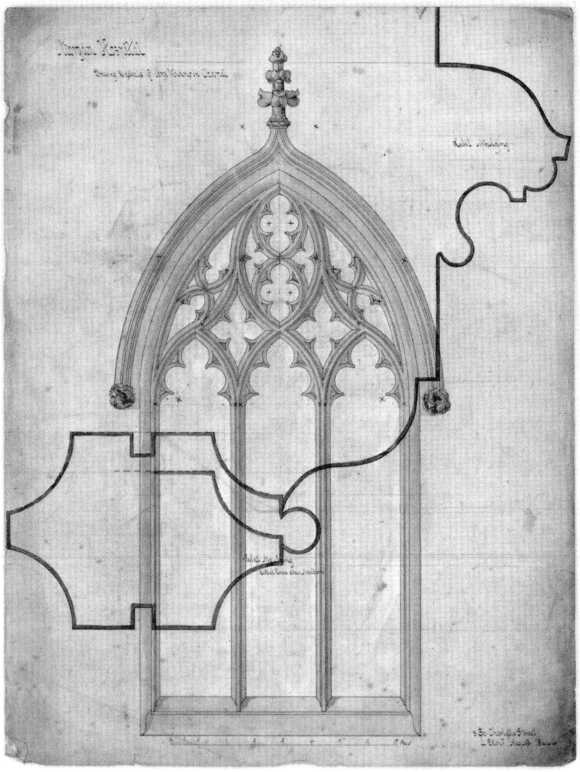

Details of chapel window, Morgan Academy, Forfar Road, Dundee by Peddie & Kinnear, c.1863-65, from the Dick Peddie & McKay Collection. [SC643740]

include furniture specialists from an Edinburgh auction house who used the Scott Morton Collection to identify pieces that had entered their showroom, an antiques dealer who consulted photographs of Thomas Haddon fireplaces in the Lorimer & Matthew Collection, and research staff from the University of St Andrews who are compiling a dictionary of Scottish architects. Several authors, including the writers of the *Illustrated Architectural Guides* and *Buildings of Scotland* series, consulted the collections.

The Shearer & Annand Collection proved useful to students from varying disciplines undertaking research at Honours level. In 2001 a student from Duncan of Jordanstone, Dundee, consulted drawings of Shearer's fire station in Dunfermline as part of her final year project, which demonstrated how the building could be converted into a hotel. In the same year an architectural history student from the University of Edinburgh embarked on a work placement with SAPPP and wrote her placement report on James Shearer's town planning work. The same student later joined the staff of the project and published her report in the SAPPP volume of *Architectural Heritage*.

Other examples of academic projects aided by the collections include an investigation of farm buildings in the North-East of Scotland for which a Strathclyde University architecture student consulted papers from the Duncan & Munro Collection; a group study of the streets centred around the Denburn Viaduct area of Aberdeen where fifth-year students at the Scott Sutherland School of Architecture visited Aberdeen City Archives to see George Bennett Mitchell & Son drawings; and a student from St Andrews University who used the Dick Peddie & McKay Collection extensively in the research for his PhD on Peddie & Kinnear.

The educational use of the collections was further increased by the projects' substantial contribution of images to the web-based projects SCRAN (the Scottish Cultural Resources Access Network), aimed at life-long learners, and the Dundee University-based Drawn Evidence project, aimed at the higher education sector. In 2004 some 2,500 items from the projects were made available online as digital images on CANMORE.

The collections have proved to be of great use to the general public, both by civic groups exploring their local heritage, and by individuals carrying out personal research into the history of their own house. The collections have also attracted interest from the families of featured architects, including relatives of James M Monro & Son (Monro & Partners), J & F Johnston and Sinclair Macdonald. The American descendants of John Dick Peddie gained new information on their ancestors after an internet search that led to the Dick Peddie & McKay website exhibition.

Other public users included a local group interested in the conservation and promotion of Rosyth garden city, Fife, much of which was designed by A H Mottram (Dunn & Findlay Collection) and an enquirer from Australia who had discovered that his Scottish Baronial house had been built from plans brought over from Scotland in the 1850s and was trying to establish the identity of the architects, whom he believed to be Peddie & Kinnear (Dick Peddie & McKay Collection).

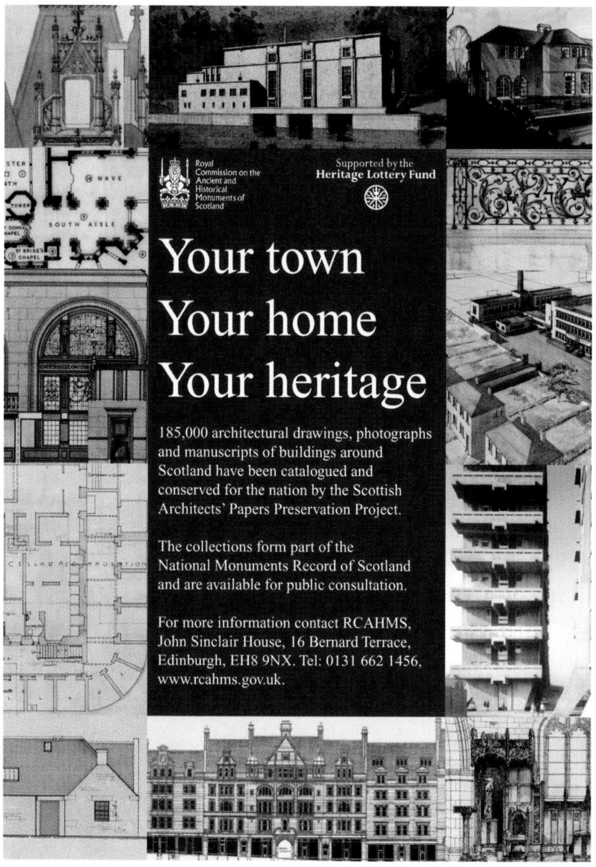

This poster advertising the projects was sent to archives and libraries throughout Scotland in 2003.

Comment

Architects' papers, and drawings in particular, are generally intended to be ephemeral: after all, they exist primarily as the means to a greater end – the construction of buildings. There are, of course, exceptions, but even in architects' minds, the proper appreciation of the historical value of working drawings and file documentation, alongside the more easily enjoyed coloured perspectives, is taking some time to achieve. Indeed, it is part of a shifting cultural change of attitudes towards our past.

History, it seems, often values the records of the everyday, rather than the special and high-profile event or production. In this context, the work of Charles McKean in rescuing drawings collections at risk during the 1980s and early 1990s, and the willingness of RCAHMS to take these under their wing, must be particularly commended. Following McKean's lead, the Royal Incorporation of Architects in Scotland (RIAS) collaborated in the Scottish Survey of Architectural Practices, and the RIAS publishing wing, The Rutland Press, published the results of the Survey in *Scottish Architects' Papers – a source book* (1996). The advent of the Lottery at that time, and its commitment to good causes, including the heritage through the Heritage Lottery Fund, then provided an opportunity to properly catalogue and preserve the large number of substantial practice collections then held by RIAS and RCAHMS. Initially led by the RIAS, with a cash contribution from members' subscriptions of £20,000 – a large sum in RIAS terms – the bid to the Heritage Lottery Fund for the Scottish Architects' Papers Preservation Project was ultimately lodged by RCAHMS.

In order to satisfy Lottery criteria, the Incorporation later agreed on the donation of the RIAS collections that formed part of the bid, collectively named the McKean Collection, to the Commission for safekeeping in perpetuity.

Why did the RIAS make such a level of commitment? Because it was the only responsible thing to do! Not to have properly catalogued the drawings, and identified where remedial work was necessary, would have kept the material from the public indefinitely. The RIAS Charter obligations include the aim to promote a better understanding of Scottish architecture, through activities that encourage access and learning. Architectural drawings comprise a distillation of many aspects of contemporary society. From the type of building designed, through its layout, use of technology and form, much can be learned of the priorities of the society of the time – in contemporary terms, the environmental, social, economic and cultural aspects.

Moreover, architectural drawings can in some instances show the thought processes of the design team in arriving at their completed solutions; in other cases, drawings indicate what was never built, or what has subsequently been demolished and is thus not available in three dimensions. Where files and correspondence have been saved, the human aspect of relationships between client, designer, contractor and others can inform an understanding of what was built, how and why.

The Incorporation believes it right to celebrate the conclusion of the SAPP Project, so ably led by the staff at the Royal Commission. This is, in current parlance, an exemplar of partnership working for the long-term common good.

And what of the future? Apart from the use which we hope will be made of these collections, the Incorporation looks forward to future collaborative work with those who share this part of its ambition. For many years the Scottish Drawings Working Group was led and hosted by the Incorporation, engaging the interests of many in the archival sector. The Incorporation wishes to maintain these strong links through the transformed Architectural Archives Forum, to maintain best practice and to keep reminding architects and design teams of the worth of their archives. While there is doubtless a lot more drawn material to collect, the future holds different challenges in the way in which drawings are both produced and stored. It is our hope that the importance and use of architectural drawings can be kept within the close watch of the developing Policy on Architecture for Scotland.

Sebastian Tombs,
Secretary and Chief Executive,
Royal Incorporation of
Architects in Scotland

Collection essays

The 25 collection essays in this report are largely based on accounts written by project staff on the completion of cataloguing work, with the assistance of Professor David Walker and Yvonne Hillyard of the Dictionary of Scottish Architects at the University of St Andrews.

The essays detail the provenance, practice history, and content of each collection. The bibliographic references include further sources available for consultation at the NMRS and elsewhere, such as unpublished documents and related collections of material, as well as newspaper cuttings, periodicals and books, some of which were written by the architects whose work is included within the collections.

One of the advantages of geo-referencing the catalogue of architects' papers is the ability to present the distribution of sites for a specific collection or body of material on a map. In this publication a map showing all of the places represented in each collection is included with each essay. Each black dot indicates a city, town, village or rural site where there is a project or projects for which there is collection material. The place where the practice was based for the greatest part of their lifespan is indicated by a red dot. The map on page 26 shows the geographic spread of all 25 collections, demonstrating how the collections span the length and breadth of Scotland.

As a whole, the essays reveal the connections formed by the transmission of drawings between practices and the career paths of the architects that created them. It is possible to see work on a particular building in more than one collection, such as George Watson's College, Edinburgh, which was built by James B Dunn (*c.*1927-34) and extended by J & F Johnston & Partners (*c.*1965-67); or the Reform Co-operative Society Limited, Durie Street, Leven, for which there are drawings for an unexecuted scheme in the Sydney Mitchell & Wilson Collection (1905) and papers for alterations to the premises as built, along with an extension, in the Haxton & Watson Collection (1920-51).

The acquisition of both original drawings and mechanically produced copies from other architects is apparent in many of the collections, the Cowie & Seaton collection, for example, contains drawings by Dick Peddie & McKay, Lorimer & Matthew, and Leslie Grahame Thomson (MacDougall), as well as those by several other practices whose collections do not form part of the SAPP Project.

The movement of architects between practices during their training and throughout their careers can be traced through the collections. Major practices attracted large numbers of apprentices, many of whom went on to be distinguished architects in their own right: Sydney Mitchell (1856-1930), George Wilson (1844-1912), Sir Robert Lorimer (1864-1929), Burnet Napier Henderson Orphoot (1880-1964) and Sir Basil Spence (1907-1976) all passed through Sir Robert Rowand Anderson's Edinburgh office at various stages of its history.

An example of an architect who moved from one practice to another during his career is James Alexander Arnott (1871-1950), who worked for Kinnear & Peddie (see Dick Peddie & McKay Collection) between 1888 and 1898 before gaining employment with Dunn & Findlay (see Dunn & Findlay Collection). He later took over the Sydney Mitchell & Wilson practice with Ernest Arthur Auldjo Jamieson (*c.*1880-1937). Lindsay Auldjo Jamieson (1904-*c.*1960), who worked for Arnott and his father, later became a partner in Dick Peddie & McKay, thereby bringing together the Sydney Mitchell & Wilson and Dick Peddie & McKay Collections.

Collaboration between practices across Scotland is also evident. Although Leadbetter & Fairley (see Cowie & Seaton Collection) designed the Carnegie Library, Wick (*c.*1895-98), it was the Thurso-based Sinclair Macdonald practice who were the executant architects on the project, and it is for this reason that papers for the building exist in the Sinclair Macdonald & Son Collection.

Architectural competition entries also connect the collections. For example, the Leslie Grahame Thomson (MacDougall) Collection contains his unsuccessful competition drawings for Coventry Cathedral (1950). These can be compared with photographic copies of the winning entry drawings by Sir Basil Spence & Partners, included in the Spence Glover & Ferguson Collection (1951-58).

It is not possible to document all of the relationships between the collections in this volume but cross-references between collections are included at the end of each essay.

Unless otherwise stated the dates cited for projects are the range given on drawings in the collections.

An extended version of each essay can be consulted in the NMRS library based at RCAHMS, John Sinclair House, 16 Bernard Terrace, Edinburgh EH8 9NX or online at www.rcahms.gov.uk

Catalogue entries for drawings, photographs and manuscripts from the collections can be found on the RCAHMS database CANMORE at www.rcahms.gov.uk. The collections, unless otherwise stated, can be viewed in the NMRS public search room at John Sinclair House (Monday to Friday, 9.30am – 4.30pm). Enquiries can also be made by telephone (0131 662 1456), fax (0131 662 1499) or e-mail nmrs@rcahms.gov.uk

General References

For general reading on Scottish architects' papers see:

Bailey, R M 1993 Manuscript files for the Scottish Survey of Architectural Practices, unpublished source, available for consultation at the NMRS.

Bailey, R M ed. 1996 *Preserving Scottish Architects' Papers: Attic to Archive. Architect Heritage VII.* Edinburgh: Edinburgh Univ Press.

Bailey, R M 1996 *Scottish Architects' Papers – a source book.* Edinburgh: Rutland Press.

Bailey, R M ed. 2003 *Architect Heritage XIV.* Edinburgh: Edinburgh Univ Press

Many buildings included in SAPPP have entries in the RIAS *Illustrated Architectural Guides* (Rutland Press, Edinburgh) and the *Buildings of Scotlan*d series (Penguin, Yale). For general reading on Scottish architecture see:

Dunbar, J G 1978 *The Architecture of Scotland.* London: B T Batsford.

Glendinning, M, MacInnes, R and Mackechnie, A 1996 *A History of Scottish Architecture.* Edinburgh: Edinburgh Univ Press.

Glendinning, M and Mackechnie, A 2004 *Scottish Architecture.* London: Thames & Hudson.

Abbreviations

Aberdeen Univ Press	Aberdeen University Press
Accounting Hist New Series	Accounting History New Series
Architect Heritage	Architectural Heritage
Architect Heritage Soc Scot Mag	Architectural Heritage Society of Scotland Magazine
Architect Prospect	Architectural Prospect
Architect Rev	Architectural Review
Architects J	The Architects' Journal
Bull Heriot Watt Univ	Bulletin of Heriot Watt University
CANMORE	Computer Application for the National Monuments Record Enquiries
Edinburgh Architect Ass Year Book	Edinburgh Architectural Association Year Book
Edinburgh Univ Press	Edinburgh University Press
GIS	Geographic Information Systems
ISAD (G)	General International Standard Archival Description
J Garden Hist Soc	Journal of the Garden History Society
J Roy Inst Brit Architect	Journal of the Royal Institute of British Architects
NMRS	National Monuments Record of Scotland
RCAHMS	Royal Commission on the Ancient and Historical Monuments of Scotland
RIAS	Royal Incorporation of Architects in Scotland
RIAS Calendar and Annu Rep	Royal Incorporation of Architects in Scotland Calendar and Annual Report
RIAS Quart	Royal Incorporation of Architects in Scotland Quarterly
RIBA J	Journal of the Royal Institute of British Architects
SAPPP	Scottish Architects' Papers Preservation Project
Scot Art Rev	Scottish Art Review
Soc Friends Dunblane Cathedral	Society of Friends of Dunblane Cathedral
SSAP	Scottish Survey of Architectural Practices
SSCR J	Scottish Society for Conservation and Restoration Journal
Trans Edinburgh Architect Ass	Transactions of the Edinburgh Architectural Association
Trans Scot Eccles Soc	Transactions of the Scottish Ecclesiological Society

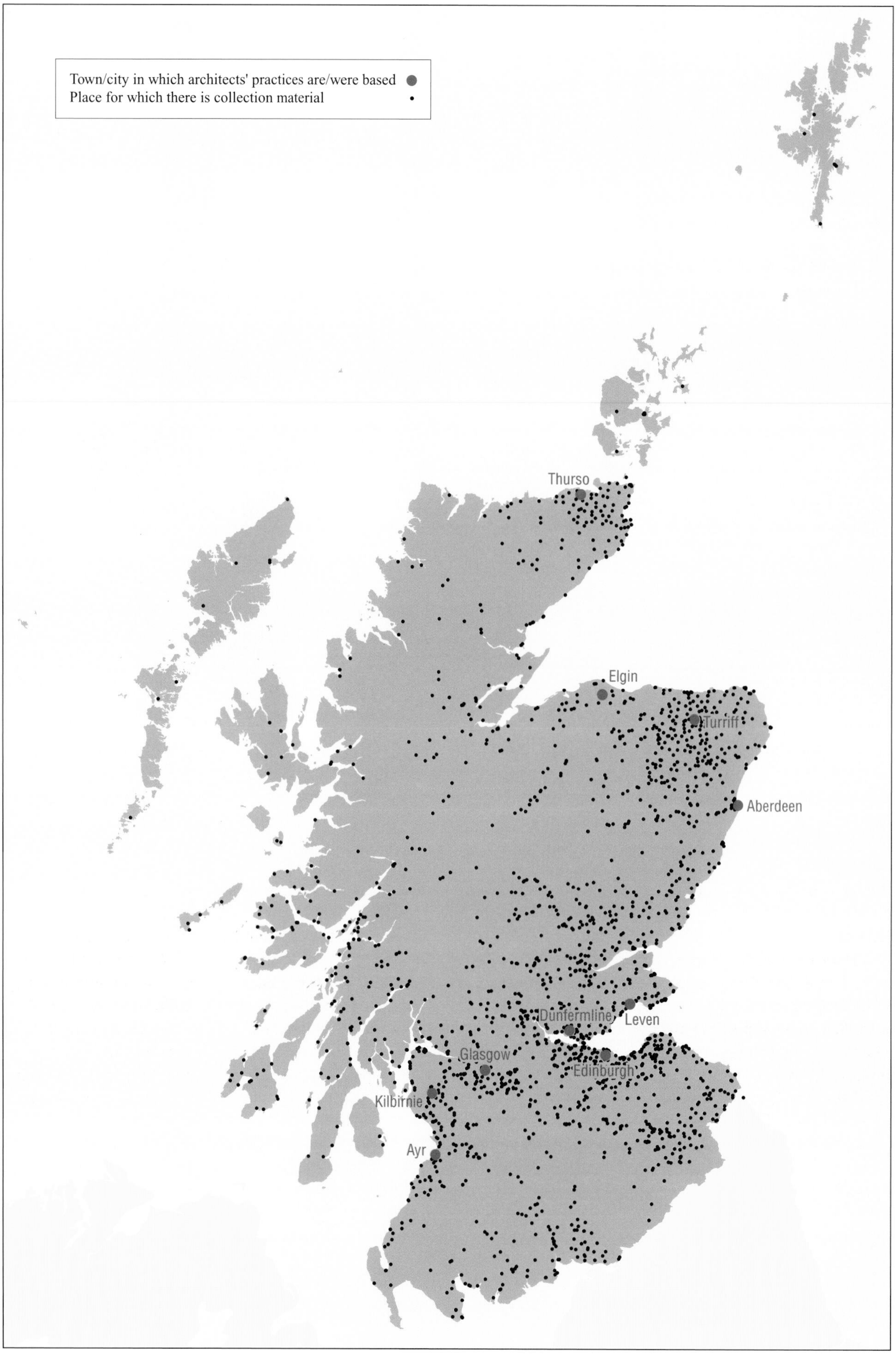

Distribution map showing where the practices were based and places for which there is collection material.

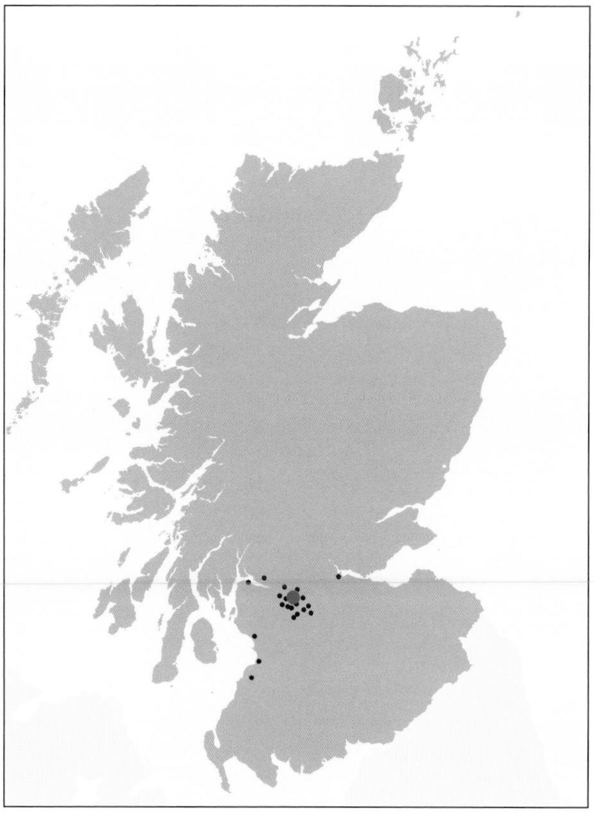

Buchanan Campbell

Provenance
The Buchanan Campbell Collection (Accession No. 1995/8) was gifted to RCAHMS in 1995 by Alexander Buchanan Campbell following the closure of the practice at 1 Royal Crescent, Glasgow. Forty-eight books and periodicals, covering a wide range of architectural subjects, were donated in addition to the drawings and practice papers.

History
Alexander Buchanan Campbell was born 14 June 1914. In the early 1930s he worked as an assistant at the Gillespie Kidd & Coia practice during which time he studied architecture four nights a week at Glasgow School of Architecture, first at Glasgow School of Art, where Jack Coia (1898-1981) taught, before changing to full-time study at the Royal Technical College of Science and Technology.

Campbell registered with the RIAS as an architect in 1937. The following year T Harold Hughes engaged him as a studio instructor at Glasgow School of Architecture for six months. He then gained employment in Liverpool with Cunard as a designer on the *Queen Elizabeth*. In 1939 Campbell returned to Glasgow and was called up for military service, working for a time in the Design and Inspection Branch of War Office Prefabrication in London.

After the war Campbell returned to the Glasgow City Architect's office before establishing his own practice in 1950, the same year that he became a governor of Glasgow School of Architecture. The practice moved from 128 Elderslie Street to 1 Royal Crescent *c.*1966-7. During this period Campbell's elder brother John worked at the practice for a short period following his retirement from the Education Department of Glasgow Corporation. By 1995 the practice had closed.

Scope and Content
The Buchanan Campbell Collection consists of approximately 11,300 items of which 5,481 items have been catalogued, encompassing 53 projects undertaken by the practice. The remainder have been hand-listed.

The Collection contains all projects commissioned by East Kilbride Town Council and the neighbouring 5th District Council of Blantyre; these projects constitute almost 40% of the catalogued material and show the development of public facilities in the New Town during the 1960s. Included are acquired papers from the East Kilbride Development Corporation for the provision and layout of leisure space, and the allocation of bus shelters, throughout the town; Campbell's designs for a library and public hall for the Murray district (*c.*1961-64); and designs for the town cleansing depot with its accompanying office at Dundas Street (1964-67). Approximately 1,275 drawings dating from *c.*1961 to 1969 document comprehensively Campbell's best known project, the Dollan Baths, Brouster Hill, East Kilbride (1961-69). There are a further 585 drawings for the adjacent Key Experimental Youth Centre (1966-70).

The remainder of catalogued papers range in date from the late 1940s to the early 1990s. The earliest drawings by Campbell himself are predominantly of

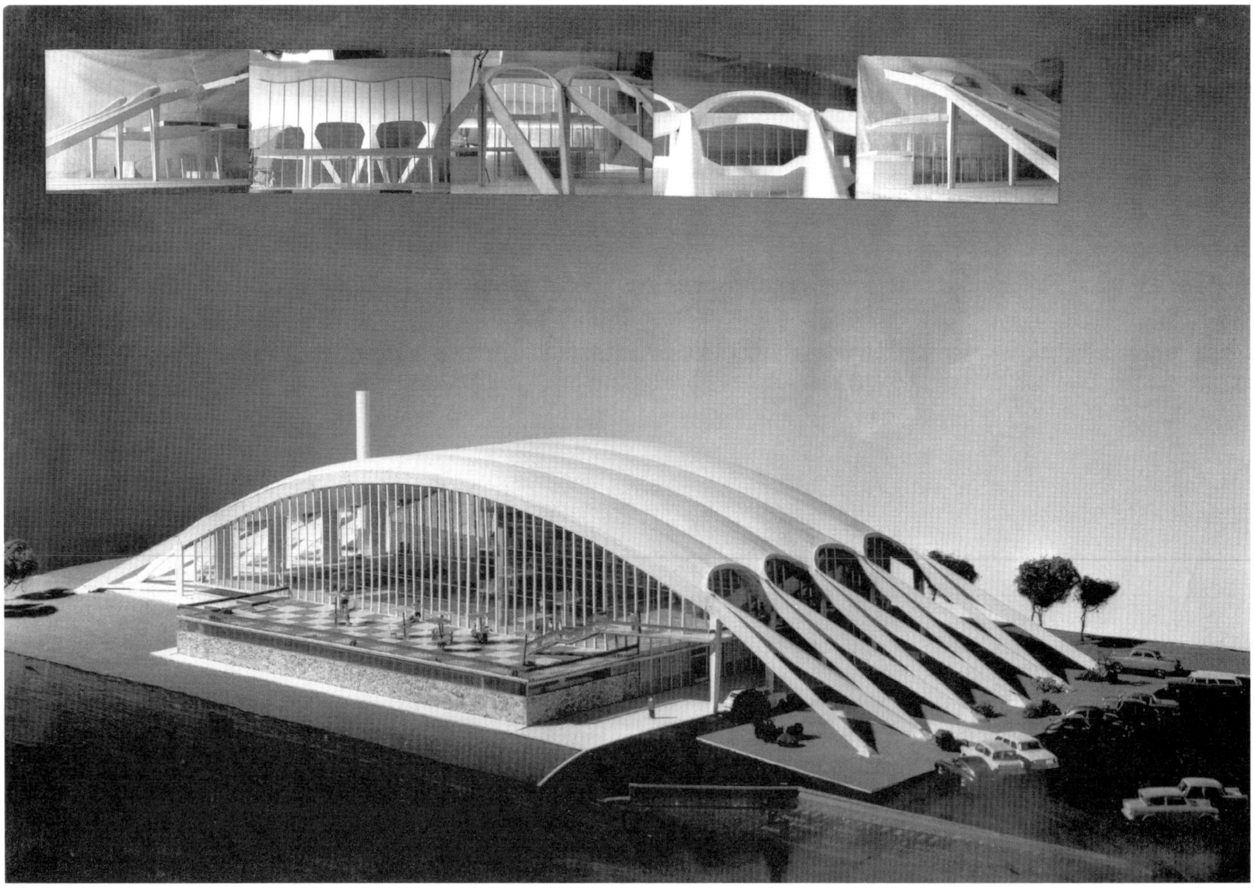

Photographic views of model for Dollan Baths, Brouster Hill, East Kilbride by Alexander Buchanan Campbell, c.1961-66, from the Buchanan Campbell Collection. [SC883762]

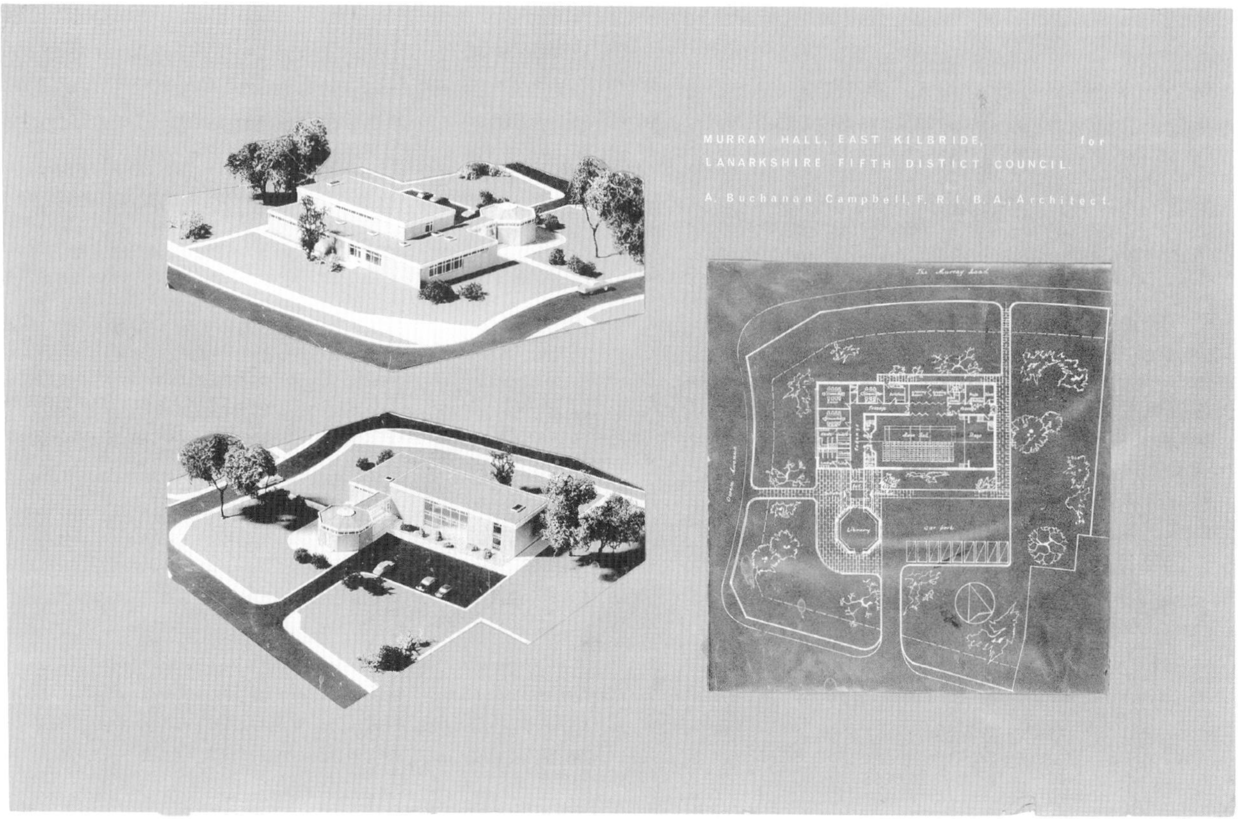

Plan and photographic views of a model of Murray Hall, Liddell Grove, East Kilbride by Alexander Buchanan Campbell, c.1963, from the Buchanan Campbell Collection. [SC883758]

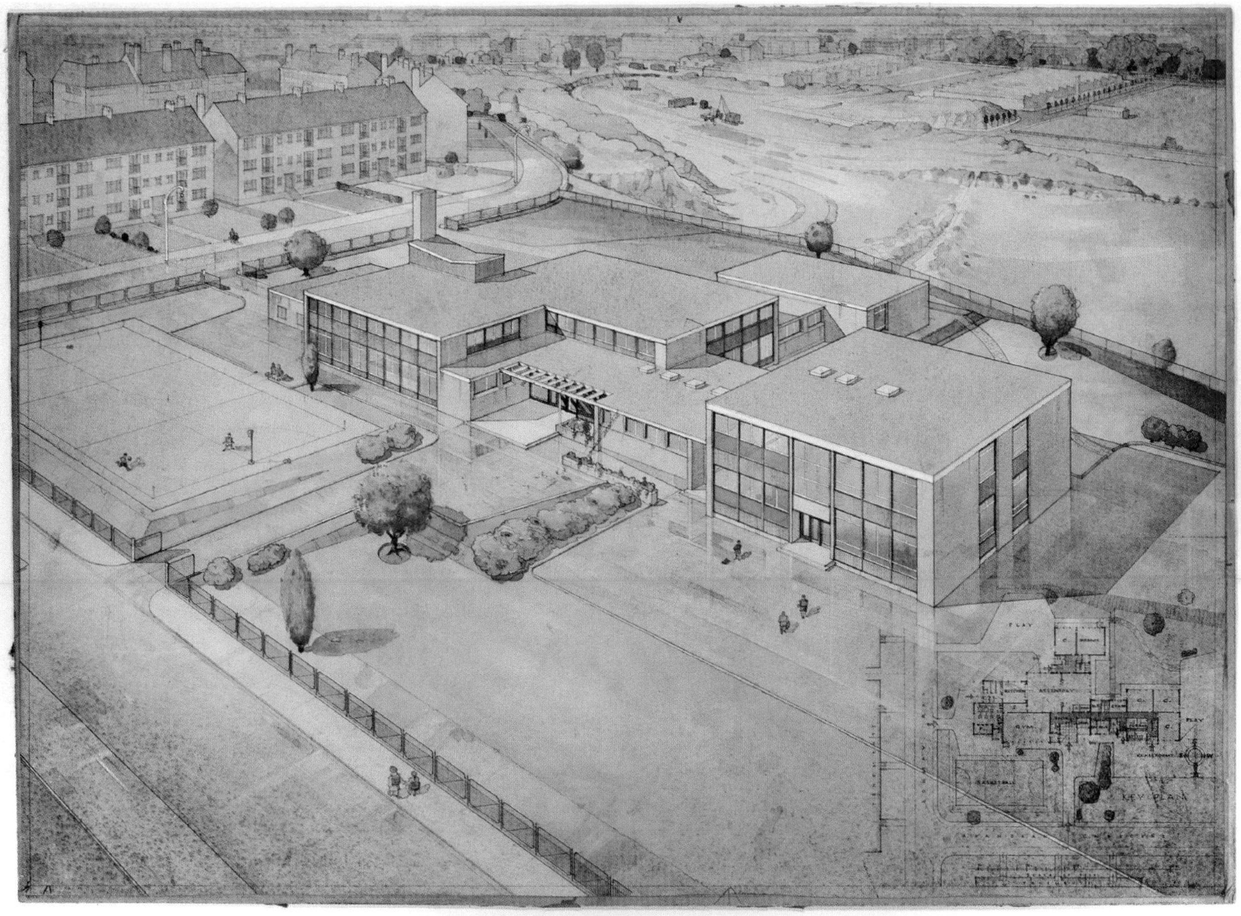

Perspective view and plan of Queenslie Primary School, Easterhouse, Glasgow by Alexander Buchanan Campbell, 1957, from the Buchanan Campbell Collection. [SC883730]

exhibition stands and commercial interiors, including Gentles & Morrison Ltd at 348 Sauchiehall Street, Glasgow (1954-63), which was part of Alexander 'Greek' Thomson's Grecian Chambers (1867-68).

Churches designed by the practice for the Roman Catholic Diocese of Motherwell date from the 1950s and include a temporary church at Glebe Street, East Kilbride (1954-55); St Bride's Church, Fallside Road, Bothwell (1955-56); and St Mary's RC Church, Cadzow Street, Hamilton (1957). Two later commissions for the Church of Scotland – Priesthill Church, Priesthill Road, Glasgow (*c*.1964-72) and St George's and St Peter's Church, Boyndie Street, Glasgow (*c*.1972-73) – are also included.

As a result of his work in the City Architect's office, Campbell received many commissions during the 1950s and early 1960s designing schools for the Corporation of Glasgow. Examples in the Collection include the Ladyloan Primary School, Drumchapel (1955-57, now demolished); Queenslie Primary School, Easterhouse, Glasgow (1957-58, now demolished); and St Teresa's RC Primary School (1959-64). The practice's designs for the Vale of Leven Academy, Middleton Street, Alexandria (*c*.1956-64) for the Dunbartonshire County Council have also been catalogued.

A significant client during the 1960s was the Scottish Council for the Training of Teachers. There are 954 papers showing all phases of Craigie College, Ayr (*c*.1963-71), which was one of the first new training colleges to be built in Scotland for over 40 years and for which Campbell received a Class I award from the Civic Trust in 1966. The project includes alterations to the 18th century Craigie house, also part of the campus. The Collection also contains papers showing alterations to Gillespie Kidd & Coia's Notre Dame College, at Bearsden (1977-88).

Within the section of the Collection that remains uncatalogued there are drawings for other educational commissions such as Callendar Park College, Falkirk (opened 1964); an extension to Ardrossan Academy, Ardrossan (*c*.1969); the renovation of the swimming pool at Jordanhill College of Education, Glasgow (*c*.1971); and alterations and additions to the Roman Catholic Notre Dame College of Education, Dowanhill, Glasgow (*c*.1960-80).

In the early 1950s Frank Mickel (b.1908) of the Mactaggart & Mickel building company appointed Campbell as company architect. The Mactaggart & Mickel Collection (Accession No. 2000/98), gifted to RCAHMS by the building company of the same name, contains many copies of drawings by the Campbell practice for housing such as Broom Housing Estate, Renfrewshire (*c*.1953-73); housing at Eaglesham, Renfrewshire (*c*.1955-65); six-storey flats at Great Western Road, Glasgow (*c*.1953-60, unexecuted); and Ascot Flats, Kelvinside, Glasgow (*c*.1981-85). To avoid duplication, no housing designed by Campbell for Mactaggart & Mickel was catalogued during the project except for a scheme for a cinema and shop complex, Carmunnock Road, Glasgow (1953-54).

Other projects that have only been listed but not catalogued include flats at Garscadden Policies,

Drumchapel, Glasgow (*c.*1961-70); Glenochil Young Offenders' Institute (*c.*1973); Church at Baljaffray, Bearsden, Glasgow for the Church of Scotland Home Board (*c.*1973-78); and rehabilitation work for the West of Scotland Housing Association at Keppochhill Road, Springburn, Glasgow (*c.*1984-87).

Only six drawings for Wishaw Shopping Centre, designed by the practice in the 1970s, were found in the Collection. These have been catalogued.

The Collection includes 16 acquired drawings (1928-30) of the Gillespie & Kidd Ca d'Oro extension to John Honeyman's F & J Smith warehouses, Gordon Street and Union Street, Glasgow, detailing fourth floor catering and dancehall facilities added during the late 1920s and removed after fire damage in the late 1980s.

References

NMRS Sources

- Taped interview with Mr Alexander Buchanan Campbell carried out by Neil Gregory and Diane Watters in August 2003.
- Photographs of the removal of the Collection from Glasgow to Edinburgh in 1995.
- 48 books from the Buchanan Campbell Collection office in the NMRS library.

Glendinning, M and Watters, D (eds) 1999 *Home Builders: Mactaggart and Mickel and the Scottish Housebuilding Industry.* Edinburgh: RCAHMS.
Glendinning, M, MacInnes, R and Page, D 1993 *Scotland the Brave New World: Scotland Rebuilt, 1945-1970*. Edinburgh: RIAS.
Rogerson, R W K C 1986 *Jack Coia: His Life and His Work.* Glasgow: Robert W K C Rogerson.
Spring, M 1995 'Splash Hit', *Building Renewal,* 9 June 1995.

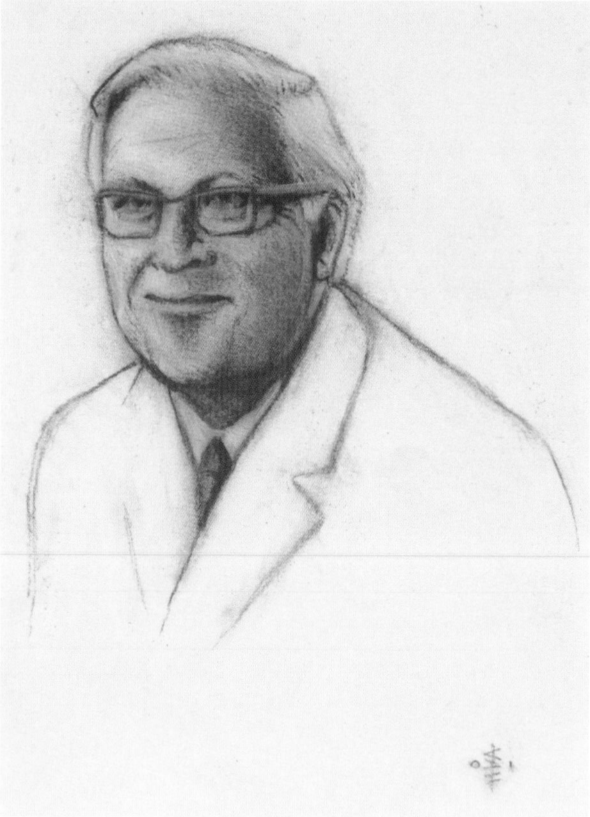

Alexander Buchanan Campbell (b.1914). [DP002564]

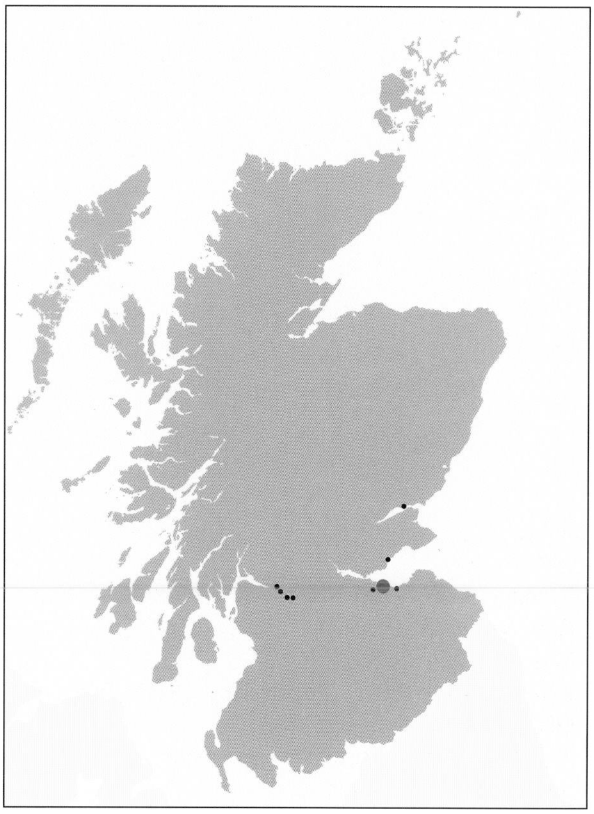

Carr & Matthew

Provenance
The Carr & Matthew Collection (Accession No. 2001/75) was deposited by Stewart Tod, senior partner in David Carr Architects, at the RIAS in 1982. It was later transferred to RCAHMS as part of the McKean Collection in 1999. In 1994, a further gift of photographs and drawings was made to RCAHMS.

History
The practice of Carr & Howard was formed in 1936 when David Carr (1905-1986) went into partnership with W F Howard following a successful joint competition entry for the design of Kirkcaldy Municipal Buildings. The two men had met earlier, in 1934, in the office of Sir Herbert Baker (1862-1946) in London and worked together on competition entries. The partnership did not become official until 1936 when it moved to 30 Rutland Square, Edinburgh. Howard remained based in England for the duration of their partnership.

In 1950 Carr moved to 14 Lynedoch Place, Edinburgh, and formed an additional partnership with Stuart Russell Matthew (1912-1996). The son of John Fraser Matthew (1875-1955), Stuart Matthew had taken over Lorimer & Matthew's office (17 Great Stuart Street, Edinburgh) from his father in 1946. Known as Carr & Matthew, the two architects worked together until 1959. Carr continued his partnership concurrently with Howard from the same address.

In 1959 David Carr Architects was set up at 43 Manor Place, Edinburgh. In 1955, during the partnership with Matthew, Carr had begun to work with Stewart Tod. Tod became a partner in 1970. Carr retired in 1977 and in 1985 the practice was renamed Stewart Tod & Partners.

Scope and Content
The Collection comprises 544 drawings and 591 photographs dating from the 1920s to the 1980s and including projects by both Carr & Howard and Carr & Matthew.

The photographs consist of survey and construction images as well as copies of competition entries for public buildings by Carr & Howard in the 1930s. The practice's best known project, Kirkcaldy Municipal Buildings, is represented in the Collection by 20 photographs of plans, sections and elevations from 1938 and photographic views from when the building was finished in 1956. Other examples in the Collection include photographic copies of designs for Parliament House, Zimbabwe [then Rhodesia] (1936); St Georges Hospital, London (1939); and a number of English civic centres including Tunbridge Wells (1934), Newport (1936) and Scunthorpe (1937). Also included are survey and construction photographs of Hopetoun House Mausoleum (*c.*1950); Daniel Stewart's College, Edinburgh (*c.*1969); and Forsyth's, 26-30 Princes Street, Edinburgh (1950-70).

In 1938, the threat of war instigated a government policy to commission designs from civilian architects for new housing developments, anticipating an increased need immediately after the war. Carr & Howard designed several schemes for the Scottish Special Housing Association (SSHA), and the

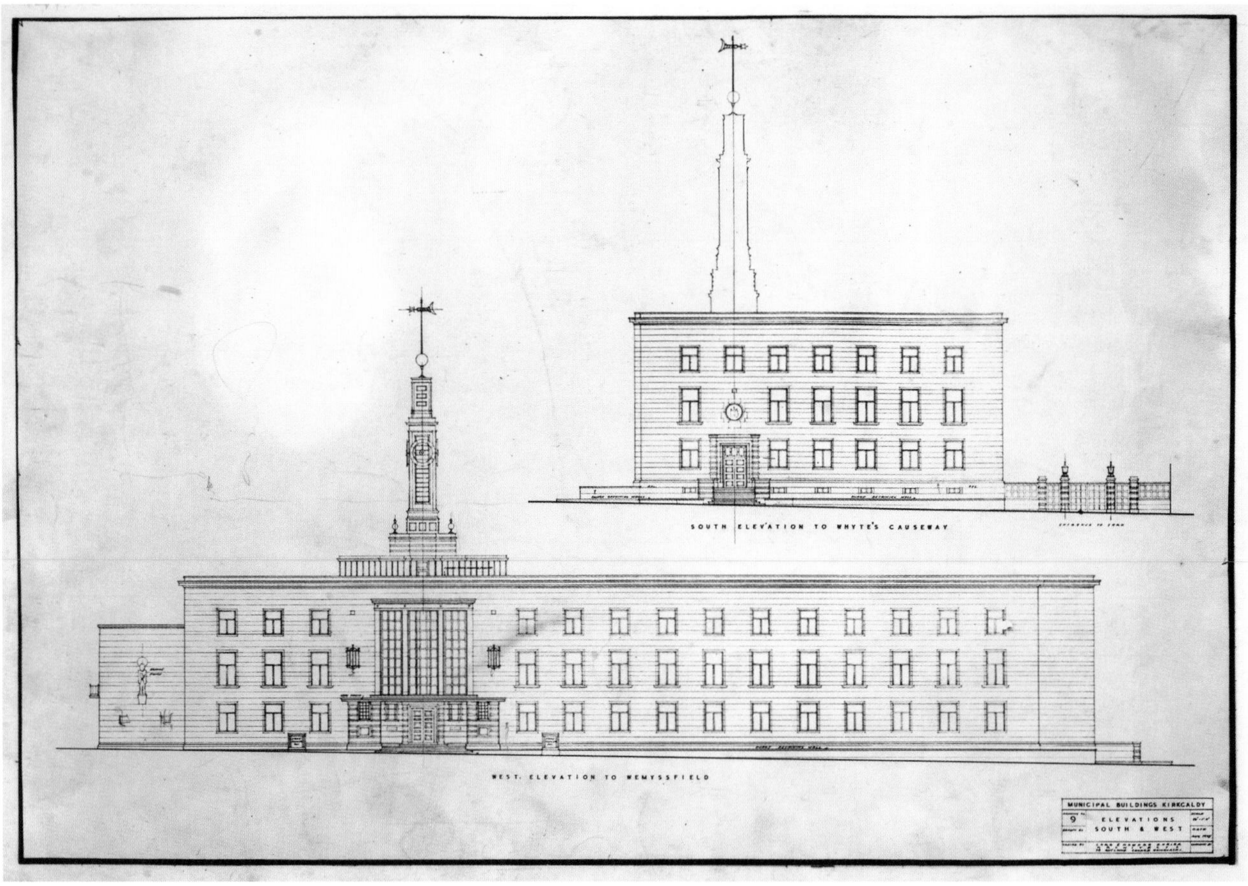

South and West elevations of Kirkcaldy Municipal Buildings by Carr & Howard, 1938, from the Carr & Matthew Collection. [DP002280]

Competition design for Newport Civic Centre, Wales by Carr & Howard, 1936, from the Carr & Matthew Collection. [DP001865]

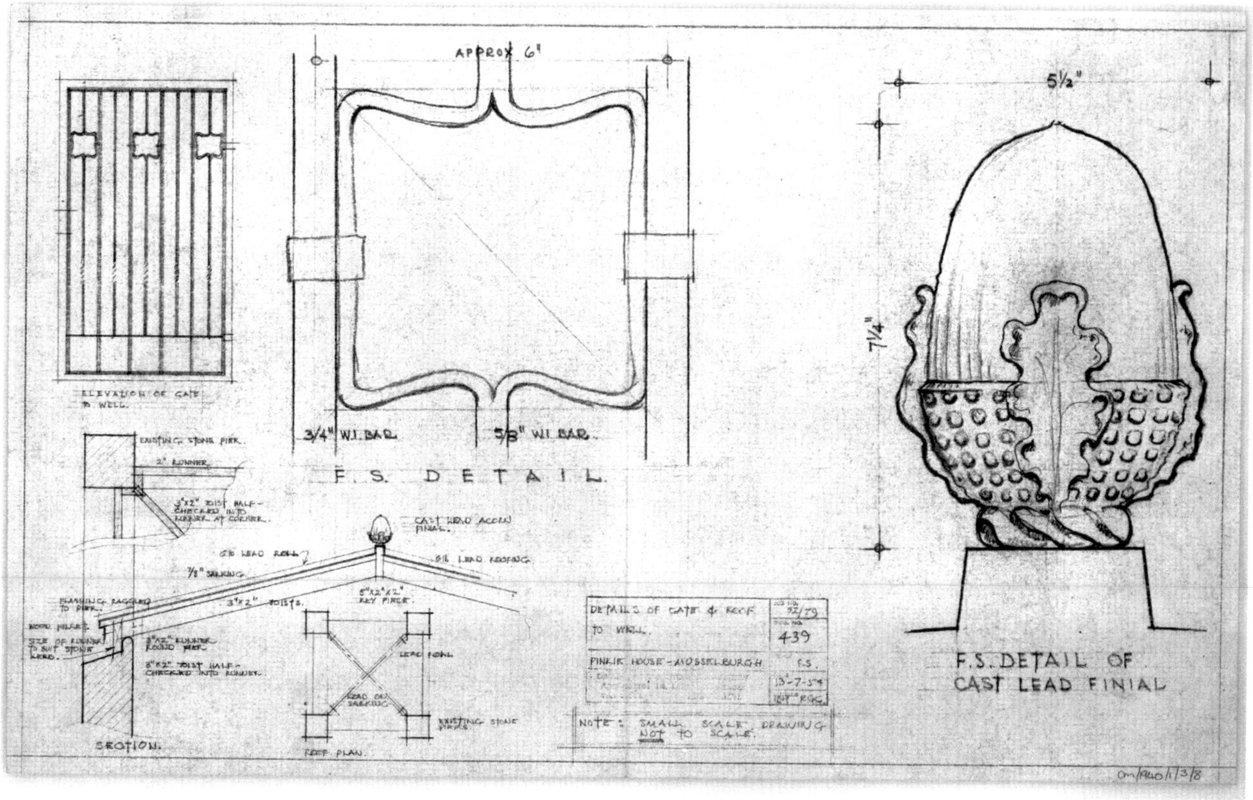

Details of gate and roof to well at Pinkie House, Musselburgh by David Carr & Stuart Matthew, 1954, from the Carr & Matthew Collection. [SC758642]

Stuart Matthew (1912-1996). [SC892408]

Collection contains photographic copies of drawings for economical timber houses in Polbeth, West Calder and Kirknewton (1938). The Collection also contains drawings of housing schemes in war-damaged Clydebank by Carr & Matthew for Nairn Street (1953-58), Mountblow (1959-61), and Perth Crescent (1960-67).

Within the Collection there are drawings for one of the practice's major clients, Loretto School (formerly Pinkie House), Musselburgh. Dating from 1947 to 1961 the material includes work from the office of Lorimer & Matthew. Many other post-1945 projects by Carr & Matthew, including The Royal Blind Asylum, Edinburgh (1950-56), are held in the Lorimer & Matthew Collection.

The Collection includes drawings by Dick Peddie & Walker Todd for Merchiston Castle School (1926-29), where Carr & Matthew carried out alterations and additions from 1956 onwards.

References

NMRS Sources

- A collection of David Carr's papers was purchased by NMRS in 1995 (Accession No. 1995/47).

Anon. 1996 'Obituary: Stuart Matthew', *The Scotsman*, 25 May 1996.

Matthew, S 1988 *The Knights and Chapel of the Most Ancient and Most Noble Order of the Thistle: a Panoramic View*. Edinburgh: Eaglebank Publications.

Thomas, J 1999 'Lorimer Papers Saved for Scotland', *Architect Heritage Soc Scot Mag*, no. 8 (Summer 1999), 26. Edinburgh.

Related practices/personnel:
Lorimer & Matthew Collection

For other Carr & Matthew papers:
Dick Peddie & McKay Collection
Lorimer & Matthew Collection

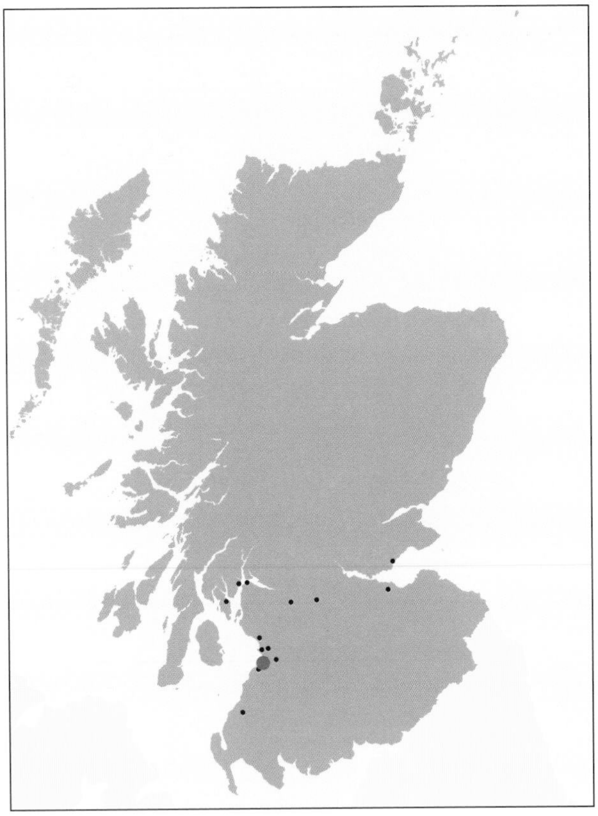

J & J A Carrick

Provenance
The J & J A Carrick Collection (Accession No. 2001/68) was gifted to RIAS by J A Carrick in February 1985 and was transferred to RCAHMS as part of the McKean Collection in 1999.

History
James Carrick (1880-1940) was articled to the Glasgow-based practice of Peter Macgregor Chalmers (1859-1922) in 1893 and six years later became an assistant to James Kennedy Hunter (1863-1929). In 1900 he joined James Miller's (1860-1947) Glasgow office to assist with the Glasgow International Exhibition of 1901, returning to Hunter in 1903. During this time he studied at Glasgow School of Art and at the Glasgow and West of Scotland Technical College under Charles Gourlay (1865-1926) and Alexander MacGibbon (1861-1939). By 1910 he became associate-in-charge (a very early instance of such an arrangement) at Hunter's office, based at 57 Sandgate, Ayr and was elected LRIBA on 19 December of the same year. In 1914 the practice moved to Kingarth, St Leonards Road, Ayr. Hunter retired and Carrick became sole partner in 1928, the same year that the practice moved to Wellington House, 7 Alloway Place, Ayr.

Carrick's son, James Andrew Carrick (1911-1989), was assumed into partnership in 1935, although his name appears on drawings from as early as 1931. Carrick trained at James Miller's practice where he worked under Richard M M Gunn (1889-1933). The practice continued operating throughout central and southern Scotland as J & J A Carrick until 1982 when it merged with Cowie Torry & Partners to become Carrick Cowie Torry. The new partnership took over the practice of T K Irving & Partners of Stranraer in 1985 and in 1999 changed its name to Carricks.

Scope and Content
The Collection represents a selection from the office archive, comprising 100 drawings, including several presentation drawings, and 53 photographs. This material encompasses 14 projects from the West of Scotland dating 1931 to 1939, and includes villas in Greenfield Avenue, Alloway (built 1930-34); premises for the Irvine and Fullarton Co-operative Society Limited, High Street, Irvine (1931); Coatbridge public baths and swimming pool (1934); the restoration of Stair House, Ayrshire (begun 1934); Cragburn Pavilion, Gourock (1935); Ayr Ice Rink (1937); Rothesay Pavilion, Bute (1937); and a villa on Ottoline Drive, Troon (1938).

References
NMRS Sources
- A job list detailing over 300 projects undertaken by the practice, many of which are not in the Collection, is available for consultation.

Perspective view of Cragburn Pavilion, Albert Road, Gourock by J & J A Carrick, 1935, from the J & J A Carrick Collection. [SC407227]

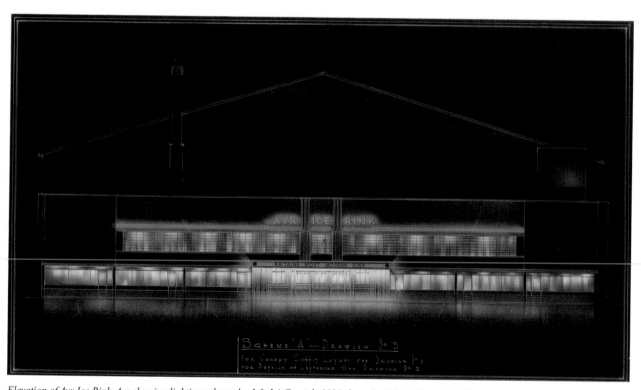

Elevation of Ayr Ice Rink, Ayr showing lighting scheme by J & J A Carrick, 1938, from the J & J A Carrick Collection. [SC752246]

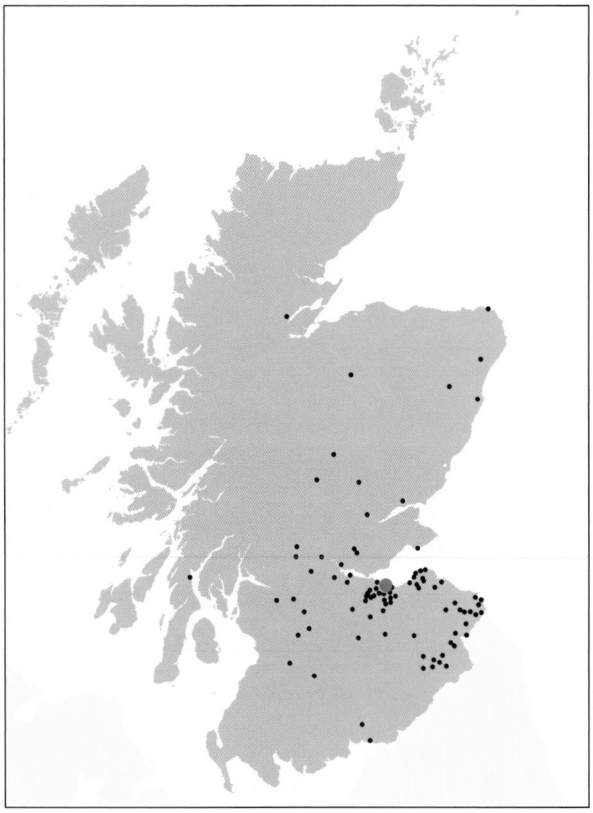

Cowie & Seaton

Provenance

The Cowie & Seaton Collection (Accession No. 1992/52) was gifted to RIAS by Douglas William Seaton on his retirement in 1993 and transferred to RCAHMS as part of the McKean Collection in 1999. The Collection consists of material from the Leadbetter Fairley & Reid; Morton J H Cowie; Cowie & D Gardiner Hardie; and Cowie & Seaton practices.

All papers dating before 1960 in the Collection had evidently been stored flat. Newspapers dated Spring 1970 had been used to separate projects from each other, suggesting that reorganisation of the Collection had perhaps taken place around the time of Morton J H Cowie's retirement.

History

The practice was established by Thomas Greenshields Leadbetter (1859-1931), who set up practice in 1884 at 122 George Street, Edinburgh, a building that was owned by John Dick Peddie (1824-1891) and also occupied by Sydney Mitchell (1856-1930) around the same date. Leadbetter's family were Lanarkshire and Roxburghshire landed gentry, and most of his work consisted of country house commissions for friends and relations. James McLellan Fairley (1860-1942) was born in 1860 and apprenticed to Hippolyte Jean Blanc (1844-1917) in 1875. Thereafter he spent five years in the offices of Wardrop & Reid, Archibald Macpherson, Walter Wood Robertson of the Office of Works and Sydney Mitchell. He passed the RIBA qualifying exam in 1886 and became an associate on 21 June of that year, his proposers being Arthur Cates (1829-1901), George Washington Browne (1853-1939), John Kinross (1855-1931) and Leadbetter (although seemingly not a fellow of the institute). Fairley seems to have begun practice on his own account by 1886 although the inclusion of Leadbetter's name on his nomination form suggests that he may have been assisting with Leadbetter's practice.

In 1895 Fairley went into partnership with Leadbetter shortly after he moved to 17 Young Street, Edinburgh. Leadbetter remained an active partner in the new firm of Leadbetter & Fairley until about 1909, continuing to be responsible for projects in which he had a particular interest beyond that date. Following Leadbetter's retirement, Fairley took Robert Stirling Reid (1883-1947) into partnership. Prior to this Reid had been apprenticed to Leadbetter & Fairley from 1901 to 1905 and had also spent some years with Dick Peddie & George Washington Browne, and Dick Peddie & Forbes Smith.

At some point during the 1930s Morton J H Cowie (d.1972) joined the practice. Cowie, a student member of the RIAS between 1930 and 1932, qualified as an architect in 1933 and carried out a small amount of business from his parents' home at 'Durrisdeere', 30 St John's Road, Edinburgh. Between 1935 and 1940 he was involved in a part-time partnership with D Gardiner Hardie based in a boarding house at 11 Melville Street, Leith.

In 1946 Reid retired from Leadbetter Fairley & Reid, dying shortly afterwards. Cowie, who had returned to the practice after service in the war, moved business

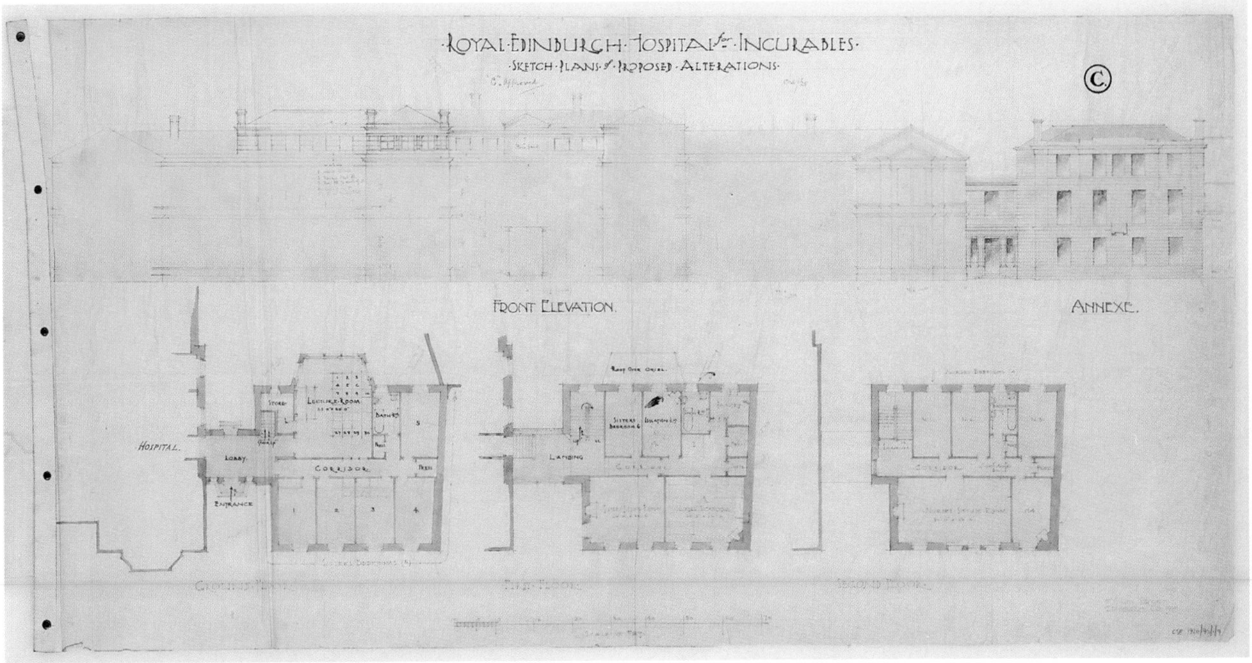

Plans and elevation showing alterations to Longmore Hospital, Salisbury Place, Edinburgh by Leadbetter Fairley & Reid, 1923-4, from the Cowie & Seaton Collection. [SC709060]

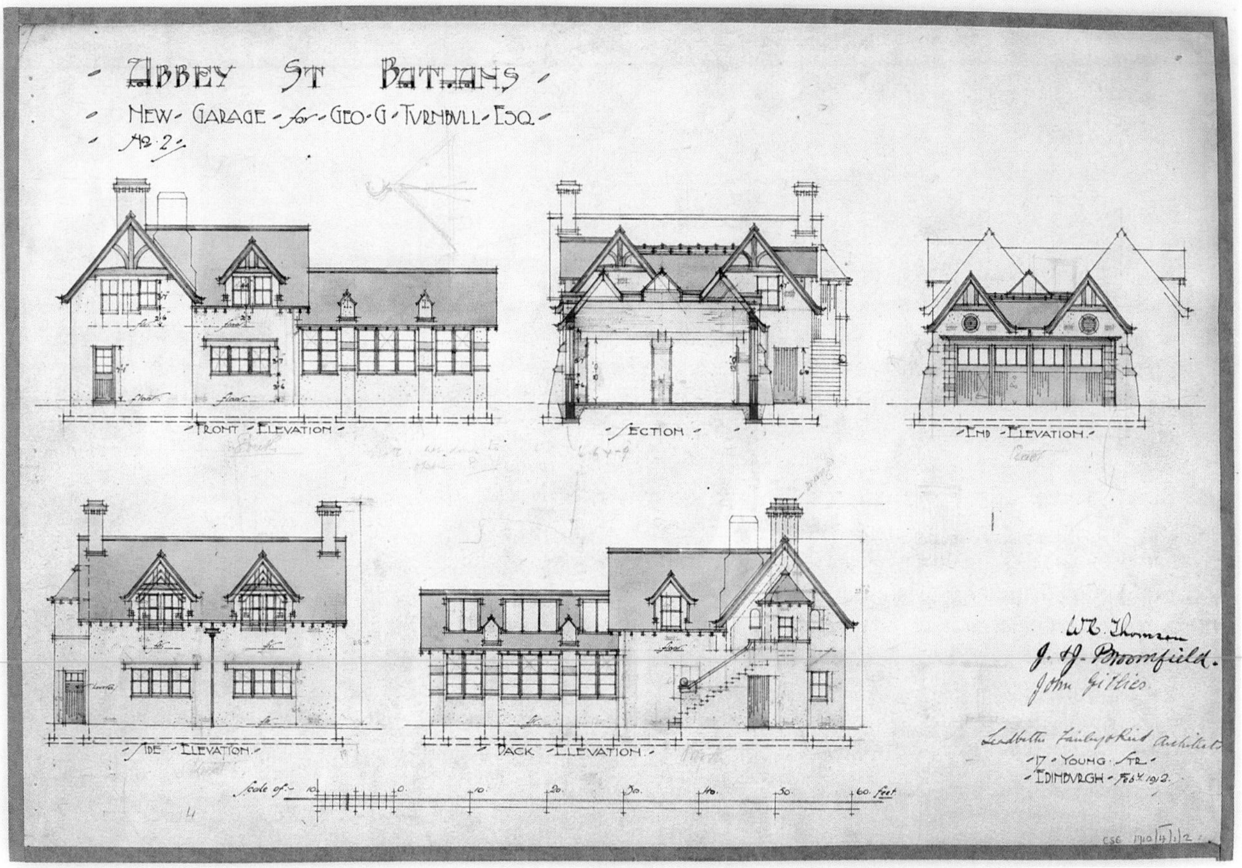

Section and elevations of garage at Abbey St Bathans, Berwickshire by Leadbetter Fairley & Reid, 1912, from the Cowie & Seaton Collection. [SC709073]

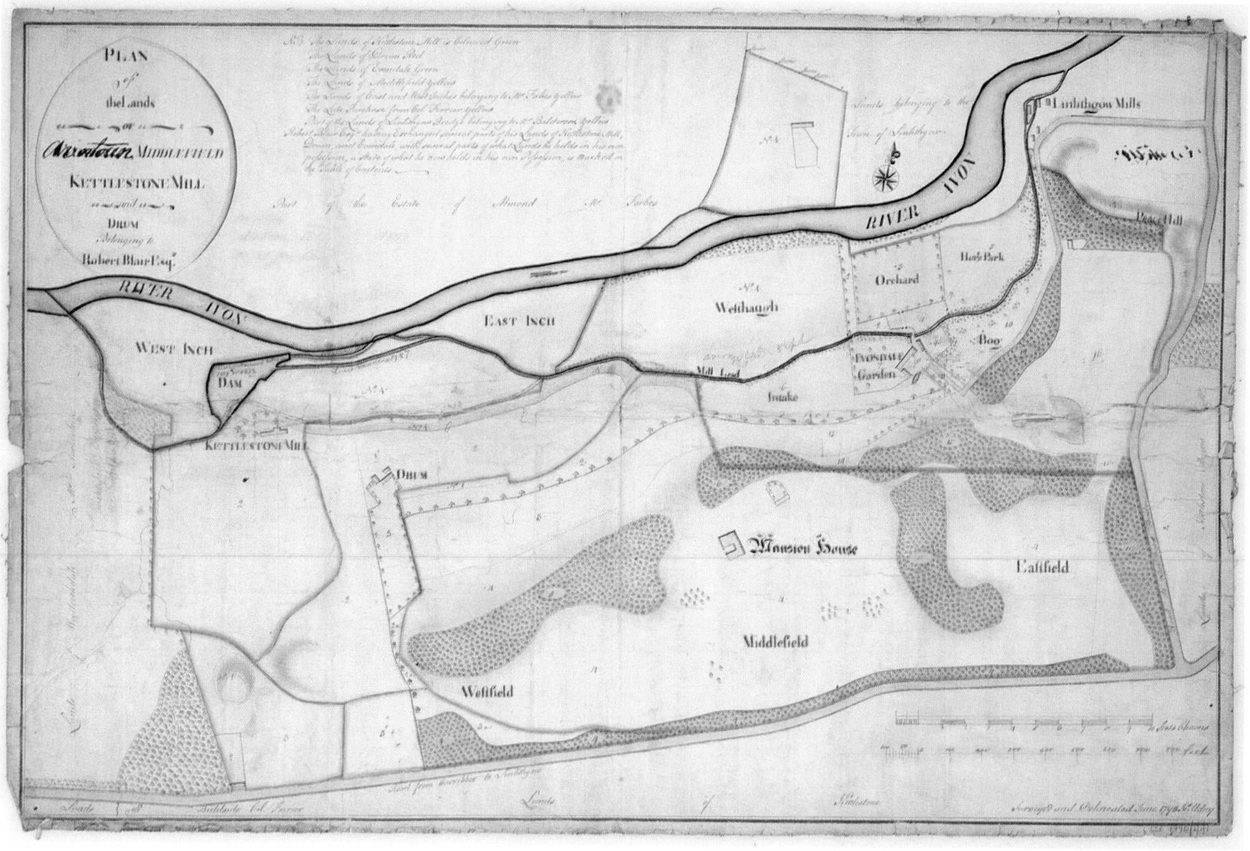

Plan showing the lands of Avontoun, Middlefield, Kettlestone Mill and Drum, West Lothian by Joseph Udny, 1793, from the Cowie & Seaton Collection. This is the earliest drawing in the SAPPP collections and shows the original location of J & G Cox Glue Works, a client of Cowie & Seaton. [SC709208]

in the Summer of 1948 to 53 Manor Place, Edinburgh, premises which had been altered by Leadbetter Fairley & Reid to form offices in 1947. The practice was renamed Morton J H Cowie. In 1961 Cowie took Douglas William Seaton into partnership to form Morton J H Cowie & Seaton. Cowie retired in 1970 and Seaton continued the practice under the same name until his own retirement from offices in Castle Terrace.

Scope and Content

5,801 papers from the Cowie & Seaton Collection have been catalogued during the project from a total of 10,388. The catalogued material comprises all projects by Leadbetter Fairley & Reid as well as all projects begun by them in the mid-1940s and finished by the new firm of Morton J H Cowie. Eight Morton J H Cowie projects with acquired drawings of historic interest were also catalogued. The remainder, along with all work by Cowie & Seaton, has been hand-listed.

Approximately 10% of the Collection comprises drawings of various buildings for Edinburgh Academy, Henderson Row, including the library (1899, altered 1930) and a war memorial building with gymnasium and workshops (1922-23). The Collection also features a commission from the North of Scotland Town and Country Bank to convert 24 Charlotte Square, Edinburgh into bank premises (1922-45), along with alterations and improvements to three Edinburgh hospitals: the Deaconess Hospital, 142-144 Pleasance (1924); Longmore Hospital, Salisbury Place (1923-37); and Liberton Cottage Hospital (1924-27). A significant client represented in the Collection is J & G Cox's Glue Works, Gorgie Mills, Edinburgh for whom the practice worked between 1926 and 1960.

The firm carried out a large amount of improvement work to houses in Edinburgh and the surrounding area including many properties in Edinburgh's New Town. This included sanitary improvements, garage accommodation, and the sub-division into flats of properties in the capital's suburbs. Country house work featured in the Collection includes an extension and improvements to Auchendinny House, Midlothian (1914-30); alterations to Bonkyl Lodge, Berwickshire (1935-40); and the restoration of the late 18th century Chesters House in Roxburghshire (1934-40).

From 1939 Cowie & Hardie were involved in the design and construction of air raid shelters across Edinburgh and in 1940 Hardie patented his own shelter design. Cowie's involvement in this work lead to Leadbetter Fairley & Reid providing air raid shelters across the capital and several examples are featured in the Collection.

A particular feature of the Collection is the large number of acquired drawings from other architectural practices, many of which are of national significance, including two drawings by David Bryce (1803-1876) acquired during alteration work at Bourhouse, East Lothian (1939). Seven drawings for Dean Park House, Edinburgh by F T Pilkington (1832-1899) were acquired when Leadbetter Fairley & Reid converted the building into extra school accommodation for Stewart Melville's College for the Merchant Company (1942-46).

Leadbetter Fairley & Reid, and the subsequent practice of Morton J H Cowie, made alterations and

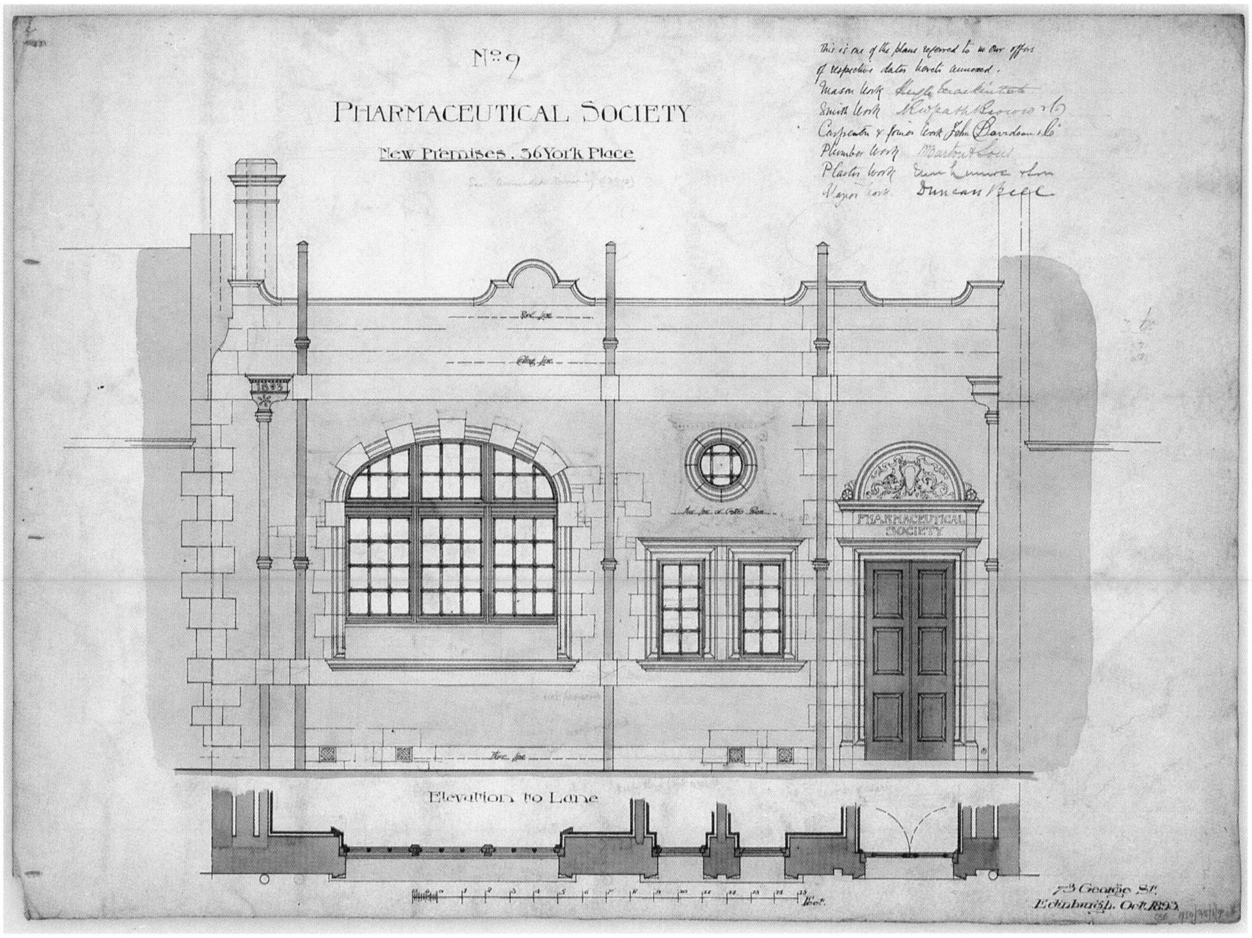

Elevation of the Pharmaceutical Society, 36 York Place, Edinburgh by J Hippolyte Blanc, 1893, from the Cowie & Seaton Collection. The building was extended to the rear by Leadbetter Fairley & Reid, 1934-35. [SC709093]

additions to several buildings that had previously been worked on by the Dick Peddie & McKay practice in its various guises. This is reflected in the Collection which includes drawings by John More Dick Peddie (1853-1921) and James Forbes Smith (1875-1957) for alterations to 7-8 Moray Place and 6 Western Terrace, Edinburgh. There are also 1940s drawings by Dick Peddie McKay & Jamieson for the Viewfield Hotel, Bo'ness and Arthur Lodge on Old Dalkeith Road, Edinburgh, both projects later for Morton J H Cowie.

The Collection also includes drawings of Loretto College, Musselburgh by Robert S Lorimer (1864-1929) that were acquired during work on the East Gate Lodge (*c.*1946), North Esk Lodge (1946-47) and Holme House (*c.*1947); and a bound set of drawings for the Royal Pharmaceutical Society at 36 York Place (1893) by Hippolyte J Blanc (1844-1917) which was extended to the rear by Leadbetter Fairley & Reid (1931-35). Other architectural practices featured in the Collection include Alexander Nisbet Paterson, Rowand Anderson & Paul, Gillespie Kidd & Coia, and Leslie Grahame Thomson (MacDougall).

There are many projects from the first three decades of the Leadbetter Fairley & Reid practice that are not included in the Collection, the bulk of the drawings being from the 1920s onwards. This missing material includes the restoration of Cessnock Castle, Ayrshire (1890); an extension to Craigcrook Castle, Edinburgh (1891); additions to Grandtully Castle, Perthshire and Blairs Castle, Ayrshire (both 1892); and the East Lodge for Dunalastair, Perthshire (1893). Also missing are drawings for Carnegie Library, Wick (*c.*1895-98), although some feature in the Sinclair Macdonald & Son Collection.

Related practices/personnel:
Dick Peddie & McKay Collection

For other Leadbetter Fairley & Reid papers:
Ian G Lindsay Collection
Sinclair Macdonald & Son Collection

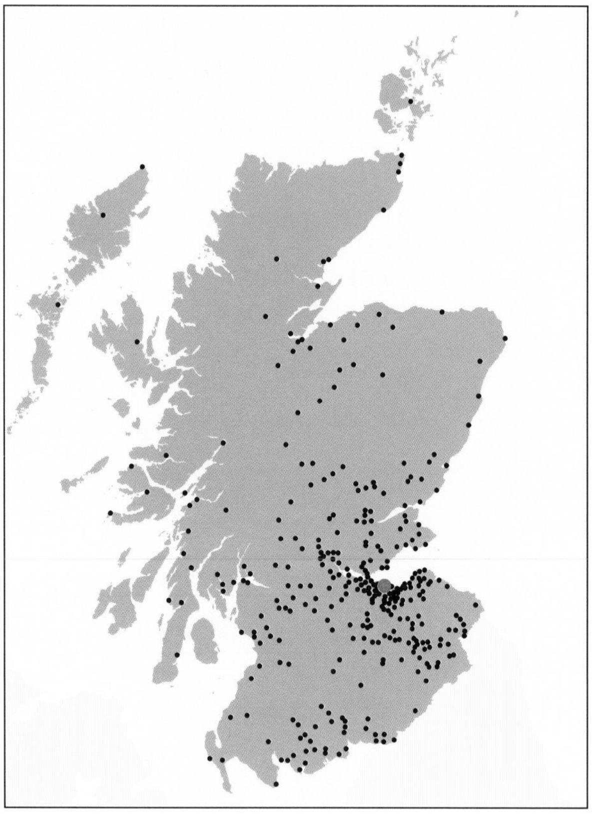

Dick Peddie & McKay

Provenance

In 1999 the Dick Peddie & McKay Collection (Accession No. 1999/90) was acquired by RCAHMS with a purchase grant from the Heritage Lottery Fund. The drawings had been organised in a system that had originated during the early phase of the practice when it was based at 3 South Charlotte Street, Edinburgh, 1860-96. The bins in the wine cellar were numbered and used for storing rolled drawings, which were wrapped in brown paper and tied with string. They were later stored in clear plastic bags. Hand-written labels described the name and address of the project, the number of its original bin location, and its bag number.

The drawings were subsequently moved to the attic of 8 Albyn Place, Edinburgh, where the same numbering system was employed. A hand list was made in 1975-76, which was revised and updated in 1982 and 1996. Further lists were compiled prior to the Collection's removal from 99 Giles Street, Leith to RCAHMS in 1999.

History

The practice was established by John Dick Peddie (1824-1891), an Edinburgh University graduate who became an articled apprentice to David Rhind (1808-1883). Peddie set up independent practice at 36 Albany Street, Edinburgh in 1845 after winning the competition for the United Presbyterian Synod Hall, 4-6 Queen Street, Edinburgh (1845-50). Three years later he moved his practice to 1 George Street, Edinburgh. Around 1854 Peddie was joined by Charles George Hood Kinnear (1830-1894), whose architectural career began when he was articled to David Bryce (1803-1876) in 1849. Peddie & Kinnear became partners in 1856.

Peddie's eldest son, John More Dick Peddie (1853-1921), received his initial training within the practice and then gained wider experience with George Gilbert Scott (1839-1897) in London before setting off on a Grand Tour. He returned to Edinburgh in 1875 and became partner in 1877, the practice becoming Peddie Kinnear & Peddie. Around 1880 his father retired and the practice was renamed Kinnear & Peddie.

In 1896 George Washington Browne (1853-1939), a former partner of Sir Rowand Anderson (1834-1921), joined J M Dick Peddie in a loose partnership to form Peddie & Washington Browne. Working in the practice throughout the 1880s and 1890s was Peddie's younger brother, Walter Lockhart Dick Peddie (1865-1902) and John Wilson (1877-1959). Browne left the practice in 1908, and James Forbes Smith (1875-1957), who had trained in the offices of George Beattie & Son and Sir Robert Rowand Anderson, became a partner.

In 1920 Smith was replaced by William James Walker Todd (1884-1944), who had begun his career as an articled apprentice to T P Marwick (1854-1927) and had previously had his own practice in partnership with Sydney Houghton Miller (1883-1938). Miller was for a time also a partner in Dick Peddie & Walker Todd, but he withdrew and in the 1930s Todd was joined by partners David John Chisholm (1885-1949) and George Lindsay Auldjo Jamieson (1905-*c.*1960). Jamieson had previously worked within his father's practice, Jamieson

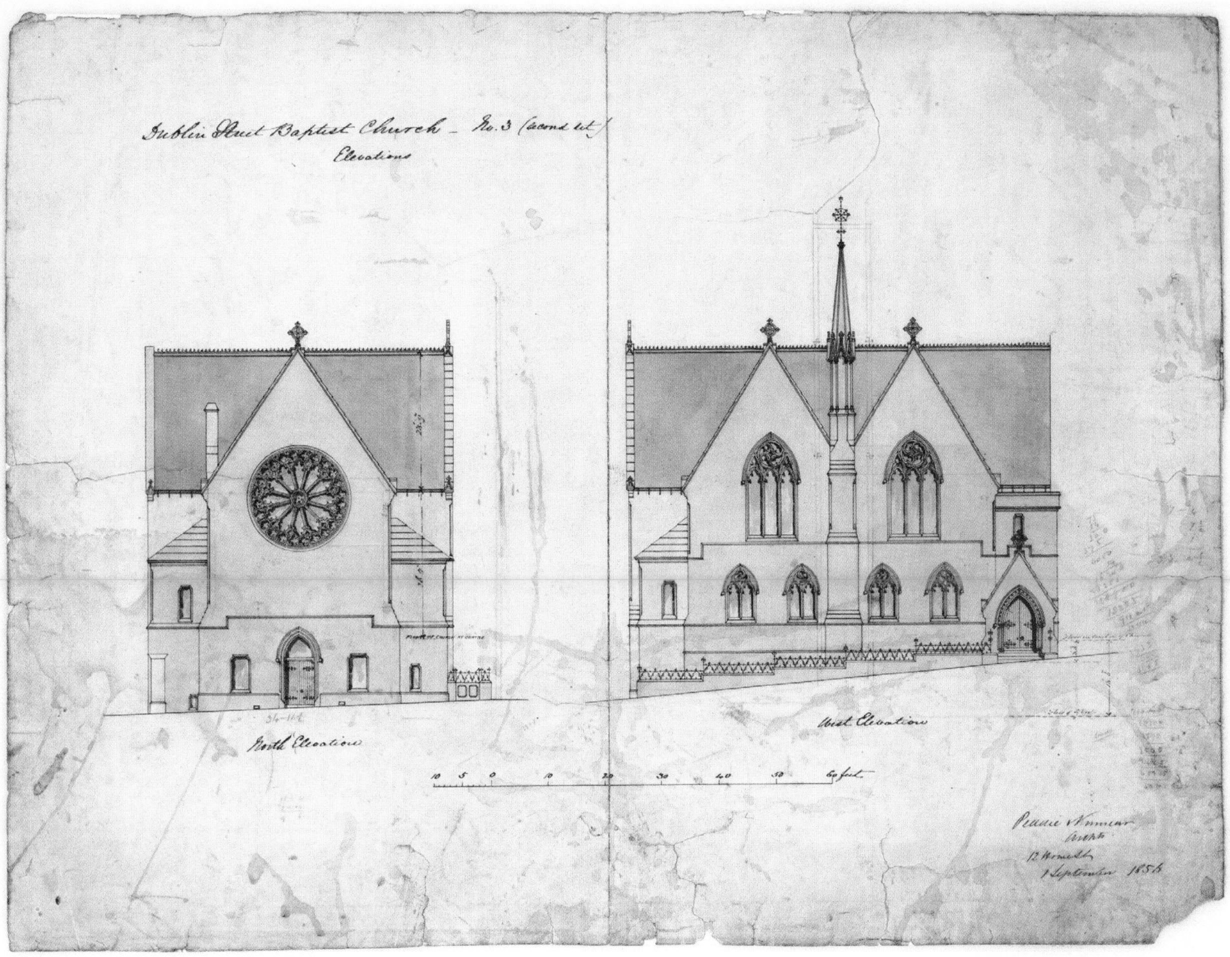

Elevations of the Baptist Church, Dublin Street, Edinburgh by Peddie & Kinnear, 1856, from the Dick Peddie & McKay Collection. [SC672036]

& Arnott at 13 Young Street, Edinburgh, which had taken over the practice of Sydney Mitchell & Wilson when Mitchell retired in 1911.

In 1942 Dick Peddie Todd & Jamieson merged with the practice of John Ross McKay (1884-1962). McKay had previously studied at the Edinburgh College of Art and trained with Sir Robert Lorimer (1864-1929) before forming a partnership in 1920 with James S Richardson (1883-1970), also from Lorimer's office, the practice name being Richardson & McKay. Richardson became full-time principal inspector of Ancient Monuments in the same year but remained a partner in the practice.

From 1942 to the mid 1950s the practice was called Dick Peddie McKay & Jamieson. In this period, two licentiates, Stanley Kennedy and Stanley W Edgar (1920-1991) worked under the direction of Jamieson and McKay respectively. In *c.*1954, Jamieson retired early and McKay became ill. Edgar became senior partner and the practice then became known as Dick Peddie & McKay. Later partners included Ian Scott-Duncan (d.1986), Ronald R Malcolm, Colin R Campbell, Norman J Miller, and Michael C Henderson, who joined the practice in 1974.

In 1987 the practice moved to 44 Constitution Street, Leith and in 1995 to 99 Giles Street, Leith. In October 1998 Dick Peddie & McKay moved to Society Place, West Calder, West Lothian.

Scope and Content

The Dick Peddie & McKay Collection consists of 36,134 drawings, which are a testimony to the practice's reputation as one of Scotland's leading architects of the mid- to late-19th century. The firm worked on a huge variety of building types, and although an Edinburgh-based practice, it is not difficult to find at least one building designed, or significantly altered, by the practice in every major town in Scotland. Within the Collection there are 147 manuscript items, including building specifications, letters, feu contracts and trade literature. The earliest specifications are for the United Presbyterian Church, Anstruther, prepared in 1850.

The Collection includes a number of unsuccessful competition designs, including the Wallace Monument, Stirling (1859) and St Mary's Episcopal Cathedral, Edinburgh (1874). It contains several examples of urban and suburban developments including the development of Chalmers Street, Lauriston, Edinburgh (1854) with terraced houses and flats; and Laverockbank, Trinity, Edinburgh (1843-64) with detached and semi-detached villas. Peddie & Kinnear's role as developers as well as designers is evident, with drawings for Cockburn Street, Edinburgh (*c.*1858-73) – a mixture of commercial and residential accommodation in the Scots Baronial style – and designs for a large proportion of Edinburgh's West End. The Collection also includes later housing schemes, such as Todd's Preston Cross Housing Scheme, Prestonpans (1936-37).

Many country houses feature in the Collection,

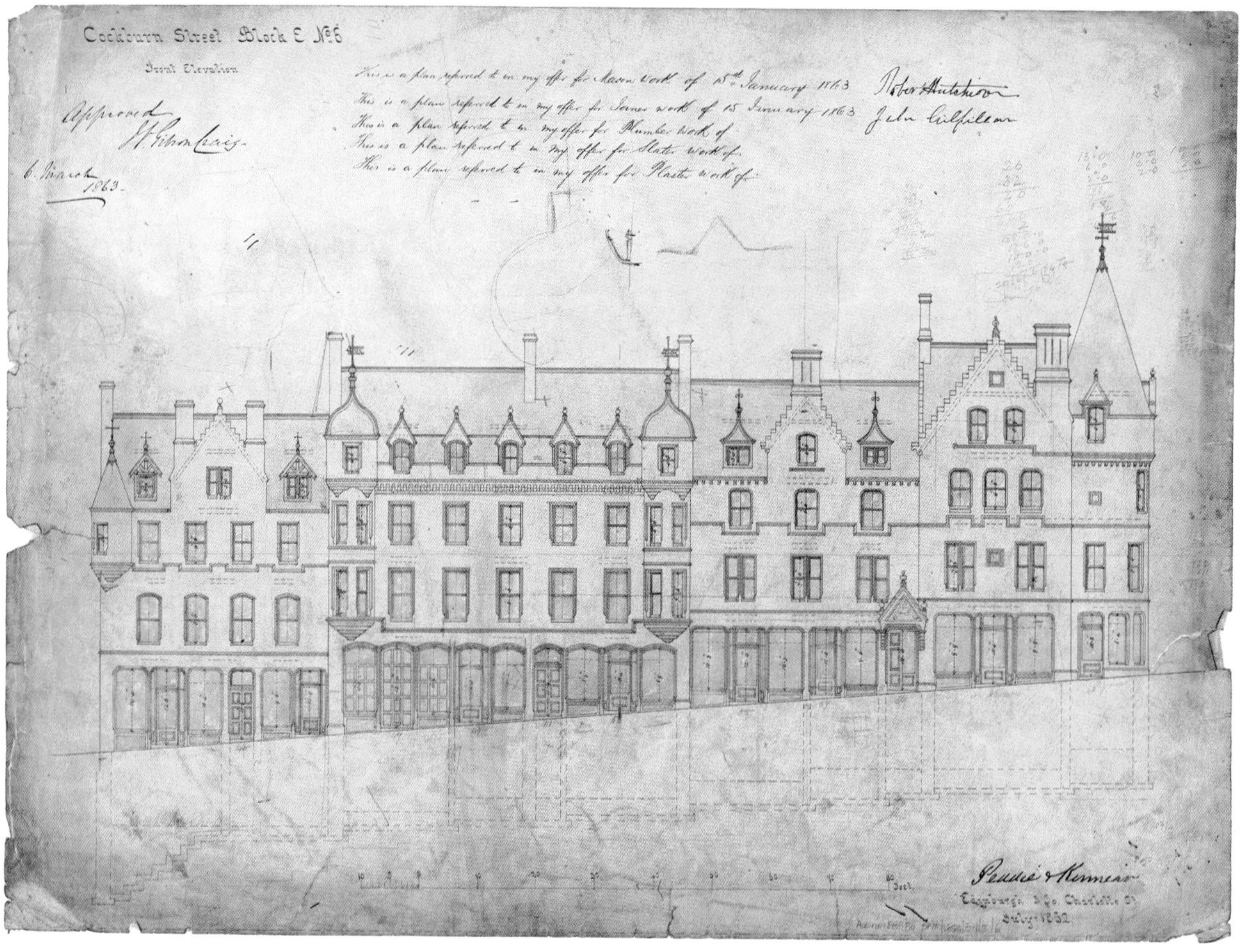

Elevation of Cockburn Street, Edinburgh by Peddie & Kinnear, 1862, from the Dick Peddie & McKay Collection. [SC600868]

including Sorne, subsequently renamed Glengorm, on Mull (1858); the remodelling of Kinnear's family seat at Kinloch, Fife (1859-60, extended 1880-81); Lathallan near Colinsburgh (1864); The Binn, Burntisland (1865); Kinnettles near Forfar (1865); Glenmayne near Galashiels (1866-68); Threave near Castle Douglas (1871); and Drygrange near Melrose (1887).

The church designs in the Collection reflect the great range of plan-types and styles adopted in Scotland. The influence of the Peddie family in the United Presbyterian Church, and the Kinnear family amongst related land-owning families, resulted in many commissions for churches and the practice gained a reputation for church design for a range of Christian denominations. This can be seen in Kinnear & Peddie's designs for Southwick Parish Church, Dumfriesshire (1889-90); the United Presbyterian Church at Sydney Place, Edinburgh (1857); and Dublin Street Baptist Church, Edinburgh (1856-57), which was the first church in Scotland to have a double transept arrangement. The Collection also contains J M Dick Peddie's designs for churches at Coldstream (1906); Melrose (1911); and the Holy Cross Episcopal Church at Davidson's Mains, Edinburgh (1912); as well as the work of McKay as the consulting architect for the Church of Scotland.

Many examples of the practice's designs for schools are included in the Collection, including early commissions undertaken by Peddie at West Linton (1851) and Leith (1853); Peddie & Kinnear's Morgan's Hospital, Dundee (1860-67); designs for Edinburgh College of Art by J M Dick Peddie & Forbes Smith (*c*.1905-27); and Todd's Merchiston Castle School, Edinburgh (1925-30).

The Collection records the practice's commissions for civic buildings, such as Peddie & Kinnear's Greenock Court House on Nelson Street, Greenock (1864-68) and Aberdeen Municipal Buildings on Castle Street and Broad Street (1861-71). In 1935 the practice converted the poorhouse at Peebles into County Buildings and a year later designed the Linlithgow County Buildings, commissioning a presentation drawing from Basil Spence (1907-1976).

The range of hospital work carried out by the practice is represented in the Collection by, for example, Chalmers Hospital, Lauriston Place, Edinburgh (1855-1927); Edinburgh Hospital for Incurables, Salisbury Place, Edinburgh (1878-1947); and Liberton Hospital, Lasswade Road, Edinburgh (1903-14). The Collection contains designs for asylums at Haddington (1860) and Stratheden, Cupar (1863); and poorhouses including South Leith (1848-49), Inveresk (1853,1860) and Stirling (1855).

Commissions from banks and insurance companies are well represented and include 1850s designs for the Royal Bank of Scotland, 1860-70s designs for the Bank of Scotland, and 1890s designs for the British Linen Bank. The period of the Washington Browne and Forbes Smith partnerships was especially rich in large headquarters buildings: included in the Collection are designs for the Edinburgh offices of Standard Life, 3-11 George Street (1897-1901); Scottish Equitable Life at 27-28 St Andrew Square (1897-99); and the Scottish

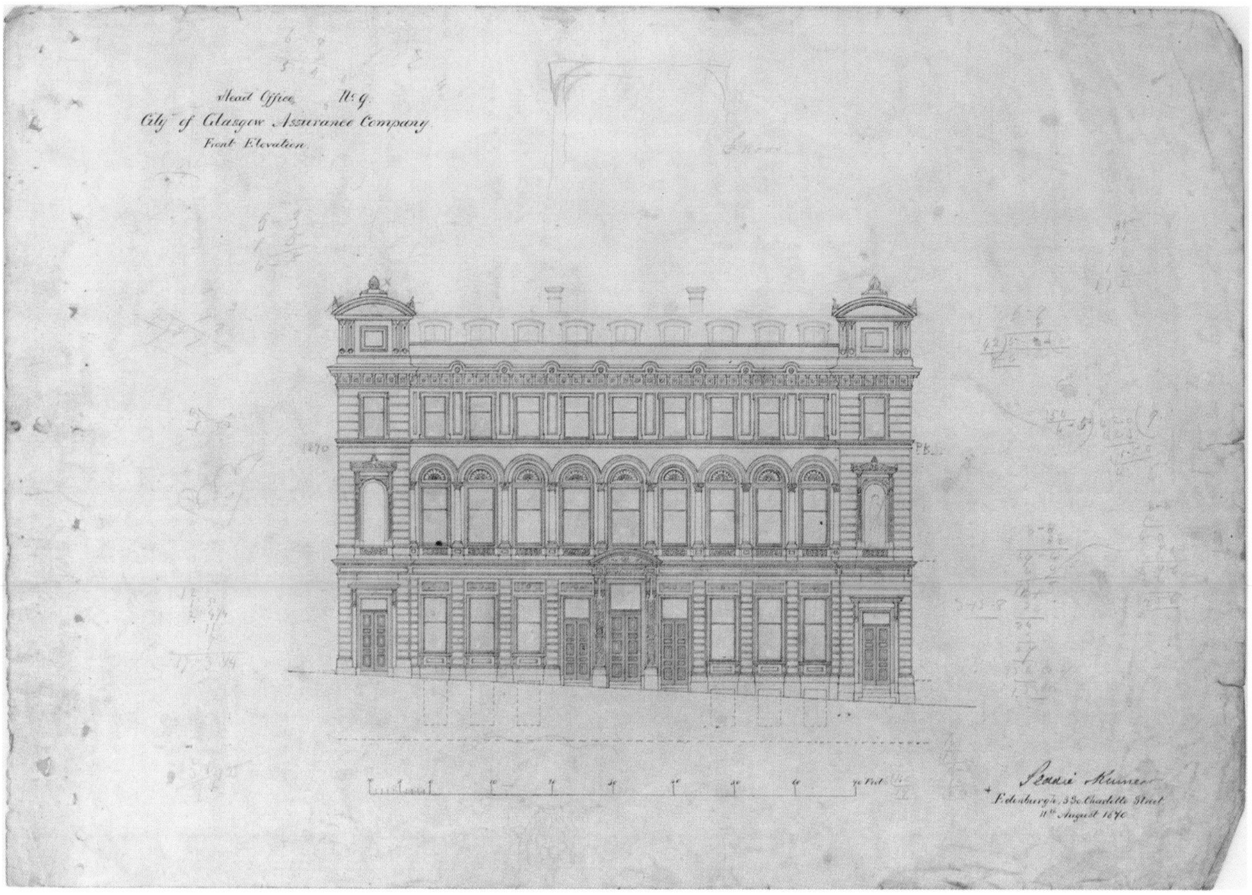

Elevation of the City of Glasgow Assurance Company, 30-40 St Vincent Place, Glasgow by Peddie & Kinnear, 1870, from the Dick Peddie & McKay Collection. [SC879082]

Provident Institute in St Vincent Place, Glasgow (1906). Bank designs from the Todd period include the Royal Bank in Hope Street, Edinburgh (1922-30), while from Dick Peddie & McKay's office came Edgar's redevelopment of the Scottish Equitable Life Assurance Company's offices at 24 St Andrew Square, Edinburgh (1968-73).

The Collection documents the practice's involvement with the 1870s boom in hydropathic institutions, made possible through the expanding railway network. Within five years, the practice designed Dunblane Hydropathic Institution (1874-77); Craiglockhart Hydropathic Institution, Edinburgh (1877-92); and Callendar Hydropathic (1879). They also converted the Jacobean mansion that J T Rochead (1814-1878) had built for Robert Napier into the West Shandon Hydropathic, Shore Road, Dumbarton (1877-78).

Hotels are represented with Peddie's University Club at 127-128 Princes Street (1865) and Blythswoodholme Hotel, 97-99 Hope Street, Glasgow (1876-79). Built to service the passengers alighting at Central Station, Blythswoodholme was the largest hotel in Scotland, its internal court accommodating a shopping arcade with a glazed roof. The practice also designed Edinburgh's equivalent: the Caledonian Railway Station and Hotel (1848-1923).

Changes in shop design are well illustrated, particularly from the 1930s onwards, and the Collection includes J R McKay's Binns department store, Princes Street, Edinburgh (*c.*1934). After the war the practice designed shop fronts and modern interiors for companies such as Blyths Ltd on the corner of Earl Grey Street and Fountainbridge (1953-57) and Messrs Darling & Co, 124-125 Princes Street, Edinburgh (*c.*1954-57), the latter incorporating a building Kinnear had built as an investment in 1866. From the 1940s to the 1960s the practice modernised many shops for William Low & Co.

In the 20th century the practice had strong connections with the brewing industry in Edinburgh, undertaking various alterations and additions for companies such as Wm Younger & Co Ltd (1902-54). Cinemas and garages also feature as well as post-Second World War commercial projects. Military commissions are represented by the pre-Second World War army headquarters at Liberton, Edinburgh (1938) and Turnhouse Road, Edinburgh (1939).

The Collection contains a significant number of drawings from other architects, principally from the Sydney Mitchell & Wilson practice. Approximately 15% of the Collection was acquired from the J R McKay practice, and there are also 310 drawings by A E Horsfield who commenced practice *c.*1906 and merged with J R McKay's practice *c.*1930. There are drawings by David Bryce, William Burn (1789-1870), John Lessels (1809-1883), Thomas P Marwick (1854-1927), Hippolyte J Blanc (1844-1917), Charles Wilson (1810-1863), David Rhind and Wardrop Anderson & Browne.

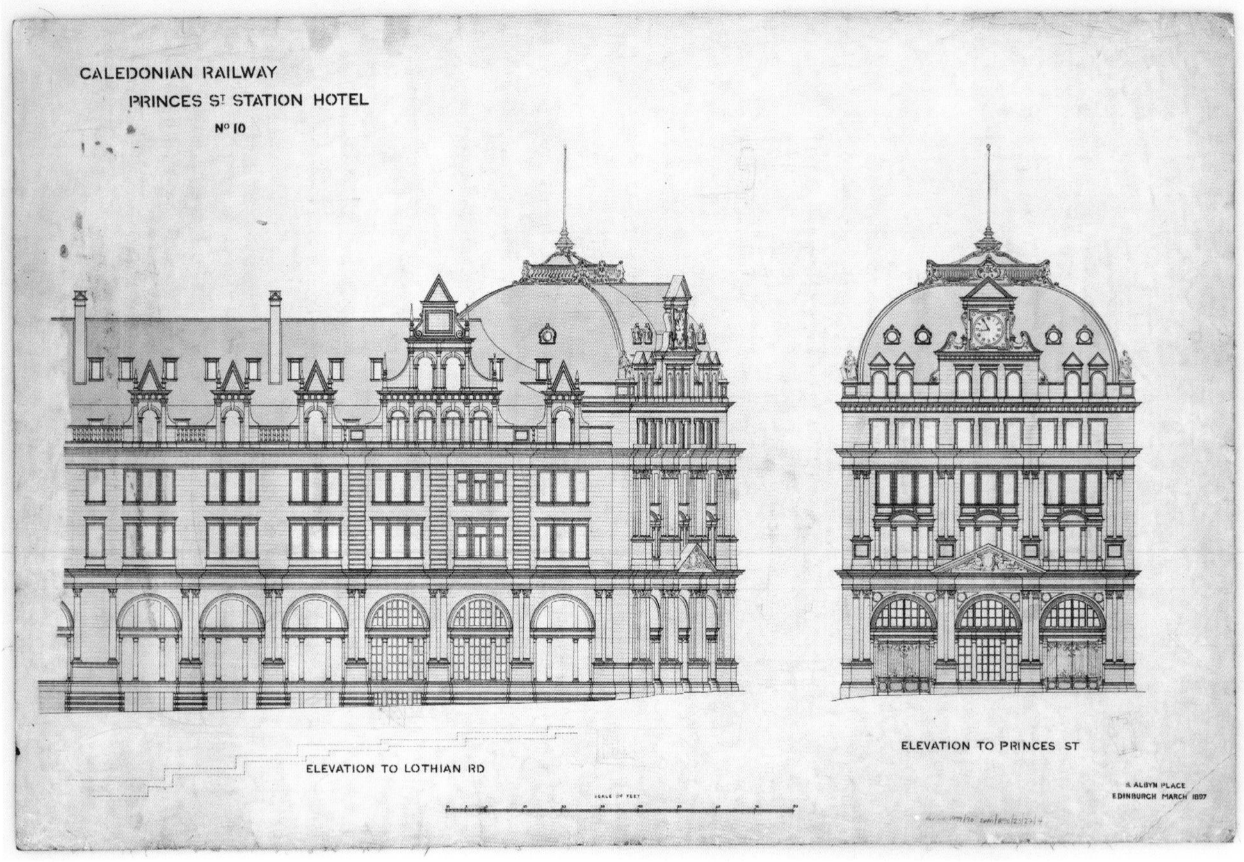

Elevations of the Caledonian Hotel, Princes Street, Edinburgh by Peddie & Washington Browne, 1897, from the Dick Peddie & McKay Collection. [SC672038]

Interior of 'The Grotto', 24-25 Abercromby Place, Edinburgh by Dick Peddie & McKay, c.1967, from the Dick Peddie & McKay Collection. [SC879077]

John Dick Peddie (1824-1891). Image courtesy of the Scottish Photography Collection, Scottish National Portrait Gallery. [DP002391]

References

NMRS Sources

- Handlists compiled by Richard Emerson, Kitty Cruft, David W Walker and Veronica Steele prior to the Collection's removal to RCAHMS in 1999.
- 187 drawings by Peddie & Kinnear and Sydney Mitchell & Wilson purchased by NMRS in 1968 (Accession No:1968/5).
- A competition perspective of St Mary's Cathedral, Palmerston Place, Edinburgh by Peddie & Kinnear, 1872, purchased by the NMRS in 1991 with assistance from the National Art Collections Fund (Accession No: 1991/76).
- Four negatives of plans and elevations of Sutherland Technical School, Golspie donated by Elizabeth Beaton in 1993 (Accession No: 1994/40).
- A perspective view by Basil Spence of Linlithgow County Buildings, 1937, purchased by NMRS in 2000 (Accession No: 2000/68).
- Interview with John Jackson, who worked for Dick Peddie & McKay from 1951 to *c*.1953, by Siobhan McConnachie and Hannah Shaw, 12 November 2002 (MS 926/4/7).

Anon. 1939 'Obituary: Sir George Browne', *The Times*, 16 June 1939.

Anon. 1962 'Obituary: Mr John McKay', *The Scotsman*, 4 August 1962.

Anon. 2001 'History in the Making', *The Courier and Advertiser*, 5 April 2001.

Browne, G W 1889 'Modern Architecture', *Scot Art Rev*, vol. 1, 57.

Christian, E 1872 Report on the Competitive Designs of St Mary's Cathedral, Edinburgh, 30 October 1872.

McAuley, P 2002 'Restoration of the Ross Fountain', *SSCR J*, vol. 13.

MacMillan, L 2001 'A Lasting Impression', *Edinburgh Evening News*, 1 August 2001.

Shaw, H 2004 'War Work: The Dick Peddie & McKay Collection 1939-45', *Architect Heritage Soc Scot Mag*, no. 16/17 (Spring 2004), 50-51. Edinburgh.

Todd, W J W 1922 'Obituary: John More Dick Peddie', *RIAS Quart*, winter, 6-9.

Wilson, J 1939 'Obituary: Sir George Washington Browne', *J Roy Inst Brit Architect*, 17 June 1939.

Walker, D W 2002 Peddie and Kinnear, PhD thesis presented to St Andrew's Univ.

Walker, D W 2003 'Peddie and Kinnear's Hydropathics', *Architect Heritage XIV*. Edinburgh: Edinburgh University Press, 22-44.

Walker, S 1996 'The Criminal Upperworld', *Accounting Hist New Series, vol. 1*, no. 2, 1

Related practices/personnel:
Lorimer & Matthew Collection
Sydney Mitchell & Wilson Collection
Scott Morton Collection

For other Dick Peddie & McKay papers (from the practice in all its guises):
Cowie & Seaton Collection

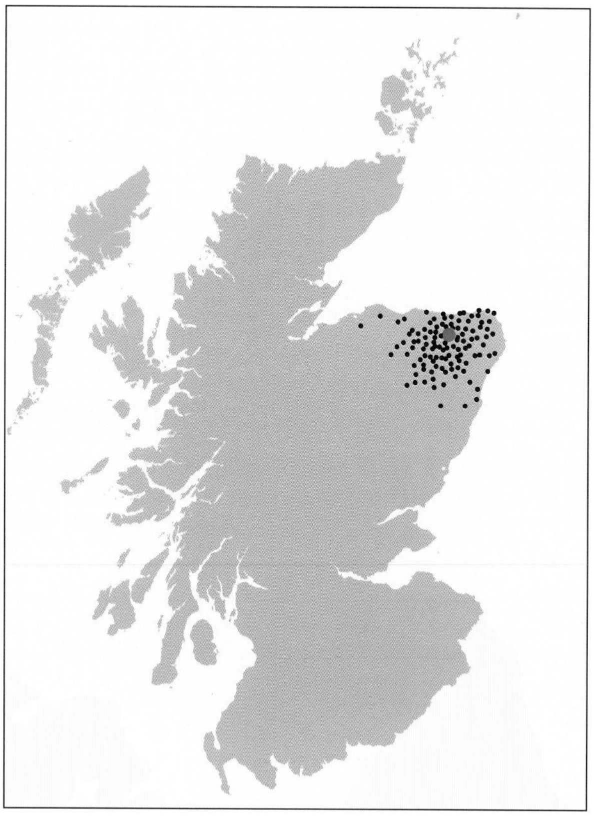

Duncan & Munro

Provenance

The Duncan & Munro Collection (Accession No. 2000/245) was initially stored in rolls in the office wing of the house in Victoria Terrace, Turriff, of the architect James Munro (d.2001). The Turriff-based architect Alan Keir subsequently acquired the Collection and his colleague David Smith presented it to RCAHMS following the SSAP.

Until 1996 the Collection was stored in the attic of a solicitors' office in Turriff. It was then taken into the care of Aberdeenshire Council and moved to storage premises in Mintlaw, Aberdeenshire. The Collection was moved to RCAHMS, Edinburgh, in December 1999 to be conserved and catalogued.

The Collection is owned by RCAHMS and held at Aberdeen City Archives under a Charge and Superintendence Agreement.

History

James Duncan (1828-1907) was the son of George Duncan, a Turriff mason. He commenced practice as an architect *c.*1860, the school at Cuminestown (1862) being his first known work. His son William Liddle Duncan (1870-1951) studied at Robert Gordon's College in Aberdeen and was apprenticed to his father in 1887, before completing his architectural education in Edinburgh. In 1897 he was taken into partnership in his father's practice and until 1907 the firm was known as James Duncan & Son.

After James Duncan's death the practice became William Duncan and remained so for the subsequent 40 years. William Duncan was admitted LRIBA on 20 July 1911, his proposers including Arthur Clyne (1852-1923) and Arthur H L Mackinnon (1870-1937). In 1947 the practice was renamed W L Duncan & Munro, the latter being James Munro of Victoria Terrace, Turriff, who had worked for Duncan from *c.*1930 onwards.

Following William Liddle Duncan's death in 1951, James Munro took over the practice until his retirement in 1975.

Scope and Content

The Duncan & Munro Collection consists of 4,500 drawings and 1,400 manuscripts relating to buildings in the North East of Scotland, with projects ranging from the Banffshire coast north of Turriff, to lands surrounding Forres in the northwest, to Dyce just north of Aberdeen. It includes a significant number of farm buildings, testament to the vast agricultural expansion that occurred between 1860 and 1975. Alterations to schools, houses and shops reflect an improvement in general living conditions in the rural communities of the North East during this time.

Many of the commissions undertaken by the practice were from estate owners in the region. This not only included work on farm buildings and workers' housing but also larger commissions such as the alteration of substantial houses. Notable examples are Scobbath House, on the Ardmiddle estate, where James Duncan worked in the 1870s; Fyvie Castle, where Duncan provided designs for a tennis court and bowling alley in the 1880s; and Muiresk House where alterations took place in the 1930s.

Commercial buildings for which the firm provided

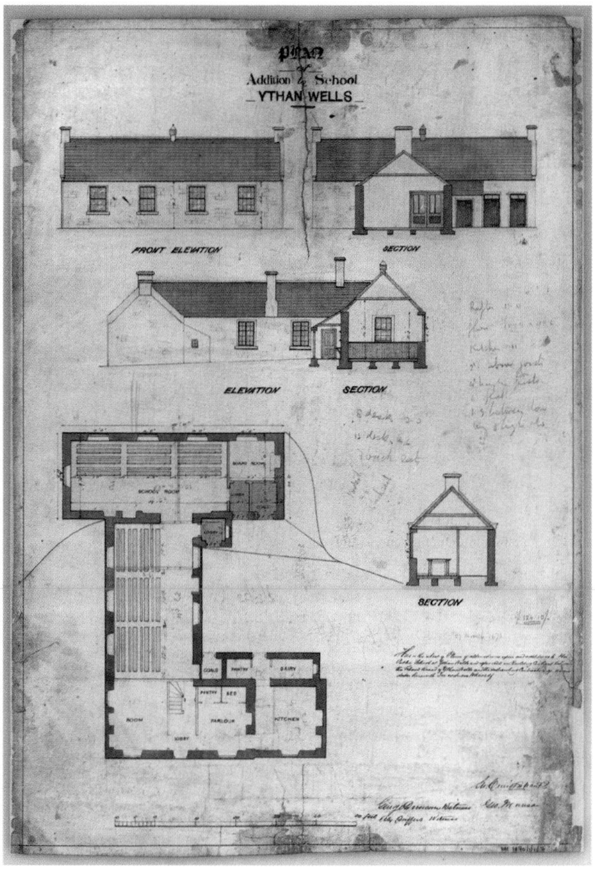

Plan, section and elevations showing additions to Ythanwells School, Aberdeenshire by James Duncan, 1871, from the Duncan & Munro Collection. [SC638703]

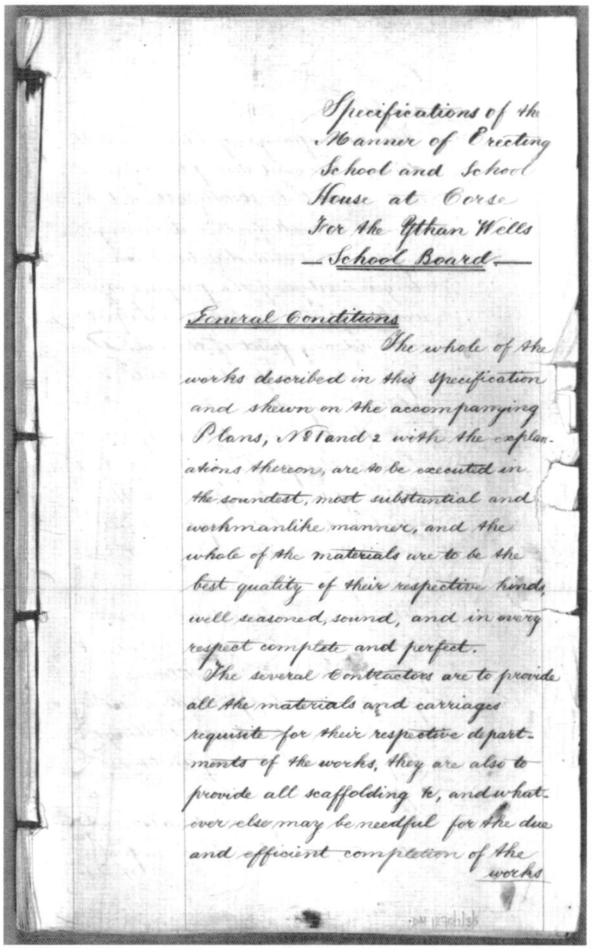

Specifications of the Manner of Erecting School and School House at Corse For the Ythan Wells School Board.

General Conditions

The whole of the works described in this Specification and shewn on the accompanying Plans, No 1 and 2 with the explanations thereon, are to be executed in the soundest, most substantial and workmanlike manner, and the whole of the materials are to be the best quality of their respective kinds, well seasoned, sound, and in every respect complete and perfect.

The several Contractors are to provide all the materials and carriages requisite for their respective departments of the works, they are also to provide all scaffolding &c, and whatever else may be needful for the due and efficient completion of the works

Specifications for additions to Ythanwells School, Aberdeenshire, 1871, from the Duncan & Munro Collection. [SC879063]

a number of drawings include Turriff Central Auction Mart and the Glenglasshaugh Distillery near Portsoy, Banffshire, both begun in the 1880s. There were also a number of jobs to which the firm returned. This is particularly notable in small parish schools, such as Ythanwells in the parish of Forgue where work began in the 1870s, and larger town schools such as The Gordon Schools at Huntly where the practice provided alterations throughout the 1940s.

There was also a small amount of work carried out on public and private monuments. James Duncan carried out alterations in 1896 to A W Reid's 1852 Gothic mausoleum at Forglen. The practice under William Liddle Duncan produced designs shortly after the First World War for many of the parish memorials in the Turriff hinterland.

The range of projects tackled by the practice throughout its lifetime reflect the changes that were taking place in the lifestyle of the community they served. Their work on farm steadings and rural cottages at the beginning of the 20th century often included details of new water supplies, and during the 1940s the practice found itself busy working on sanitary improvements to the schools they had designed years earlier. The plans of the steadings show clearly the changes taking place in farm practice as the century progressed. The poultry houses the practice designed in the 19th century had turned into battery farming sheds by the 1940s. Cartsheds and stables were altered as the horse was replaced by the tractor. The different housing types worked on by the practice indicate the shifts taking place in the society of the time. Their early work

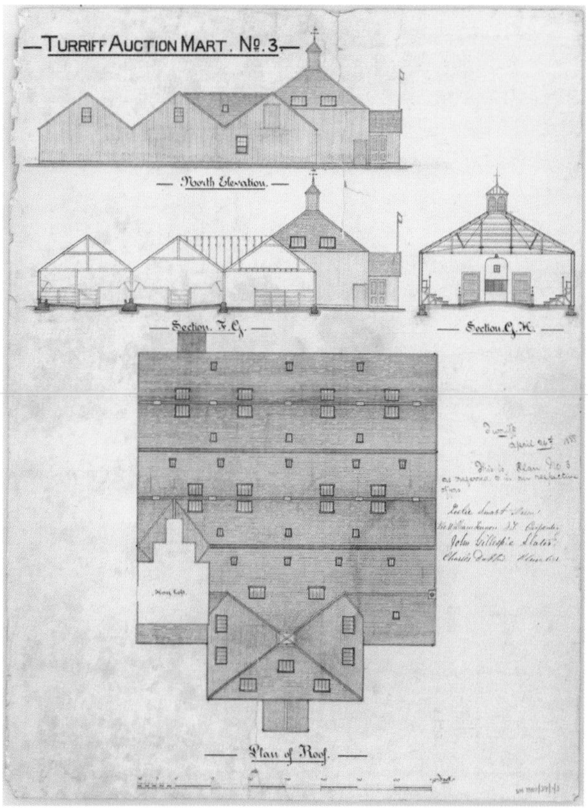

Plan, sections and elevation of the Central Auction Mart, Turriff, Aberdeenshire by James Duncan, 1888, from the Duncan & Munro Collection. [SC879050]

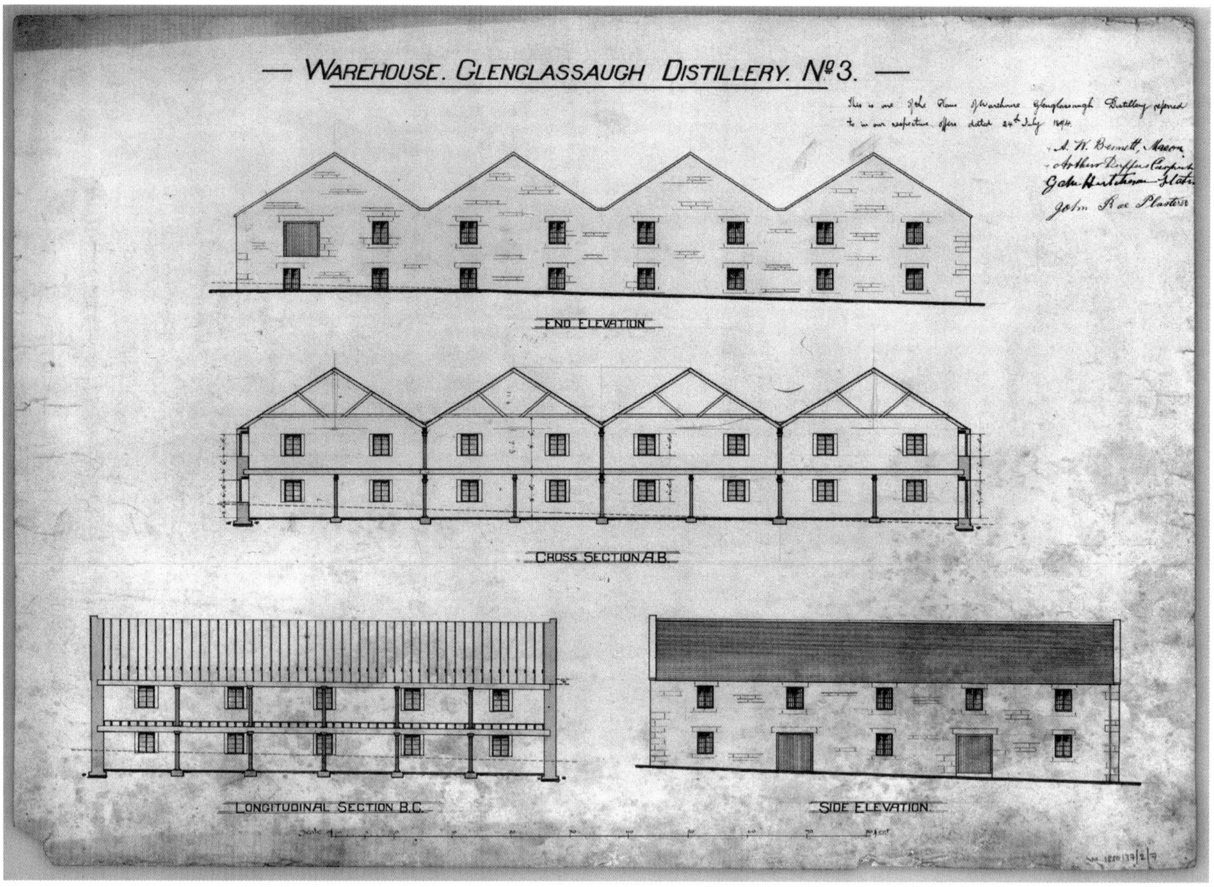

Sections and elevations of a warehouse, Glenglassaugh Distillery, Banffshire by James Duncan, 1894, from the Duncan & Munro Collection. [SC638704]

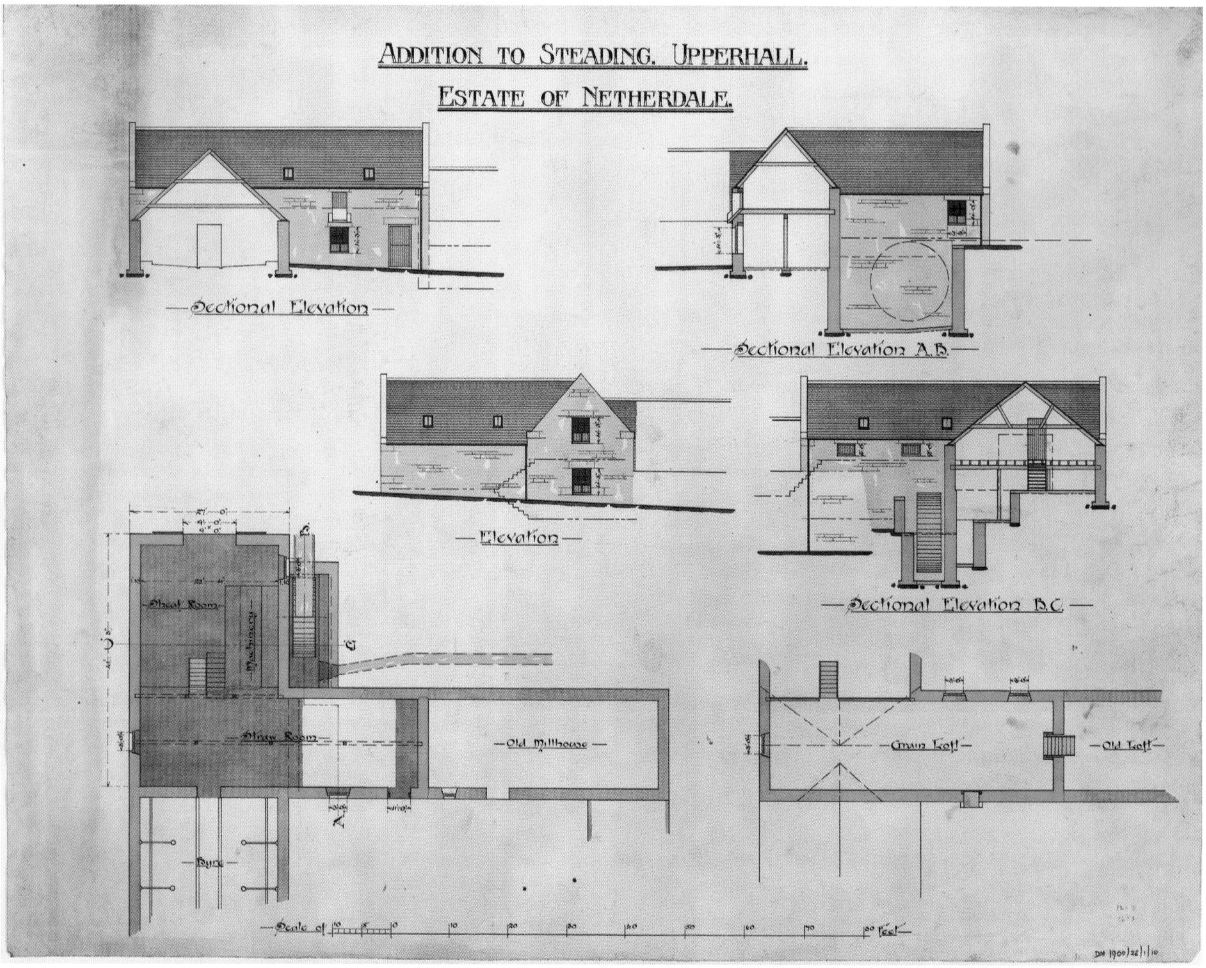

Plans, sections and elevations showing additions to a steading, Upperhall, Netherdale Estate, Aberdeenshire by James Duncan & Son, 1907, from the Duncan & Munro Collection. [SC879073]

on farm cottages was replaced by work on the suburban villas and social housing of the 1940s. The 1950s saw the car come into more general use and the practice supervised the installation of petrol pumps with their illuminated signs throughout the countryside.

The manuscripts in the Collection are chiefly specifications for the jobs undertaken by the practice, but also include letters from clients or contractors to the architect, and bills of quantities. The manuscript items are stored separately from the drawings but are linked to the drawings by a shared project number.

The Collection appears to be fairly complete in its present form although there are some omissions. There are no drawings for the Turriff municipal buildings or the impressive Bethelnie steading for which the contracts were advertised on 8 May 1872. Nor are there drawings of the medieval Mercat Cross at Turriff, for which James Duncan designed a Gothic crocketed base in 1865. The drawings for commercial buildings and county housing have suffered the most through damp and poor storage.

References

Aldred, N 2003 'From Filling the Kist to Fitted Kitchen:100 Years of Rural Housing in Scotland', *Architect Heritage XIV*, 8-21. Edinburgh: Edinburgh Univ Press.

Aldred, N and Gregory, N 2002 'Scottish Architects' Papers from Rural Practices in the Highlands and the North East', *Vernacular Buildings Working Group J*, 15-19.

Gregory, N 2001 'Scottish Architects' Papers Preservation Project: Local Collections', *Architect Heritage Soc Scot Mag*, no. 13 (Winter 2001), 28.

Hepburn, H 2002 'Preserving Turriff's History', *Turriff Gazette*, 15 February 2002.

Walker, B 1979 *Farm Buildings in the Grampian Region*, Aberdeen: Grampian Regional Council.

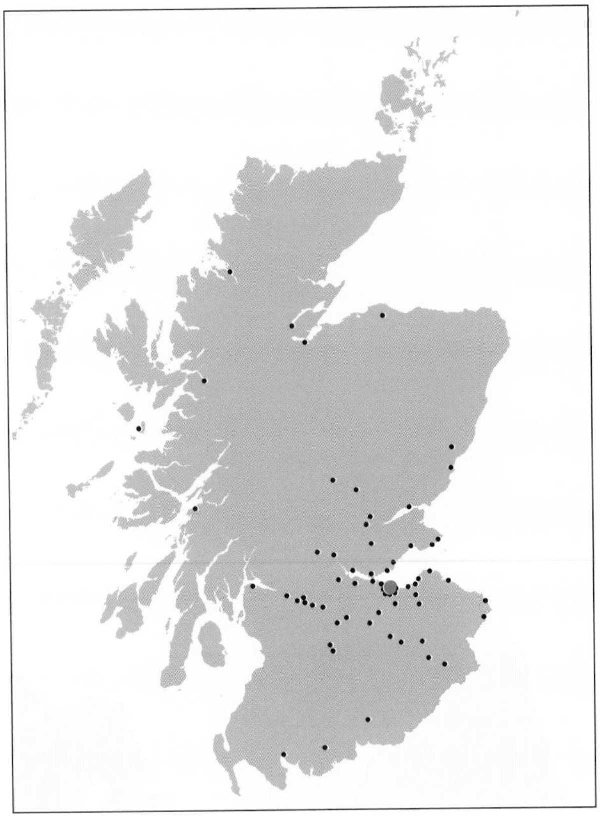

Dunn & Findlay

Provenance
The Dunn & Findlay Collection (Accession No. 1981/10) was salvaged by the NMRS from the offices of 14 Frederick Street, Edinburgh in 1981 when the Mottram Patrick & Dalgleish practice moved from the premises to new offices in Leith. The Collection is an amalgam of drawings from two distinct practices established by James Bow Dunn and Alfred Hugh Mottram respectively. The fusion of drawings seemed to occur due to the attic floor being used for storage by both practices.

Dunn & Findlay
James Bow Dunn (1861-1930) was born in Pollokshields, Glasgow, and educated at George Heriot's School, Edinburgh. As a young man he travelled widely through Europe and was articled to the Edinburgh architect, James Campbell Walker (*c.*1822-1888) in 1876. Nine years later he worked at the Burgh Engineer's Office, Edinburgh, and established a small private practice of his own at 116 George Street, Edinburgh in 1887. During the same year he entered the competition to design the Edinburgh Public Library under the pseudonym 'Triumphant Democracy' and his reputation was enhanced when Alfred Waterhouse, the competition assessor, placed his entry second to that of George Washington Browne (1853–1939). The following year Dunn won the competition for the Society of Solicitors to the Supreme Courts of Scotland premises under the pseudonym 'Wisdom, Health and Beauty', assessed by J J Burnet (1857-1938). This success enabled him to fully set up business on his own account. In 1889 he moved to 94 George Street where he remained until 1896.

In 1894 Dunn began a ten-year partnership with James Leslie Findlay (d.1952), the younger son of the *Scotsman* newspaper proprietor John Ritchie Findlay. Harrow-educated, Findlay was apprenticed to his father's architect, A G Sydney Mitchell (1856-1930), where he designed the Dean Path buildings, Edinburgh (1885) for his father. The partnership of Dunn & Findlay was probably formed for the building of the *Scotsman's* new premises but had got off to an earlier start with a competition win for the Adam Smith Memorial and Beveridge Halls and Library in Kirkcaldy (1894). From 1896 to 1902 the practice resided at 35 Frederick Street, Edinburgh before moving to 42 Frederick Street. The partnership ceased in 1903, although both architects continued to share an office for three years, during which time Dunn was admitted FRIBA (1905). After 1906, Findlay did little architectural work. During active service in the First World War he was invalided and after 1918 retired to the house he had built for himself at Muirtown, Strathspey.

In 1909 the practice moved to 45 Hanover Street, Edinburgh, and then in 1912 to 14 Frederick Street, Edinburgh, where it remained. In recognition of his contribution to architecture, Dunn was elected President of the Edinburgh Architectural Association in 1910 and 1911, Associate of the Royal Scottish Academy in 1918, an Academician in 1930, and was one of the Academy's representatives on the governing board of the Edinburgh

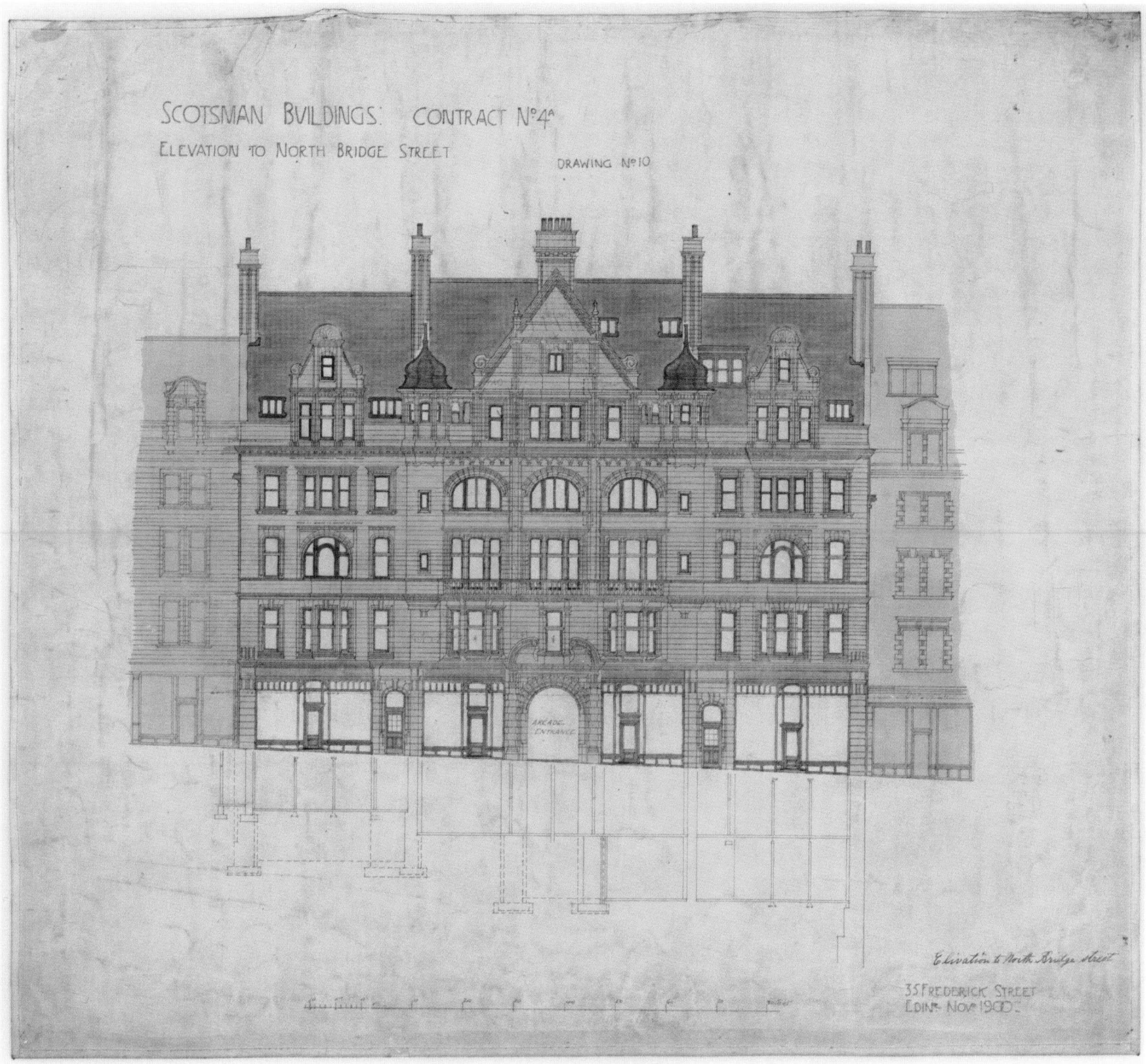

Elevation of the Scotsman Buildings, 20-26 North Bridge Street, Edinburgh by Dunn & Findlay, 1900, from the Dunn & Findlay Collection. [SC553823]

College of Art. After his death, his son Herbert G Dunn went into partnership with his former principal assistant G L Martin, to continue the practice as Dunn & Martin.

Alfred Hugh Mottram

The brother of the author R H Mottram, Alfred Hugh Mottram (1886-1953) was born in Norwich, England, and educated in Lausanne, Switzerland. In 1903 he was articled to George Faulkner Armitage of London and Manchester and remained as an assistant until 1907 when he joined Parker & Unwin. He was admitted ARIBA 4 December 1911, his proposers being Unwin, Herbert Vaughan Lanchester, and the Presbyterian church architect, Thomas Philips Figgis. Thereafter, on the strength of his garden city and town planning experience with Parker & Unwin, he obtained a post with the Housing Reform Company of Cardiff. In 1915 he took up a similar post with the Scottish National Housing Company to work as architect and town planner for the new town of Rosyth, again on Unwin's recommendation. Mottram planned the whole development, although part of the work was handed over to Greig Fairbairn & MacNiven when he was enlisted in the army.

After the war Mottram returned to the Scottish National Housing Company's office at 59 Frederick Street, Edinburgh. In 1925, due to the closure of the dockyard, the Rosyth project stalled and Mottram joined Dunn's office for a short time before establishing his own practice in the same building. Mottram was also the architect to the Edinburgh Welfare Housing Trust and the Edinburgh Housing Association. In 1950 his son James Arthur Hugh Mottram, who had completed a short apprenticeship with Dunn & Martin, became a partner and the practice was renamed A H Mottram & Son.

Also working in the office as an independent architect was Thomas Edward Patrick (b.*c*.1916), a friend of James Mottram from Edinburgh College of Art. Shortly before the death of A H Mottram on the 12 March 1953, Patrick was brought into the partnership, which in the late 1950s became Mottram & Patrick. In 1960 Andrew Martin Dalgleish, a long serving chief assistant, became a partner and by 1964 the practice was known as Mottram Patrick & Dalgleish.

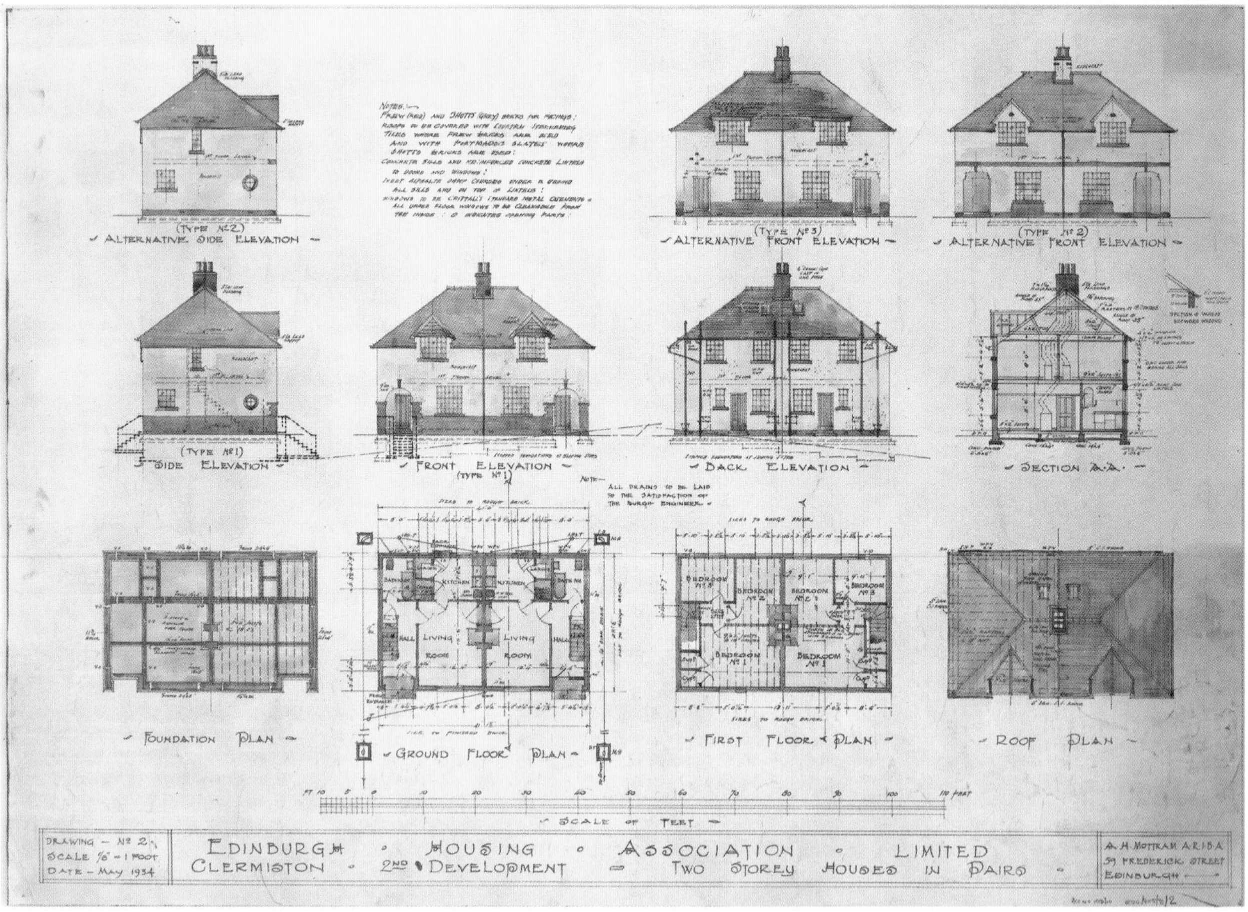

Plans, section and elevations of two storey houses, Clermiston, Edinburgh for the Edinburgh Housing Association Ltd by A H Mottram, 1934, from the Dunn & Findlay Collection. [SC879023]

Perspective view of The Ladies' Club, 14 Frederick Street by James B Dunn, c.1912, from the Dunn & Findlay Collection. [SC685044]

Throughout his career A H Mottram was a prominent member of the architectural community. He was president of the Edinburgh Architectural Association, a post his son was later to hold, and was a Scottish member of the Architect's Registration Council of the UK.

Scope and Content

The collection contains 4,182 drawings, approximately two-thirds of which originate from the James B Dunn practice, with the remainder belonging to the practice of A H Mottram. The majority of drawings are for projects based in Edinburgh.

Significant projects by the James B Dunn practice include *The Scotsman* Building (1899-1904), Jenner's Repository (1925-26), and George Watson's College (*c.*1927-34), all in Edinburgh. The Collection also includes housing developments at Plewlands in Morningside (1904-07, second phase 1920s), Barnton (1902-08, second phase 1920s) and Murrayfield Gardens (1898-1906), along with designs for several villas in East Lothian, most notably Gullane, between the 1890s and the 1920s.

Mottram's involvement in housing development is also represented strongly in the Collection, which includes drawings for his work in Rosyth (1917-25); designs for housing at Greenock for the Scottish National Housing Company (Housing Trust) Limited (1926); housing in Lanarkshire for the Scottish Special Housing Association (1937-38); and tenement housing for the Edinburgh Welfare Housing Trust Ltd (1928-

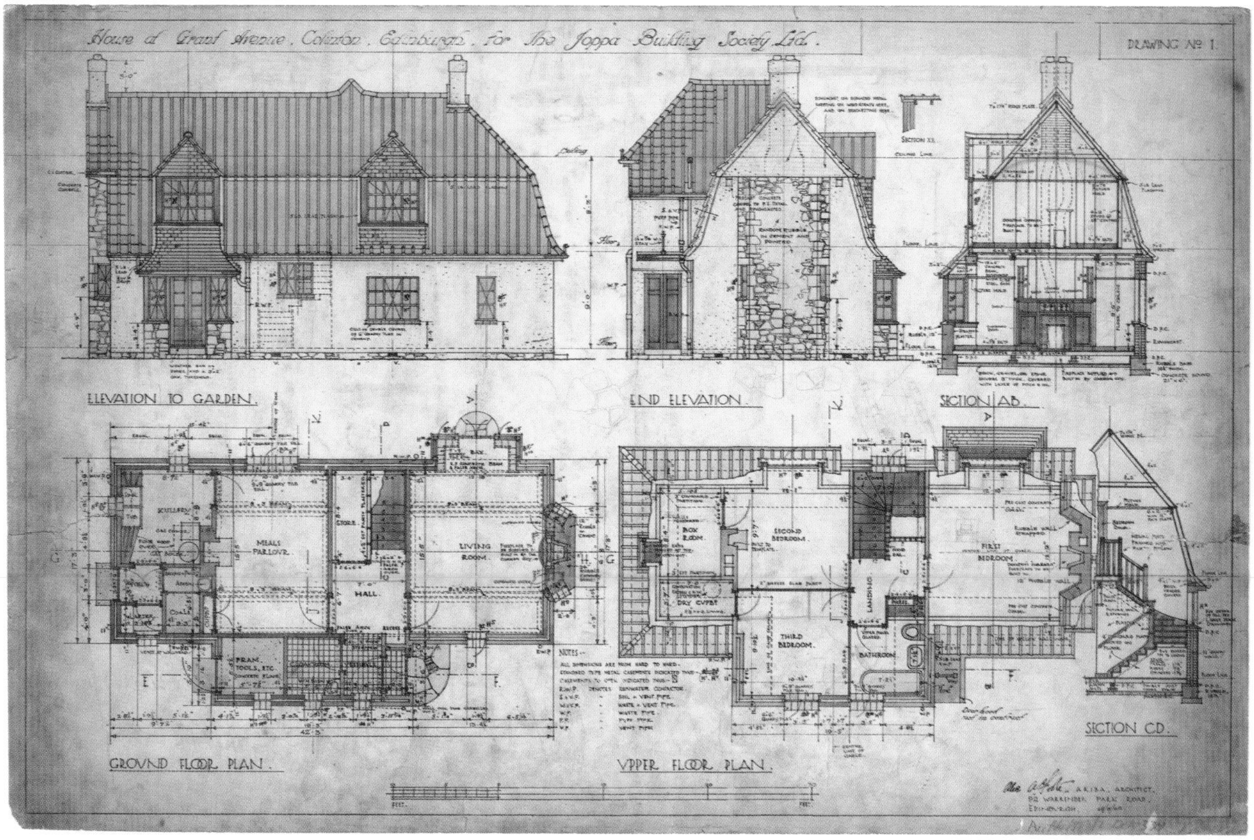

Plans, sections and elevations of a house at Grant Avenue, Colinton, Edinburgh for the Joppa Building Society Ltd by Alexander Allan Foote, 1922, from the A A Foote & Son Collection. [DP001866]

The 20 photographs in the Collection are of the Phoenix Cinema, Kirkwall; Dalserf village, Lanarkshire (1958); and South Morningside Church for which the practice provided additional hall accommodation (1968). There is also a framed presentation panel with four photographic views of housing in Barnton Loan and Davidson's Mains (*c*.1923-30).

The copy job index contains information on projects dating from 1922 to 1978 and reveals notable omissions in the Collection, such as alterations to Salvation Army premises in Edinburgh at 18a Nicolson Street (1934) and Hamilton Place (1934-38). Also not reflected is the significant number of dwellings that the practice designed for Lerwick Town Council in the 1930s and late 1940s, including 50 houses at Clickimin (started 1935) and 180 houses for the Grantfield site in Lerwick (started 1938). Non-housing commissions for Lerwick, including alteration work on Lerwick Town Hall (*c*.1937-49); new buildings for Lerwick Harbour Trust (*c*.1938-50); and Bell's Brae Infants School, Gilbertson Road (completed 1957) are also absent from the Collection.

There are no drawings for housing schemes in Galashiels, including houses for the SSHA and a number of schemes on the Melrose Road site for Wimpey and Cruden Homes (all *c*.1950-60). Other omissions include alteration work for the Merchant Company Education Board, primarily boarding accommodation at Dean Park House (1963) and new staff accommodation for Daniel Stewart's College (1966).

Interior view of a coffee room, 90A Princes Street, Edinburgh for Messrs John Sinclair Ltd by Alexander Allan Foote, perspective by H Peddie, 1937, from the A A Foote & Son Collection. [SC751799]

There are six acquired drawings in the Collection of a house at Spylaw Avenue, Edinburgh (1862) by the Dumfries-based architect James Barbour (1835-1912).

References

NMRS Sources

- A set of 68 photographic copies taken from a bound set of prints showing the practice's conversion of Calton House, Dean Street, Edinburgh to premises for the photography firm Francis C Inglis.

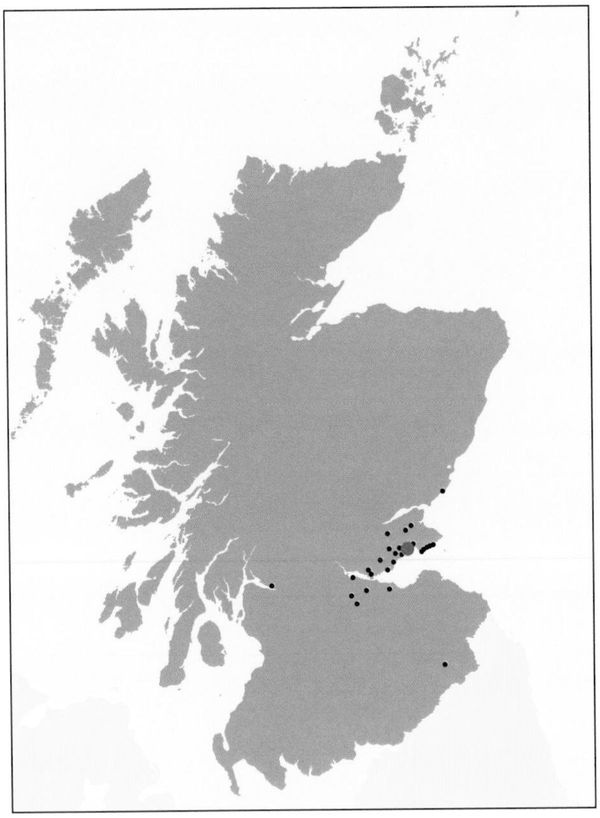

Haxton & Watson

Provenance
The Haxton & Watson Collection (Accession No. 2003/123) was presented to RCAHMS by David G Moir of David Moir, Architect (incorporating Haxton & Watson) in 1985.

History
A native of St Andrews, Andrew David Haxton (1878-1960) served a five-year apprenticeship, beginning in November 1893, with the St Andrews firm of Gillespie & Scott. He continued as an assistant for a further one and a half years during which time he attended evening classes given by art master R S Douglas and was awarded prizes by the Dundee Institute of Architects for measured drawing. This was followed by nine months as assistant to Thomas Edward Marshall (*c.*1860-1940) of Harrogate in 1900. Thomson & Sandilands of Glasgow then took him on as assistant from 1900-01. Haxton finally returned to Gillespie & Scott to serve as chief assistant between 1901-07.

William Walker (1881-1923) was articled to Gillespie & Scott in 1898 and remained as assistant, spending a total of eight years with the firm. From *c.*1906-07 he assisted J D Swanston & Syme of Kirkcaldy. After this he was briefly engaged in competition work on his own account and produced the winning entry for a block of business premises in Leven.

Haxton & Walker began independent practice in 1907 at 3 High Street, Leven. On 24 June 1912 both partners were admitted as licentiates of the Royal Institute of British Architects having been proposed by W Fleming Wilkie, President of the Dundee Institute of Architects.

After Walker's death, Haxton continued the practice under his own name, moving to Commercial Road, Leven in 1930. He was elected President of the Dundee Chapter of the RIAS from 1943 to 1945. After the war, Adam Elliot Watson (1908-1996) became a partner and the business became A D Haxton & Watson at the new address of 5 Scoonie Place, Leven.

A native of Glasgow, Watson qualified from Glasgow School of Architecture in 1935 and became Associate (later Fellow) of the RIBA in 1935, serving his apprenticeship with Wylie Shanks & Wylie of Glasgow. Whilst working for a London firm of architects he applied to join the Royal Engineers but was 'reserved' and between 1935 and 1947, undertook the building and rebuilding of factories in England. After setting up practice with Haxton, Watson became an Associate Member of the RIAS in 1948, and a Fellow in 1953.

Andrew Haxton retired around 1950 to the house that he had designed with Frank Pride, The Pines, 13 (now 28) Buchanan Gardens, St Andrews. Adam Watson retired in *c.*1973. The practice continued until *c.*1984 when it was incorporated into the practice of David Moir, Architect.

Scope and Content
The Collection comprises approximately 15,000 drawings relating to buildings in North East Fife. 7,340 drawings, dating from the 1910s to the 1960s, and with a predominance from the 1930s, have been catalogued. These include several social housing schemes built by

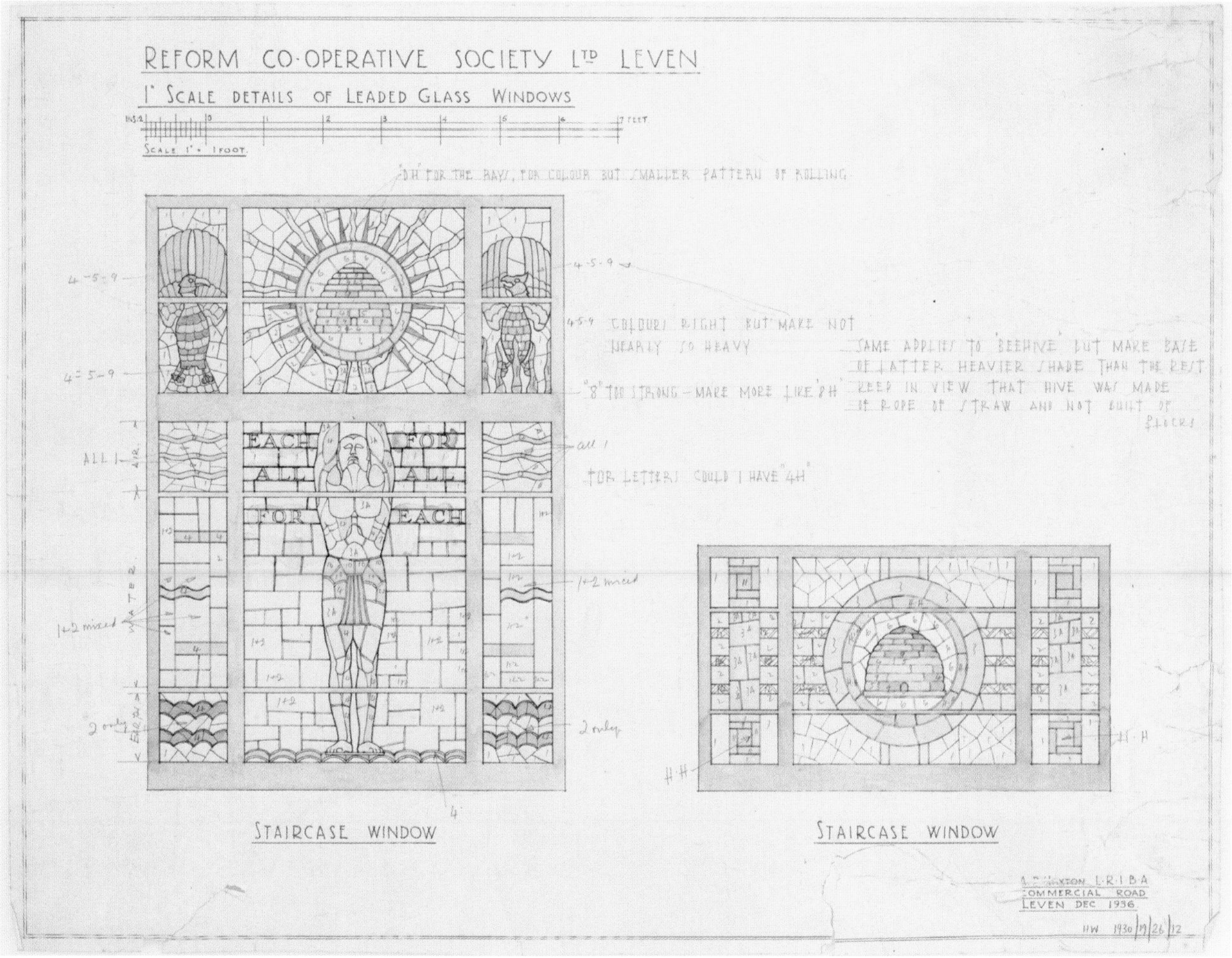

Details of stained glass windows for the Reform Co-operative Society, Durie Street, Leven by A D Haxton, 1936, from the Haxton & Watson Collection. [SC879103]

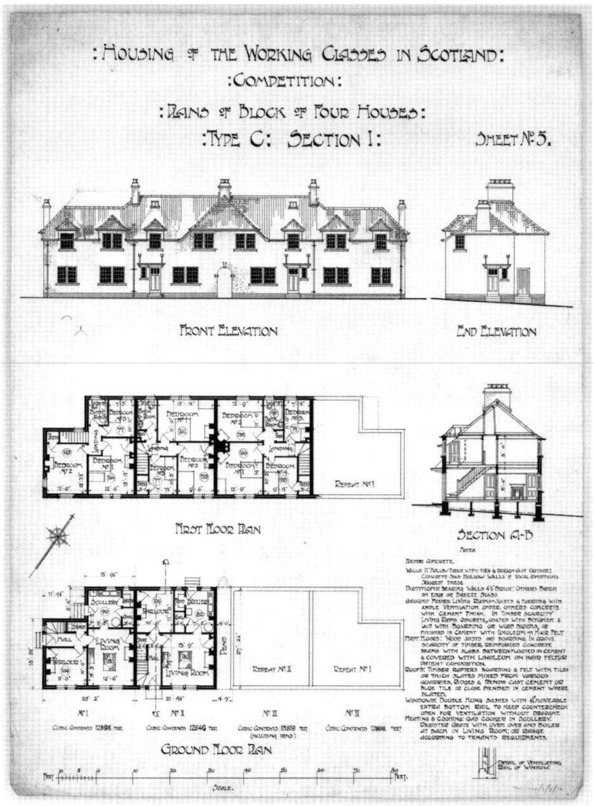

Plans, section and elevation of a block of four houses for the Housing of the Working Classes Competition by Haxton & Walker, c.1919, from the Haxton & Watson Collection. [SC879107]

the practice and all papers for cinemas, hospitals, co-operative societies, public halls, schools and churches. All uncatalogued papers have been hand-listed.

The practice commissions reflect the changes in Fife society brought about by the boom in the coal and steel industry in the middle decades of the 20th century. Social housing developments were needed to house increased numbers of workers in urban areas and these new communities required buildings to accommodate the services of health, entertainment, education and religion.

The practice established a reputation for cinema design, the majority of which were Art Deco buildings with interior decoration by M Alexander & Sons of Newcastle and lighting schemes by Claudegen Neon Signs and Franco Signs. Cinemas featured in the Collection include the Globe Electric Theatre, Buckhaven (1914-15); the All Super Imperial Cinema, Fisher Street, Methil (1925-26, 1954-55); Troxy, North Street, Leven (1934-35, 1938); and Regal cinemas at Broxburn (1936, 1941), Armadale (1937, 1946), Bathgate (1937-39, 1946), and West Calder (1938-39, 1948-55). The Collection also includes the conversion of a school into a cinema at Pittenweem (1920); alterations to existing cinemas at Bathgate (1938-39) and Bo'ness (1945-47); and unrealised schemes for cinemas at East Wemyss (1915), Arbroath (*c.*1930-39), Lochgelly (1945), and Kennoway (1949).

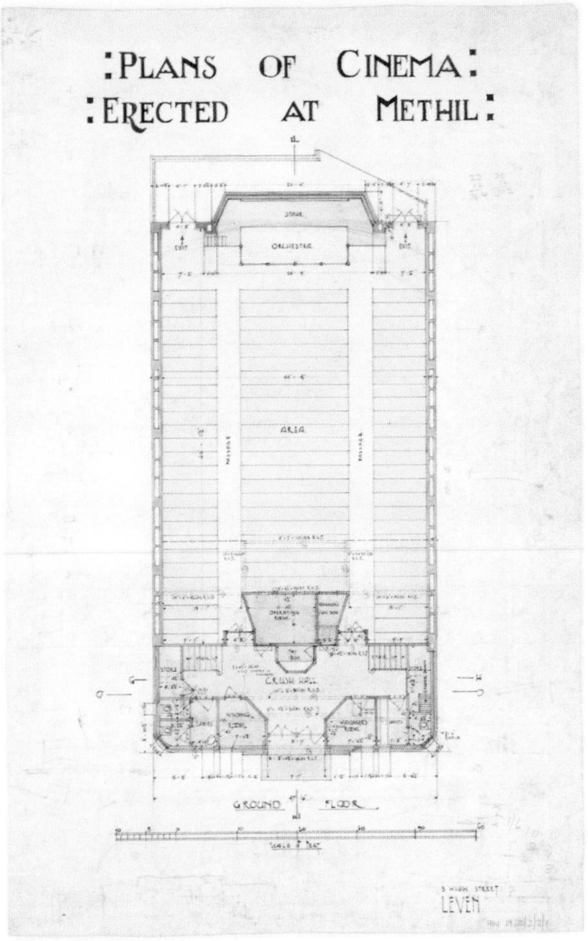

Plan of the Imperial Cinema, Fisher Street, Methil, Fife by A D Haxton, 1925, from the Haxton & Watson Collection. [SC879110]

Sketch of a decorative feature over the auditorium exit door, Regal Cinema, 24-34 North Bridge Street, Bathgate, West Lothian by A D Haxton, 1938, from the Haxton & Watson Collection. [SC800184]

Inter- and post-war social housing was a main feature of Haxton & Watson's work. State-aided housing was often for the Scottish National Housing Company Ltd or the Scottish Special Housing Association, while non state-aided housing was largely for the Fife Housing Company Ltd, one of 25 private companies providing housing in Fife during this period. The Collection documents the different phases of housing schemes in North East Fife, Leven (*c*.1919-68), some of which was designed in association with Lawrence Rolland (d.1959) of L A Rolland & Partners; Kilrenny (1919-33); Anstruther (*c*.1920-50), which includes plans for the Anstruther Slum Clearance Scheme; Elie (*c*.1930-52); and Methilhill (1937).

The Collection includes acquired material by A H Mottram (1886-1953) of Edinburgh for the Burgh of Jedburgh (1944) and housing for the workers of particular companies, including the Kinneil Cannel & Coking Coal Company, the London & North Eastern Railway and Lochgelly Iron & Coal Limited.

Commissions for co-operative societies included work on premises at Auchtermuchty (1902), Methil (1908-13), Buckhaven (1910-19), Dumbarton (1934), Lower Largo (1934) and Anstruther (1934-35). The drawings for the Reform Co-operative Society Limited, Durie Street, Leven (1920-51) include 1930s stained glass designs by Ralph Cowan who went on to become an architect, painter and Head of Architecture at Edinburgh College of Art.

The practice also provided additions, alterations, temporary structures and new builds for schools at Leven (1891-1919), Kirkcaldy (1905), St Monans (1910), Dairsie (1910-11), Lundin Links (1910-11), Upper and Lower Largo (1910-58), and Pittenweem (1911); and post-war schemes at East Wemyss (1945-47), Methil (1946-47), Thornton (1946-47), Burntisland (1946-48), Denbeath (1947), and Kinglassie (1947). The Collection also features unsuccessful competition entry drawings by Haxton for technical schools at Kirkcaldy (*c*.1926) and Dunfermline (*c*.1929).

References

NMRS Sources

- Practice job book dated 1963.

Anon. 1923 'Death of St Andrews Architect', *Fifeshire Advertiser*, 10 February 1923.

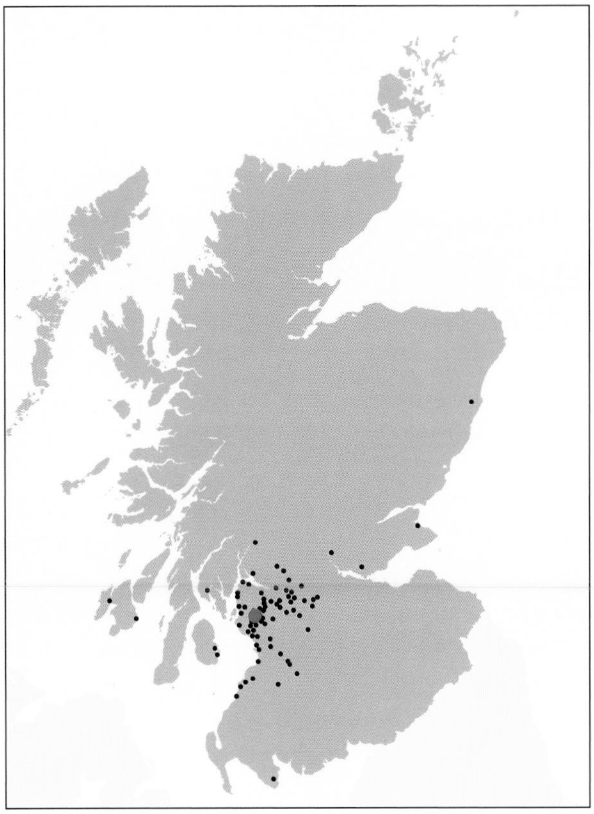

Houston & Dunlop

Provenance

The Houston & Dunlop Collection was gifted to RCAHMS by James B G Houston in two stages. The first donation, in 1989, comprised 457 drawings and manuscript material virtually all of which was related to the Moorings Café and Viking Cinema, Largs; and the Radio Cinema, Kilbirnie (Accession No. 1989/7). The remainder of the Collection was brought from the attic at the practice's Kilbirnie office to RCAHMS in 1995 as a result of the SSAP (Accession No. 2002/225).

The practice stored the Collection in rolls ordered alphabetically by client. This order has been retained.

History

James Houston JP FRIBA (1893-1966) was born into a family of Ayrshire artists that included George Houston RA (1869-1947) and Robert Houston RSW (1891-1942), both well known for their scenes of Ayrshire and the Firth of Clyde. He began his training with the Largs-based practice Fryers & Penman before attending the Glasgow School of Architecture, which was based at the Royal College of Science and Technology and Glasgow College of Art. During the first half of the 1920s he worked as an assistant tutor to Professor Charles Gourlay at the College, whilst working as an architect from Glenlogan, his family home in Kilbirnie and a number of Glasgow addresses including 8 Blythswood Square and 171 West Regent Street.

In 1925 Houston set up office on the first floor of Bridgend House in his native Kilbirnie. He had two assistants: Hugh Macdonald, who was employed at the practice for over 20 years, and Gavin MacClure, who was killed in the Second World War. In 1938, Houston demolished Bridgend House and redeveloped the site as the Radio Cinema. The practice relocated to offices nearby at 2 Schoolwynd.

Houston remained the sole partner until *c.*1956 when his son, James B G Houston, also a graduate of Glasgow School of Architecture, joined the practice and it became known as James Houston & Son. As a student he was interested in timber construction and submitted a prize-winning entry to a timber house building competition sponsored by the British Columbia Lumber Manufacturers who wanted to encourage timber construction in the UK. Along with seven other British architects, he won a trip to British Columbia where he gained experience in the uses of timber. During the late 1950s William Kelly, a retired Burgh Surveyor of Greenock, was employed in the office.

In 1972, the Ayrshire architect William MacDougall Dunlop was assumed into partnership, and a branch office was opened at 36 Kirkgate, Irvine. Dunlop had been previously employed at James Houston & Son and had also worked for the Irvine Development Corporation. In 1976 the practice changed its name to Houston & Dunlop. During the 1980s Peter Gurton became an associate in the practice. On 6 April 2001 Dunlop retired from the practice and a local architect James Harper, another former employee of James Houston & Son, agreed to join and form the new firm of Houston Harper, which still operates from 2 Schoolwynd, Kilbirnie [2004].

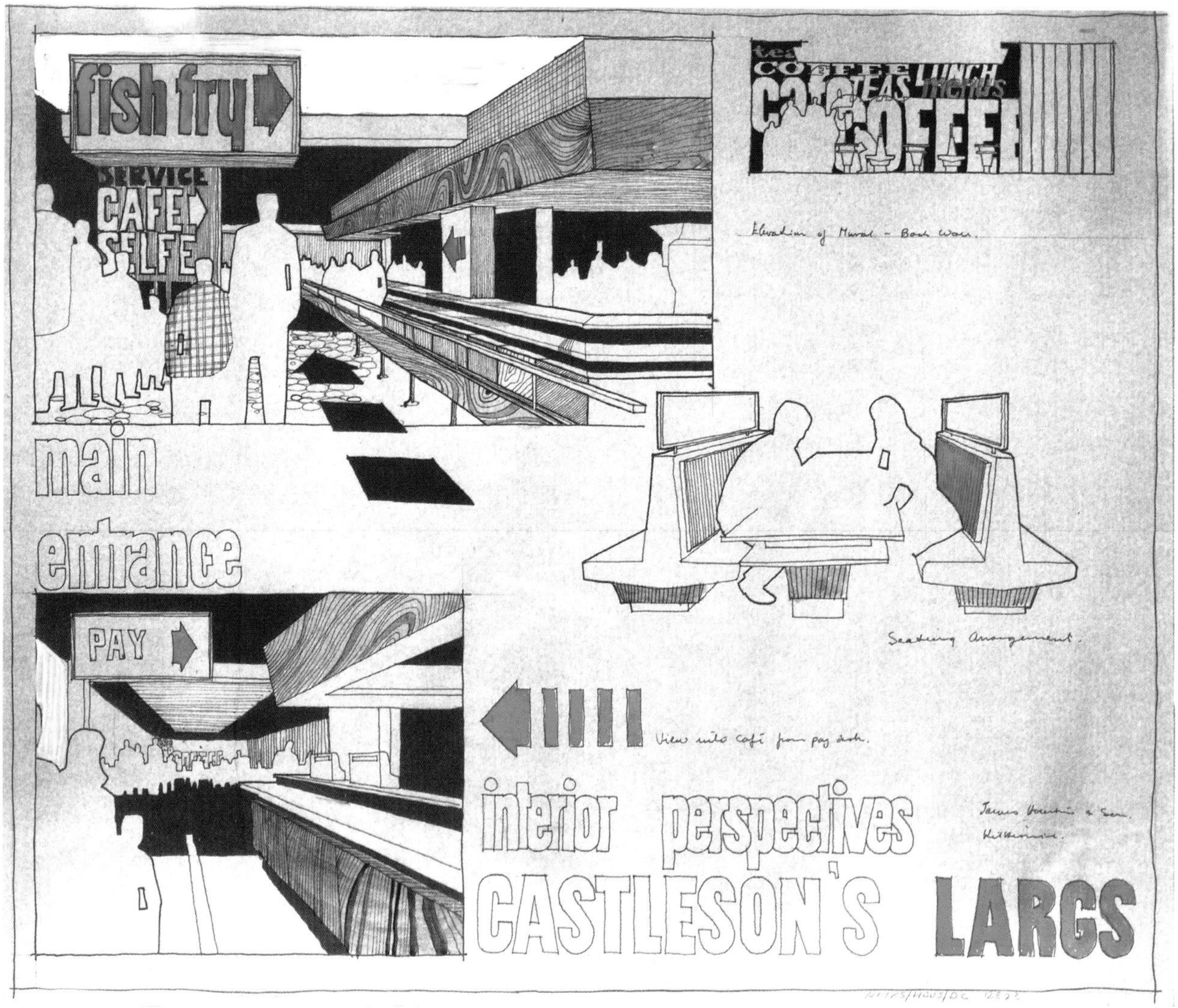

Castleson's Cafeteria, Largs by James Houston & Son, c.1965, from the Houston & Dunlop Collection. [SC883760]

Sketch details of interior design for the Radio Cinema, Bridgend, Kilbirnie by James Houston, c.1937, from the Houston & Dunlop Collection. [SC879098]

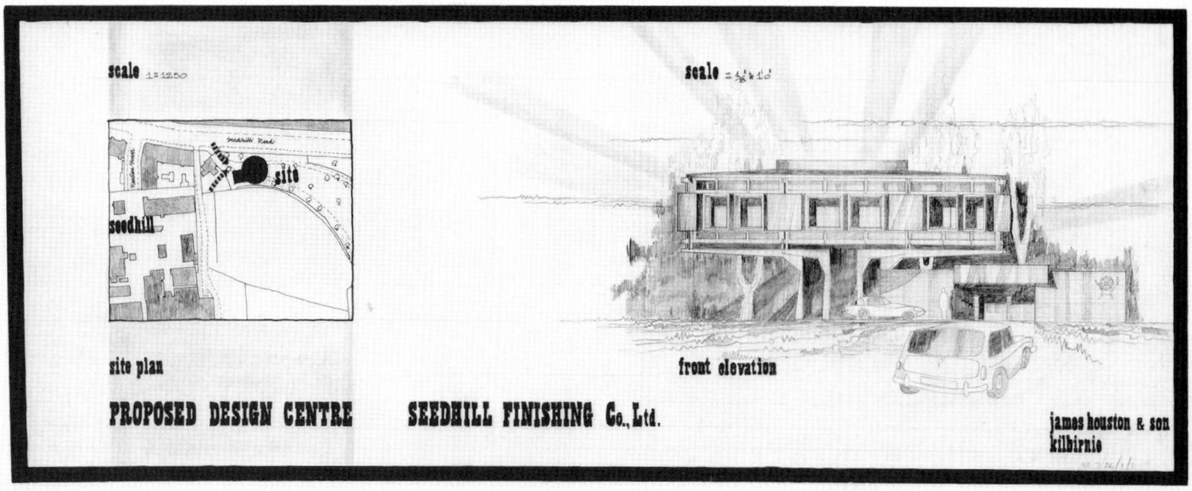

Plan and perspective view of unexecuted design centre for Seedhill Finishing Co Ltd, Paisley, by James Houston & Son, c.1960-70, from the Houston & Dunlop Collection. [SC883731]

Scope and Content

The Houston & Dunlop Collection consists of 7,166 drawings and 87 manuscript items, dating from 1919 to 1976. The projects featured within the Collection, almost all from the North Ayrshire and Renfrewshire area, illustrate the variety of building types tackled by the practice.

Within the Collection are several projects for the Ayrshire textile industry, including alterations and additions to both the Dennyholm and Stonyholm Mills, Kilbirnie for W & J Knox Ltd (1919-74); the expansion of the war-damaged Worsted Mills site, Drumfrochar Road, Greenock for Fleming, Reid & Company Ltd (1948-57); and new buildings at New Cumnock for Charles W Hall Ltd (1949-73). Other industrial projects featured in the Collection include various alterations and additions to R & W Watson Limited paper mills, Linwood (1928-29); and a factory for Fibreglass Ltd, Possilpark, Glasgow (1946-48).

Along with work for W & J Knox Ltd, the practice also provided alterations and additions to houses owned by members of the Knox family. This work features in the Collection along with designs for workers' cottages and memorial panels to at least three generations of the family.

The wealth of buildings produced by the Houston practice in all its guises for North Ayrshire and Renfrewshire's other major industry of leisure and tourism is apparent in the Collection. Perhaps the most well known examples are three themed buildings: the Radio Cinema, Kilbirnie (1938); the Moorings Café, Largs (*c*.1935, demolished 1989); and the Viking Cinema, Largs (1938-39). Later examples of the practice's specialism of themed architecture are the Ashton Hotel, Gourock (1954-58), where the practice extended the dance floor on large pilotis sunk into the seabed and created the ship-themed Davy Jones Locker Bar underneath; and several pub interiors for Scottish & Newcastle Breweries (*c*.1964-71) containing seaside imagery. Along with alterations to several hotels in the area, projects include a clubhouse at Kilbirnie Place Golf Club, Largs Road, Kilbirnie (*c*.1938-56); a golf

Perspective view of interior of Ardrossan Park Church, Stanley Road, Ardrossan by James Houston & Son, 1957, from the Houston & Dunlop Collection. [SC883767]

clubhouse at Cowal View, Gourock (1961-62); and an extension to the Royal Gourock Yacht Club, Ashton Road, Gourock (1957-69).

The Houston & Dunlop Collection contains drawings for a number of projects commissioned by Kilbirnie District Council, spanning the towns of Beith, Dalry and Kilbirnie. These include landscaping and improvements to facilities at Dalry Public Park (*c*.1925-38) and a community centre at Muirpark Road, Beith (*c*.1953-63). Gourock Town Council was also a significant client for whom commissions included a set of proposals to renovate and modernise James Carrick's 1935 Cragburn Pavilion (*c*.1966).

Commissions for both the Church of Scotland and the Roman Catholic Church feature in the Collection. For the former, there are drawings for four churches designed by James Houston & Son including Park Church, Stanley Road, Ardrossan (*c*.1955-58). For the Roman Catholic Church, there are drawings for St

James Houston (1893-1966). Image courtesy of James B G Houston. [SC896713]

James B G Houston at 2 Schoolwynd, Kilbirnie. Image courtesy of James B G Houston. [SC896715]

John's, Kilwinning Road, Stevenston, which the practice built (1958-62, extended 1970).

The Collection also includes papers for unrealised projects, including a competition design for the war memorial at Paisley (1920). Unexecuted designs for an Egyptian-style war memorial for Kilbirnie are included along with papers for a completed Neo-Greek-style memorial that was built (*c.*1920-25, altered *c.*1945-51).

The Collection contains few drawings executed after 1970 and only two small drawings from the Houston & Dunlop phase of the practice. Several major projects from the late 1960s onwards are missing from the Collection, including swimming pools in Kilbirnie, Largs, Saltcoats, Oban and Perth. Later projects include a substantial amount of work undertaken by the practice for the Glasgow Health Board between 1979 and 1988, such as the rehabilitation of Glasgow's Southern General Hospital (1981-88) and the restoration and renovation of Brooksby House, 18 Greenock Road, Largs, a convalescent home for which the practice designed all interior fittings, finishes and fabrics.

References

Additional information on the town of Kilbirnie and in particular the Knox family can be found at www.stbrigids-kilbirnie.com.

NMRS Sources

- Notes from a taped interview with James B G Houston carried out by Neil Gregory in February 2002.
- In addition to the SAPPP Houston & Dunlop Collection, the NMRS holds copies of over 100 photographs from a private collection, including the Moorings, the Radio Cinema and the Viking Cinema with building work in progress (Accession No. 1997/66). The NMRS also holds RCAHMS survey photographs of the Moorings taken just prior to demolition.

Anon. 1966 'Mr James Houston', *Glasgow Herald*, 7 September 1966.
Cameron, N M 2002 'Picture Palaces – James Houston's Themed Architecture', *Modern Painters*, January 2002, 101.

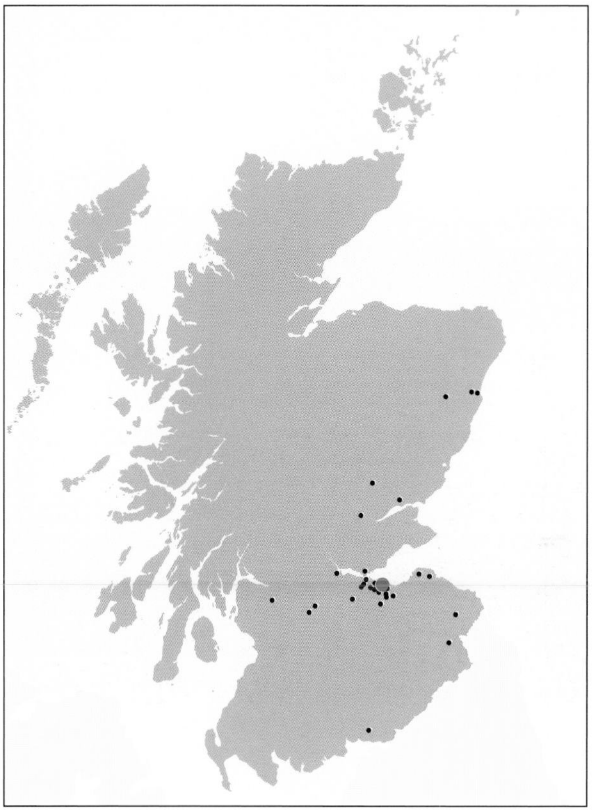

J & F Johnston & Partners

Provenance
The J & F Johnston & Partners Collection (Accession No. 1995/6) was gifted to the RCAHMS in 1994 by Sandy Brown and Robert Adams when J & F Johnston Ltd, as the practice was known from 1990, went into receivership. The drawings were stored in the attic of the office at 4-5 John's Place, Leith.

History
Joseph Marr Johnston (1871-1934) was educated at George Watson's College, Edinburgh, and was articled to Wardrop & Anderson from 1886 to 1891. He subsequently became Assistant Clerk of Works at the University of Edinburgh, a post that he probably gained through his association with Rowand Anderson's work on the McEwan's Hall, Bristo Square, Edinburgh. He was later employed as chief assistant in the Leith office of W N Thomson before setting up his own practice J M Johnston in 1900, initially based at 34 Bernard Street, Leith. Shortly afterwards the practice relocated to 56 Constitution Street, later designated 47 Queen Charlotte Street, from where they branched out into shipping and naval work during the First World War.

Around 1930, Johnston's son James (1901-1992) who had studied at Edinburgh College of Art, joined the practice, taking it over four years later in 1934 after his father's death. He was joined by his brother Frank (1906-1994) and the practice was renamed J & F Johnston.

The beginning of the 1960s saw additional partners join the practice, including Thomas Inglis (d.1988), Donald Cattanach (d.1985) and Alexander Brown (ret. 1990). Under the title J & F Johnston & Partners, the practice moved to larger premises at 4-5 John's Place, Leith. In 1969 both James and Frank Johnston retired but remained as consultants over the following decade. Additional partners, John McLaren and Tom P Craig joined in 1974. At this time, a growth of commissions in the North East of Scotland led to the opening of an additional office managed by another new partner, George Hutcheson. In 1981 George Gilbert joined the firm. Keith MacDonald, Nigel Somner and Bob Adams also became partners over the following decade. In 1994 the practice was incorporated into Fletcher Joseph Ltd of 35a Melville Street, Edinburgh.

Scope and Content
The J & F Johnston & Partners Collection comprises over 52,000 drawings of which 1,231 drawings and photographs have been catalogued. This component comprises 99 projects and includes all pre-1950 work as well as several major projects from after that date.

The practice was renowned for its school designs and the catalogued part of the Collection features papers for several Edinburgh schools built between 1930 and 1960 and includes a number of presentation drawings. Projects include Carrickvale Secondary, Stenhouse Street West (*c.*1935-36); Ainslie Park High School, Pilton, now in use as the North Campus of Telford College (begun 1938); Burdiehouse Primary (1950-55); a new science wing for Daniel Stewart College (1959-60); and the Sighthill College Complex (1966-71).

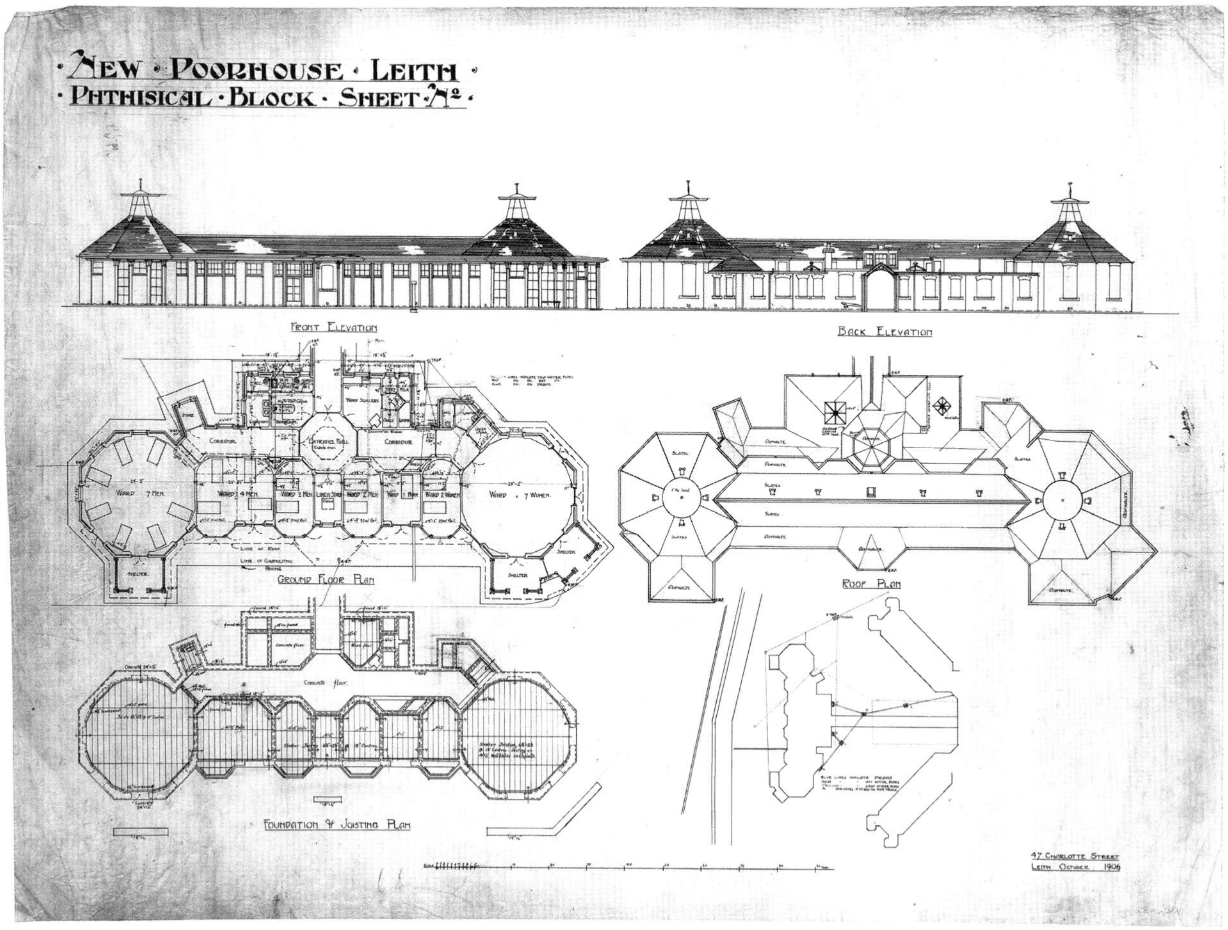

Plans and elevations of Leith Poorhouse, Seafield, Edinburgh by J M Johnston, 1906, from the J & F Johnston & Partners Collection. [SC879169]

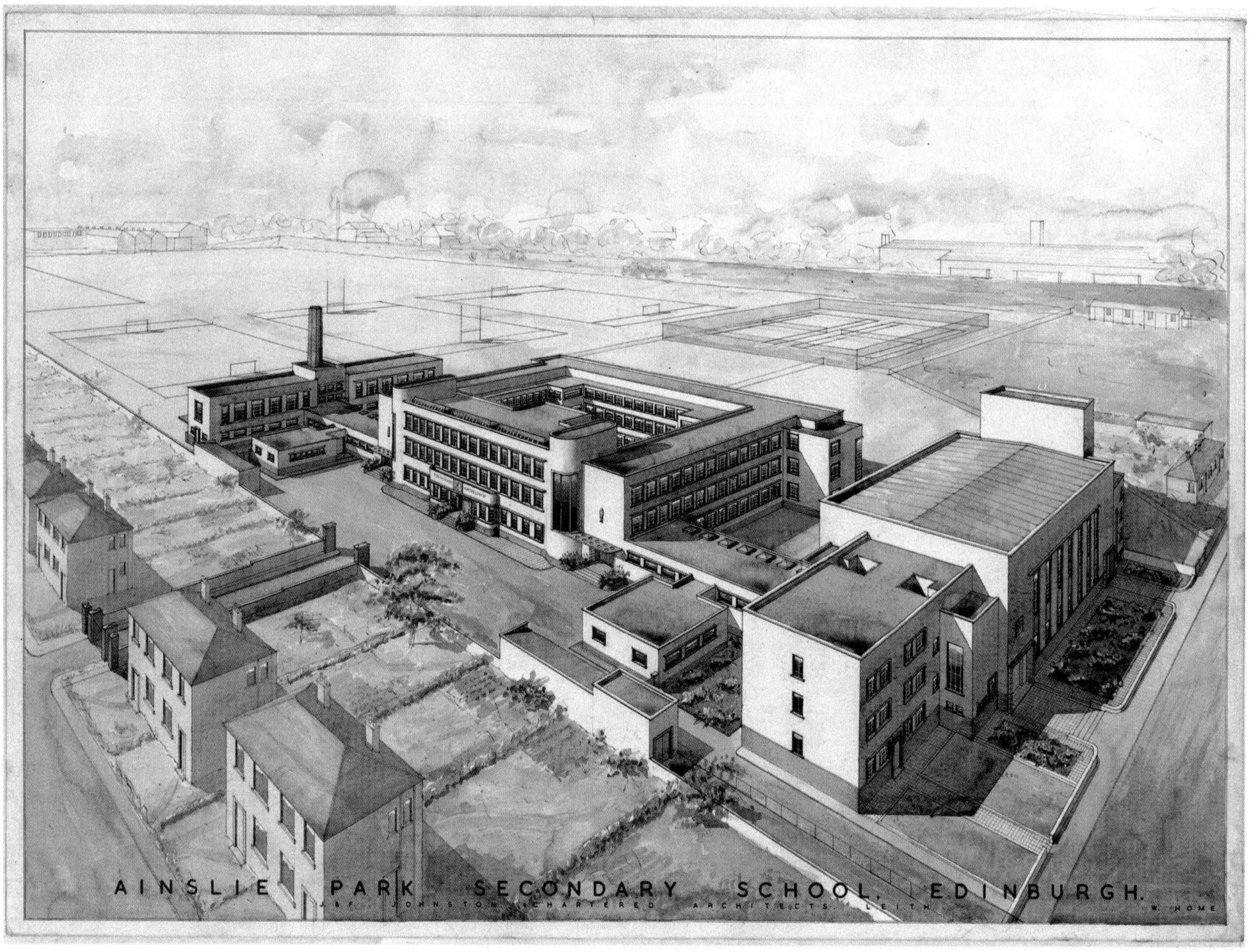

Perspective view of Ainslie Park High School, Pilton, Edinburgh by J & F Johnston, c.1938-54, from the J & F Johnston & Partners Collection. [SC756764]

Photographic view of building work in progress at George Watson's College, Colinton Road, Edinburgh, 1965, from the J & F Johnston & Partners Collection. [SC879166]

Perspective view of extension to George Watson's College, Colinton Road, Edinburgh by J & F Johnston & Partners, c.1963-67, from the J & F Johnston & Partners Collection. [SC879167]

Other catalogued projects include the Poor Law Hospital, Seafield Street, Leith (1904-23); the Alhambra Theatre, 200-204 Leith Walk, Edinburgh (opened 1914, demolished 1974); and the conversion of C & J Brown's warehouse at Bernard Terrace in Edinburgh into premises for RCAHMS (1989-92). The Collection also includes J M Johnston's personal sketchbook (1898-1925).

Drawings not catalogued include papers for Goldberg's department store, High Riggs, Edinburgh (1960) and three large factories for Golden Wonder Crisps Ltd at Widnes, Cheshire (1958); Broxburn, West Lothian (1964); and Northamptonshire (1965).

References

NMRS Sources

- The RIAS Collection, held on deposit in the NMRS, contains 15 J & F Johnston presentation drawings.
- **Johnston, J S 1979** J & F Johnston & Partners, 5 St John's Place, Leith: A Brief History of the Firm.

Anon. 1934 'Joseph Marr Johnston', *RIBA J*, 13 October 1934.

Anon. 1934 'Death of Leith Architect', *The Scotsman*, 3 September 1934.

Anon. 1988 'Mr Tom Inglis', *The Scotsman*, 18 July 1988.

Stevenson, A 2002 'J & F Johnston Collection', *Architect Heritage Soc Scot Mag*, no. 14 (Summer 2002), 29.

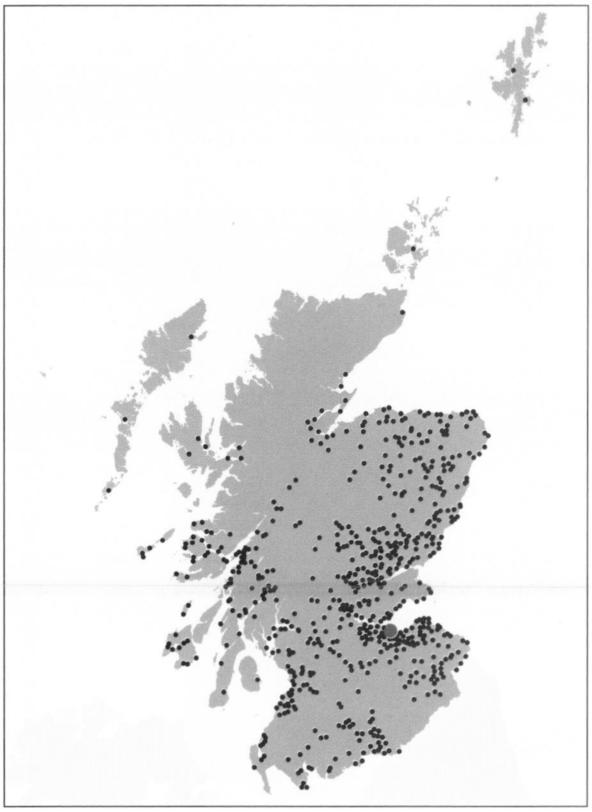

Ian G Lindsay

Provenance

The Ian G Lindsay Collection was gifted to RCAHMS by John H Reid in 1973 (Accession No. 1973/12). A subsequent gift was made in 1992 on the sale of the Slateford Road premises in Edinburgh (Accession No. 1992/50).

History

The practice of Orphoot & Whiting was established after the First World War when Burnet Napier Henderson Orphoot (1880-1964) entered into partnership with Frank Edward Whiting (b.1883). Orphoot had been apprenticed to J M Dick Peddie & Washington Browne and had studied at the Edinburgh School of Applied Art and the École des Beaux Arts in Paris. He had joined Rowand Anderson's office in Edinburgh before then gaining wider experience with Mewes & Davis and Colcutt & Hamp in London. In 1909 he established his own Edinburgh-based practice.

In 1931 Orphoot & Whiting, based at 21 Alva Street, Edinburgh, took Ian Gordon Lindsay (1906-1966) into partnership after he had completed a short apprenticeship with Reginald Fairlie (1883-1952). Edinburgh-born Lindsay was educated at Trinity College, Cambridge, where he studied architecture under David Theodore Fyfe (1875-1944). As a 20-year-old student, Lindsay published *The Cathedrals of Scotland*, the first of many architectural history publications that he wrote during his lifetime, heralding the beginning of a lifetime interest in Scotland's historic buildings, particularly churches and Burgh architecture.

Around 1937 George Hay (1911-1987), an apprentice to Scott Morton & Company, and a former employee of Lorimer & Matthew and the H M Office of Works, joined the practice, now named Orphoot Whiting & Lindsay.

During the Second World War, Orphoot gave up the Alva Street office and practiced from his home at Well House, Belmont Road, Edinburgh. Whiting, who lived mainly in Devon, left the partnership in 1948 and from then until 1952 the practice traded as Orphoot & Lindsay. The name of Ian G Lindsay & Partners was in operation from 1951, firstly at Houstoun House, Uphall, West Lothian and later at 17 Great Stuart Street, Edinburgh, to which the practice relocated in 1952. Walter Schomberg Scott (1910-1988) joined the firm in 1946 and became a partner, along with Hay, in 1953.

In 1959 John H Reid, who had joined the practice in 1952, replaced Scott as partner. The following year Hay left the practice to return to the Ministry of Public Building and Works as an Ancient Monuments architect. Ian H Marshall and Crichton W Lang joined the practice in 1963 and 1965 respectively, both becoming partners later that decade.

On Lindsay's death in 1966, John H Reid became the senior partner. In 1968 he moved the practice to Slateford House, Lanark Road, Edinburgh and in the same year the Dalgeish Lindsay Group was formed. Offices were opened in Athens, Nairobi and Lusaka to deal with the practice's overseas projects. Reid led the practice until 1984 and in 1992 the office at Slateford Road closed.

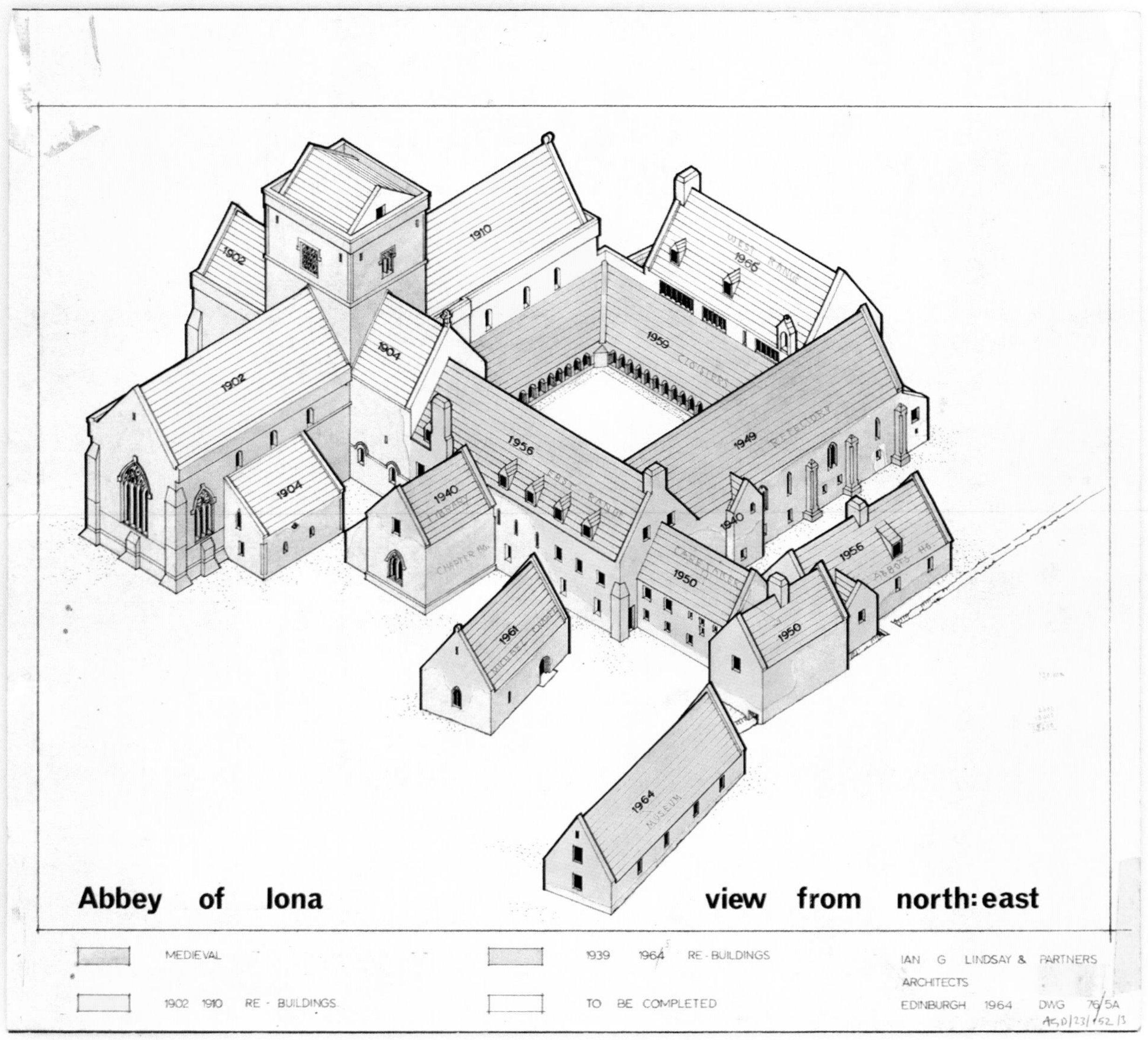

Isometric view of Iona Abbey from North East showing restoration work by Ian G Lindsay & Partners, 1964, from the Ian G Lindsay Collection. [SC742001]

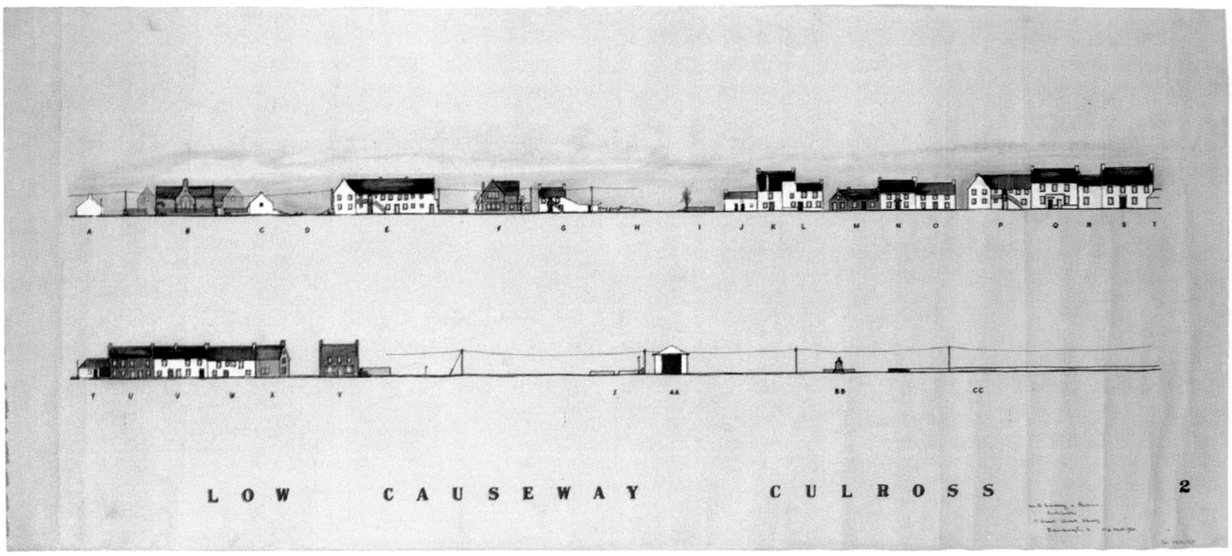

Elevations of Low Causeway, Culross, Fife by Ian G Lindsay & Partners, 1960, from the Ian G Lindsay Collection. [SC732546]

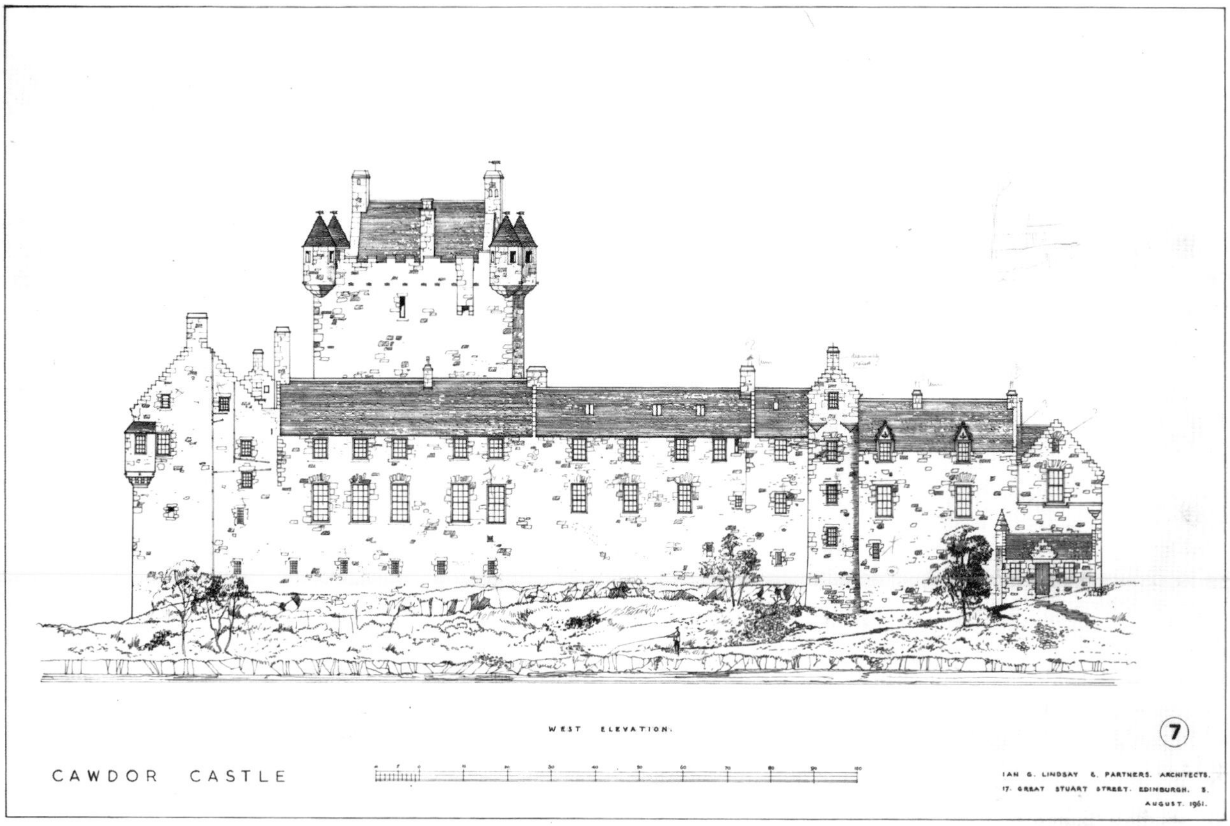

Elevation of Cawdor Castle, Nairn by Ian G Lindsay & Partners, 1961, from the Ian G Lindsay Collection. [SC879163]

Scope and Content

The Collection comprises approximately 26,000 drawings, mostly encompassing jobs undertaken during Ian Lindsay's lifetime, but also including projects from the Orphoot & Whiting phases of the practice and work carried out by Ian G Lindsay & Partners after Lindsay's death. Under the leadership of Lindsay, the practice not only pioneered the repair, restoration and conversion of buildings as an alternative to demolition, but also brought to the fore the concept that Scotland's small houses were as worthy of preservation as its great castles. Early projects in the Collection that demonstrate Lindsay's growing interest in conservation include the restoration of James Smith's 1685 Canongate Kirk, Edinburgh (*c*.1938-54); Iona Abbey for the Iona Community (*c*.1939-52); William Burn's early 19th century North Leith Parish Church, Madeira Street, Edinburgh (*c*.1946-50); and Pluscarden Priory, Morayshire (*c*.1946-63).

In the years before the Second World War, Ian Lindsay became involved with the 4th Marquis of Bute and his concern for the future of towns and villages across Scotland, where decayed old housing stock was facing demolition on sanitary grounds. Lindsay was commissioned by the Marquis to continue his work in surveying buildings worthy of conservation. The work was interrupted by the war, towards the end of which Lindsay was appointed chief investigator to implement the historic buildings legislation in the Town and Country Planning Act of 1945. His lists were adopted by the Secretary of State and form the nucleus of the listing system today. The formation of the Scottish National Buildings Record, now the NMRS, was another Bute-initiated enterprise to which Lindsay acted as expert advisor.

As a result of Lindsay's expertise in the conservation field, Ian Lindsay & Partners became specialists in the restoration and adaptation of dilapidated building stock in the small communities of Falkland, Fife (1936-48); Dunkeld, Perthshire (1953-63); the Royal Burgh of Culross, Fife (1950-67); Cramond, Edinburgh (1958-63); Kenmore, Argyll (1960-66); and Newhaven, Edinburgh (1961-79), projects which are all contained in the Collection. Also included is the complete restoration of the Duke of Argyll's 18th century planned town of Inveraray, Argyll (1955-62); and the residential buildings at Robert Owen and David Dale's industrial planned village of New Lanark (1965-73).

The Collection contains many examples of the practice's country house commissions, including Mertoun House, Berwickshire (*c*.1950-55), where the practice oversaw the demolition of the 19th century wings allowing the original work of Sir William Bruce (*c*.1630-1710) to stand proud; work on the 16th century Craignish Castle, Argyll (1954-60); Bemersyde House, Berwickshire (1959), where they carried out a programme of reduction and remodelling; and Makerstoun House, Kelso, Roxburghshire (1970-74), which was rebuilt following a fire to William Adam's original plan of 1714 and for which they received a Special Merit in 1975 as part of the European Architectural Heritage Awards. Also included are drawings for the restoration of Inveraray Castle (1950-76), a key project in Lindsay's career, that was accompanied by research, culminating in the seminal publication *Inveraray and the Dukes of Argyll*, published posthumously.

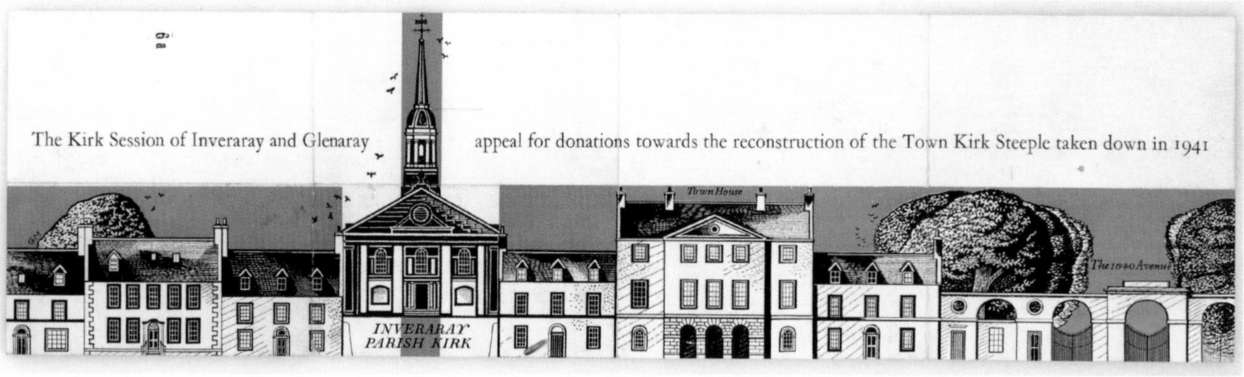

An illustration for a leaflet appealing for funds to reconstruct Inveraray Town Kirk Steeple, c.1961, from the Ian G Lindsay Collection. [SC742010]

Although the practice was well known for their conservation work, this did not prevent them working on commissions for new buildings such as Eventyr, Longniddry, East Lothian (1934-36); Allt a Bhruais, Spean Bridge (1935-38); St Finnan's RC Church, Invergarry (*c*.1936-8); Livingston Station Church (1949); Colinton Mains Church, Edinburgh (1954); and the chapel at Carberry Tower, East Lothian (1964-65); all of which are included in the Collection. New housing is well represented, with large schemes for Newhaven, Edinburgh (1961-79); and Lochgilphead, Argyll (1960-62); along with new dwellings for gap sites within conservation areas such as 2-10 Dean Path, Edinburgh (1957-63); and 20-30 Canongate, Edinburgh (1957-64).

A significant client featured in the Collection is the University of Edinburgh, for whom Ian Lindsay & Partners restored St Cecilia's Hall (*c*.1964-74), originally built for the Edinburgh Musical Society by Robert Mylne in 1762. The conversion of tenements in the late 17th century Mylne's Court and the surrounding Mound and Lawnmarket area into halls of residence, for which the practice received a Saltire Society Award in 1971, is also well documented, as are the practice's major changes to the interior of Old College to create gallery space, a Centre for European Studies, and offices (1969-73).

The Collection includes student and early professional drawings by Orphoot (*c*.1906) and many acquired drawings, including examples by Sir Robert Rowand Anderson for the McEwan Hall, Bristo Place, Edinburgh (1889); by Sydney Mitchell & Wilson for Duntreath Castle, Stirlingshire (1889-90); and by Lorimer & Matthew for St John's Church, Perth (1923-30).

References

NMRS Sources

- The NMRS holds a large collection of personal and office correspondence; press cuttings albums from 1923-82; 26 notebooks and sketchbooks from 1923, including record surveys and site notes; photograph files of works executed by the practice; a file of research material on Scottish churches; two binders of job numbers for commissions; recording drawings issued and names of draughtsmen; and a typed alphabetical index (MS 754). The NMRS also holds 31 sketchbooks from 1923-35 covering a diverse range of architectural and antiquarian subjects, presented by Mrs Lindsay in 1967; a folder of certificates for design awards from the Civic Trust and Saltire Society (1959-80), deposited by John Reid in 1983; and typescript lists of maps of 'Little Houses' in Scottish towns compiled in the late 1930s, presented by Mrs Christine McWilliam as part of the McWilliam Collection in 1989.
- **Cruft, K** Unpublished lecture on Ian G Lindsay.
- **Hay, J** Unpublished typescript about George Hay (1911-1987).
- **Lindsay, I G 1962** 'Special architectural or historic interest': or the ways and means at present operative to preserve our building heritage.
- **Lindsay, I G 1963** Visit to Australia, 1962-63.

Anon. 1964 'Obituary: Mr B N H Orphoot', *The Scotsman*, 9 April 1964.
Aldred, N 2002 'Scottish Architects' Papers Preservation Project: Ian G Lindsay Collection', *Architect Heritage Soc Scot Mag*, no. 15 (Winter 2002), 35.
Aldred, N 2003 'From Filling the Kist to Fitted Kitchen: 100 Years of Rural Housing in Scotland', *Architect Heritage XIV*, 8-21. Edinburgh: Edinburgh Univ Press.
Betjeman, J 1967 'Obituary: Ian G Lindsay', *RIBA J*, April 1967.
Lindsay, I G 1926 *The Cathedrals of Scotland*, London and Edinburgh: W and R Chambers.
Lindsay, I G 1939 *Old Edinburgh 1939*. Edinburgh: Oliver and Boyd.
Lindsay, I G *c*.1946 *Canongate Kirk: the Kirk of Holyroodhouse: the Church, Canongate Booklets No.1.* Edinburgh.
Lindsay, I G 1947 *Old Edinburgh 1947*. Edinburgh: Oliver and Boyd.

Ian G Lindsay (1906-1966). Image courtesy of The Herald & Evening Times Picture Archive.

Lindsay, I G 1948 'The Restoration of Iona Abbey and Pluscarden Priory', *Trans Scot Eccles Soc*, vol. 14, 7-17.
Lindsay, I G 1948 *St Nicholas' Kirk, Strathbrock: North Church, Uphall.*
Lindsay, I G 1948 *The Scottish Tradition in Burgh Architecture*. Edinburgh: The Saltire Society, Scottish Tradition Series.
Lindsay, I G 1948 *Architecture in Scotland*, The Arts Council of Gr Brit, catalogue to accompany exhibition.
Lindsay, I G 1948 *Georgian Edinburgh*. Edinburgh: Oliver and Boyd.
Lindsay, I G 1949 *St Cuthbert's Parish Kirk, Dalmeny*. Edinburgh.
Lindsay, I G 1949 *The Parish Kirk of Kirkliston*. Edinburgh.
Lindsay, I G 1950 'Some Notes on Renovations', *Trans Scot Eccles Soc*, vol.14, 43-5.
Lindsay, I G 1950 'The Kirks of the Diocese of Dunblane', *Soc Friends Dunblane Cathedral*, vol.6, 8-17.
Lindsay, I G 1953 *The Friary Church of Mount Carmel, South Queensferry*. Edinburgh.
Lindsay, I G 1953 'The Little Houses of Scotland: a Statement of the Work of the National Trust for Scotland', *RIAS Quart* (February 1953), 3-6.
Lindsay, I G 1956 'Face of a City', *Scotland's Mag*, vol.52, 24-27.
Lindsay, I G 1956 'The Kirk at Kilcrochet', *Architect Prospect*, November 1956, 16-20.
Lindsay, I G 1959 *The Royal Burgh of Culross*. Edinburgh: National Trust Scot.
Lindsay, I G and MacGregor, D B *c*.1960 *Pittenweem Priory*. Anstruther.
Lindsay, I G 1960 *The Scottish Parish Kirk*. Edinburgh: St Andrew Press.
Lindsay, I G and Cosh, M 1973 *Inveraray and the Dukes of Argyll*. Edinburgh: Edinburgh Univ Press.
McWilliam, C 1966 'Obituary for Ian G Lindsay', *The Scotsman*, 5 Sept 1966.

Related practices/personnel:
Lorimer & Matthew Collection
Sydney Mitchell & Wilson Collection
Scott Morton Collection
Schomberg Scott Collection

For other Ian G Lindsay papers:
Schomberg Scott Collection

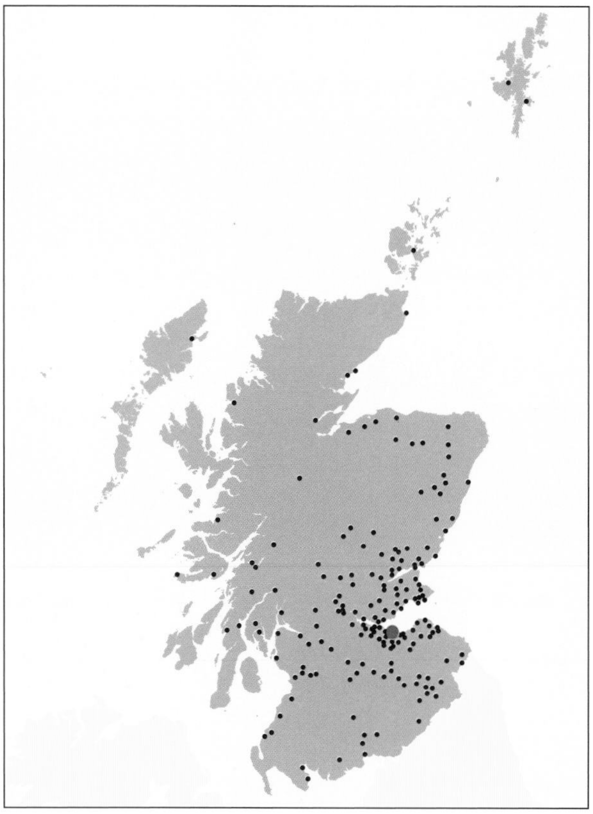

Lorimer & Matthew

Provenance

The majority of the Lorimer & Matthew Collection was presented to RCAHMS by Stuart Matthew in several phases, the first being a large proportion of the office drawings in 1968. By this time the Collection had already been moved several times to different locations in Edinburgh, including premises occupied by Robert Matthew Johnson Marshall & Partners, the practice of Stuart Matthew's brother.

In 1978 Stuart Matthew presented a further series of drawings from both the Lorimer & Matthew and Carr & Matthew practices (Accession No. 1978/20) and two years later RCAHMS purchased further material, including presentation drawings of the Thistle Chapel and the Scottish National War Memorial (Accession No. 1980/8). Stuart Matthew made a gift of photographs in 1990, mostly comprising general views and details of war memorials (Accession No. 1990/54), followed by another large collection of drawings, news-cuttings, correspondence and photographs in 1995 (Accession No. 1995/11).

In addition, the Lorimer & Matthew Collection also includes two collections of photographs presented by Peter Savage (Accession Nos. 1989/20 and 1990/30) along with plans and correspondence gifted by J W F Morton (Accession No. 1976/6) relating to Tuethur House, Carlisle; Morton Sundour Fabrics Ltd, Carlisle; and to Craigiehall House, West Lothian.

Further important accessions of office and personnel papers are all outwith the scope of SAPPP but are listed under the NMRS Sources at the end of this essay.

History

Robert Stoddart Lorimer (1864-1929) was born in Edinburgh in 1864. He was educated at Edinburgh Academy and then Edinburgh University before taking an apprenticeship in 1885 with Sir Robert Rowand Anderson (1864-1929) and his partner Hew Montgomerie Wardrop (1856-1887). In 1889 Lorimer left Edinburgh for London to join the practice of G F Bodley (1827-1907). He later briefly worked in the office of James Majoribanks MacLaren (1853-1890) before returning to Scotland having won his first commission, to restore Earlshall, Leuchars in 1891. In 1893 Lorimer opened an office at 49 Queen Street, Edinburgh where he remained until 1913.

From *c.*1913 the practice resided at 17 Great Stuart Street, Edinburgh. In 1927 Lorimer's office manager (and first apprentice) John Matthew (1875-1955) was assumed into partnership and the practice was renamed Lorimer & Matthew. On Lorimer's death in 1929, Matthew continued the practice alone until succeeded by his son Stuart Matthew (1912-1996) in 1946. Following the creation of a partnership with David Carr (1905-1986), the practice became Carr & Matthew. Previously, Carr had been in partnership with W F Howard following their winning entry for Kirkcaldy Town Hall (completed 1956). The Carr & Matthew practice resided at 14 Lynedoch Place, Edinburgh.

Scope and content

The Collection totals 35,220 items comprising 33,000 drawings and 2,220 photographs ranging in date from

Design for Air Force bay, Scottish National War Memorial, Edinburgh Castle by R S Lorimer, c.1925, from the Lorimer & Matthew Collection. [SC742115]

Photographic view of building work in progress on the North façade and shrine, Scottish National War Memorial, Edinburgh Castle, c.1924, from the Lorimer & Matthew Collection. [SC708451]

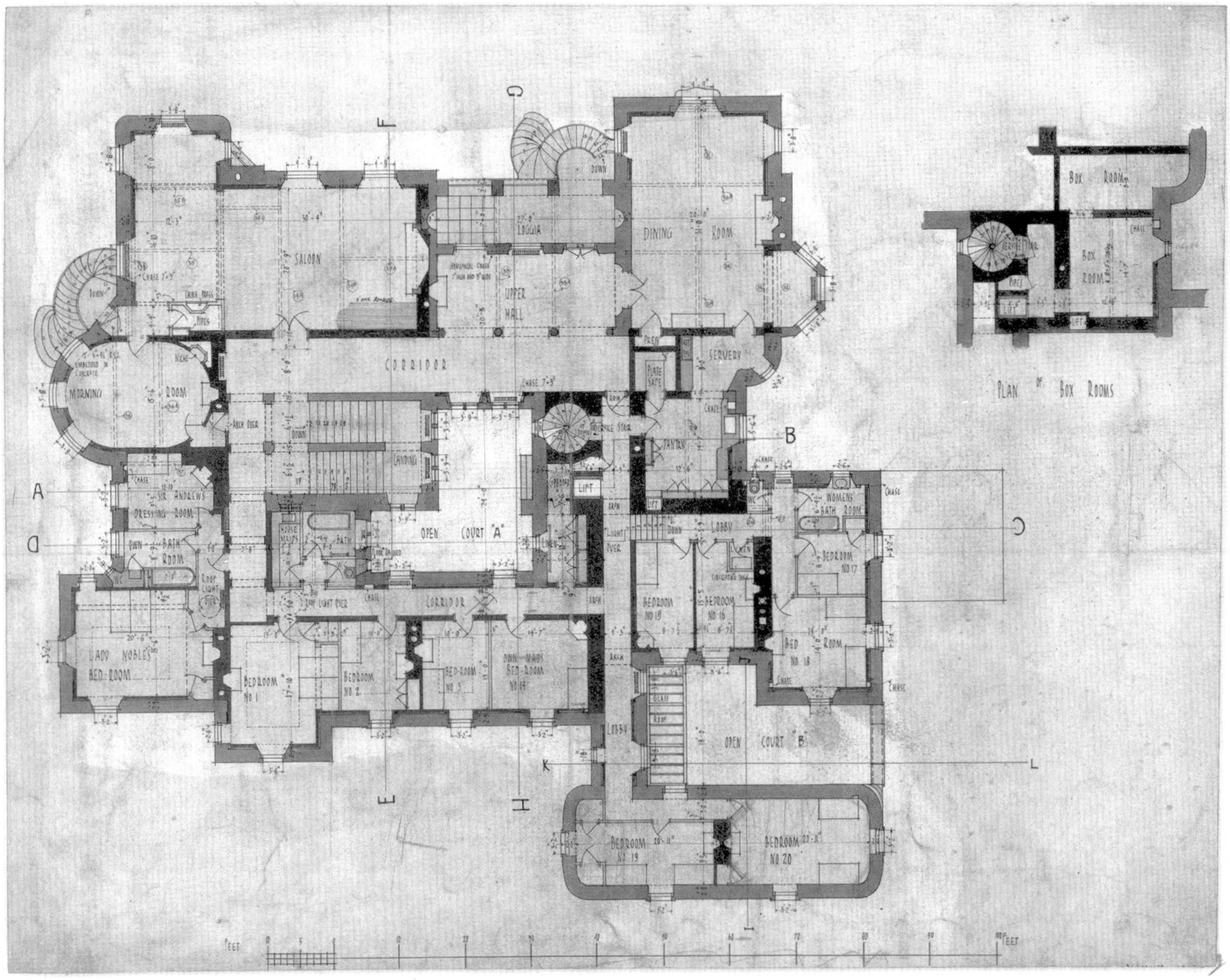

Principal floor plan of Ardkinglas, Argyll by R S Lorimer, 1906, from the Lorimer & Matthew Collection. [SC732518]

Photographic view of building work in progress at Ardkinglas, Argyll, c.1908, from the Lorimer & Matthew Collection. [SC732520]

the 1890s to the 1960s. It reflects Lorimer's position as one of Scotland's leading country house architects during the first two decades of the 20th century, with his 'traditionalist' approach of drawing influence from the past, his adherence to the Arts and Crafts ethos of simple façades built from local materials, and his rejection of highly ornamental façades that came into fashion during the mid-19th century through historicist eclecticism. These beliefs are well illustrated by papers for houses such as Rowallan, Ayrshire (*c.*1901-6); Ardkinglas, Argyll (1906-12); Rhu-Na-Haven, Aboyne, Aberdeenshire (1907-11); and Formakin, Renfrewshire (1903-20).

The Collection not only incorporates existing houses across Scotland for which Lorimer provided large extensions, such as Craigmyle, Torphins, Aberdeenshire (1901-10); Pitkerro, Broughty Ferry, Dundee (1902-10); Wemyss Hall, Fife (1904-14, now known as Hill of Tarvit); and Bardrochat, Colmonell, Ayrshire (1906-8); but also includes papers for interiors that he remodelled such as those at Aberlour House, Fife (*c.*1892) and Marchmont House, Berwickshire (*c.*1913-17). It includes drawings for fire-damaged premises that Lorimer made fit for rehabitation such as Ellary, Ardrishaig, Argyll (1894-7); The Glen, Innerleithen (1905-11); Monzie Castle, Perthshire (1908-11); and Dunrobin Castle, Sutherland (1911-20).

Lorimer's skill as an interior and furniture designer as well as an architect is also apparent in his ecclesiastical commissions: his many designs for reredos, panelling and furnishings are included in the Collection, demonstrating his close working relationship with craftsmen such as Scott Morton & Company. The prime example is the Thistle Chapel, St Giles' Cathedral, Edinburgh, a project which earned Lorimer his knighthood in 1911 and for which there are 645 drawings in the Collection. Other examples include St Andrew's Episcopal Church, Aberdeen (1910-21); Dunblane Cathedral, Perthshire (*c.*1911-29); and St John's Church, Lattingtown, USA (1921-31).

This use of craftsmen is well documented in the Collection, which contains drawings and photographs of work by many craftsmen who were contracted by the practice, including Thomas Hadden Ornamental Blacksmiths, W & A Clow, Alice Meredith Williams (*c.*1870-1934), Phoebe Traquair (1852-1936) and Scott Morton & Company. Included in the Collection are drawings for The Glen, Innerleithen by David Bryce (1803-1876) that date from *c.*1855 to 1857. Also extant within the Collection are a number of competition designs by Carr & Howard including Waverley Market, Edinburgh (1938-39), and Newcastle Town Hall (1938).

During the 1920s Lorimer received many commissions for war memorials, the largest of which, and perhaps his best known work, was the Scottish National War Memorial, Edinburgh Castle (*c.*1919-27) for which there are over 1,000 drawings and photographs. These show the complete design process from early aborted schemes to working drawings for the shrine and for the individual memorials dedicated to each Scottish regiment. Drawings for over 300 memorials to the dead from villages, towns and schools

Sketch design for a carved bull head for the Bilsland Crest, Thistle Chapel, St Giles Cathedral, Edinburgh, by Lorimer & Matthew, c.1950, from the Lorimer & Matthew Collection. [SC889799]

in Scotland and England are contained in the Collection along with papers for cemeteries in Greece, Macedonia, Italy and Egypt that Lorimer designed in his capacity as one of the official architects to the Imperial War Graves Commission.

Lorimer's work in England is well represented in the Collection and includes Barton Hartshorn, Buckinghamshire (1901-14); the renovation of Lympne Castle, Kent (1906-20); a large extension to the Morton Sundour carpet factory, Carlisle (1915-25), the architect's only industrial commission; St Andrew's Church, Aldershot (1925-6, altered 1945-52); and Stowe School Chapel, Buckinghamshire (1926-49).

The work of Lorimer's partner John Matthew is evident in the Collection which incorporates projects he continued after Lorimer's death, such as the King's Buildings, University of Edinburgh (1926-34); and St Margaret's Church, Knightswood, Glasgow (1929-34); as well as his own projects such as Granton Parish Church, Edinburgh (1934-36).

Carr & Matthew work represented in the Collection includes the Scottish National Institute for the War Blinded, Linburn, West Lothian (1946-51); and the Thistle Foundation, Craigmillar, Edinburgh (1945-50), two major projects that catered for those injured in the Second World War. The Observatory and Natural Philosophy Department, University of St Andrews (1948-58); Duddingston Primary School, Edinburgh (1950-57); an extension to Warriston Crematorium, Edinburgh (1951-61); and a large housing scheme in the Meadowbank area of Edinburgh (1952-60); are also large post-war commissions that are well represented.

R S Lorimer (1864-1929).

References

The Lorimer & Matthew office correspondence is held in the Special Collections department of University of Edinburgh Library.

NMRS Sources

The NMRS has a large amount of material relating to Sir Robert Lorimer that was largely received after SAPPP had started and was thus not catalogued as part of the Project. This includes:

- Accounts and bills for work at 54 Melville Street, Edinburgh and correspondence to Sir R S Lorimer, presented by Stuart Matthew (Accession No. 1990/25).
- A collection of papers from the Lorimer office relating to the design of the Thistle Chapel, St Giles Cathedral, Edinburgh. Includes correspondence files, specifications, receipts, invoices and a statement of 'total cost', gifted by Stuart Matthew (Accession No. 1996/14).
- Collection of material from Lorimer's office: two volumes of account books (1910-31 and 1925-30); an album of photographs of chimney-pieces and furniture with annotations by Lorimer; 14 glass plate negatives showing views of Edinburgh decorated for a royal visit (probably 1911) (Accession No. 1996/18).
- A collection of architects' papers from Alfred G Lochhead (*c.*1888-1972) largely relating to Lorimer & Matthew and including many designs for war memorials (Accession No. 1997/101).
- A large collection of material relating to the work of Lorimer & Matthew representing the remainder of the office papers as well as a cabinet of drawing instruments and maquettes for architectural sculpture. The papers include an incomplete run of office diaries (1907-34); an incomplete run of office certificate books (1892-1928); John Matthew's letter book of 1899 (unfinished); and material relating to Stuart Matthew, including his student notebooks. Purchase assisted with a grant from the Heritage Lottery Fund (Accession Nos. 1998/135 and 1999/27).
- A collection of drawings, photographs, notebooks and other papers relating to the work of George Walls (1902-1977), an apprentice and assistant with Sir Robert Lorimer from 1919-25. Presented by Dr Archie Walls (Accession No. 2000/46).
- A collection of material relating to Sir Robert Lorimer and Lorimer & Matthew including certificate books from the period 1894-1928, notebooks and ledgers, Stuart Matthew's college notebooks 1930-1932, and Sir Robert Lorimer's diaries from the period 1905-1934 (Accession No. 2000/220).
- A set of sketchbooks belonging to Robert Lorimer gifted by William Lorimer (Accession No. 2002/29).
- Savage, P The Work of Sir Robert Lorimer, ARA, 1864-1929.
- Savage, P Robert Lorimer's Colinton Manner of Design.

Anon. 1929 'Obituary: Sir Robert Lorimer, KBE, HON, LLD, ARA, RSA', *The Times*, 14 September 1929.

Anon. 1996 'Obituary: Stuart Matthew', *The Scotsman*, 25 May 1996.

Deas, F W 1933 'The Work of Sir Robert Lorimer', *Trans Edinburgh Architect Ass*, vol. 10, 113-26.

Hussey, C 1931 *The Work of Sir Robert Lorimer*. London: Country Life.

Hussey, C 1964 'Kellie Castle, Fife: the Home of Mr and Mrs Hew Lorimer', *Country Life*, vol.135, 446-9.

Lorimer, R S 1899 'On Scottish Gardens', *Architect Rev*, November 1899, 194-205.

Matthew, S 1988 *The Knights and Chapel of the Most Ancient and Most Noble Order of the Thistle: a Panoramic View*. Edinburgh: Eaglebank Publications.

Mays, D 1990 'Lorimer in Perspective', *RIBA J* (December 1990), 34-9.

McKean, C 1991 'Sketchy Outline of a Cultured Man', *The Scotsman*, 4 March 1991, 15.

Savage, P 1975 'Lorimer and the Scottish Tradition', *Weekend Scotsman*, 31 May 1975.

Savage, P 1977 'Lorimer and the Garden Heritage of Scotland', *J Garden Hist Soc*, vol.v, no.2.

Savage, P 1980 *Lorimer and the Edinburgh Craft Designers*. London and Edinburgh: Paul Harris.

Thomas, J 1999 'Lorimer Papers Saved for Scotland', *Architect Heritage Soc Scot Mag*, 8, 26.

Watters, D 2001 'The Scottish National War Mar Memorial', *Architect Heritage Soc Scot Mag*, 12 (Summer 2000), 34-35.

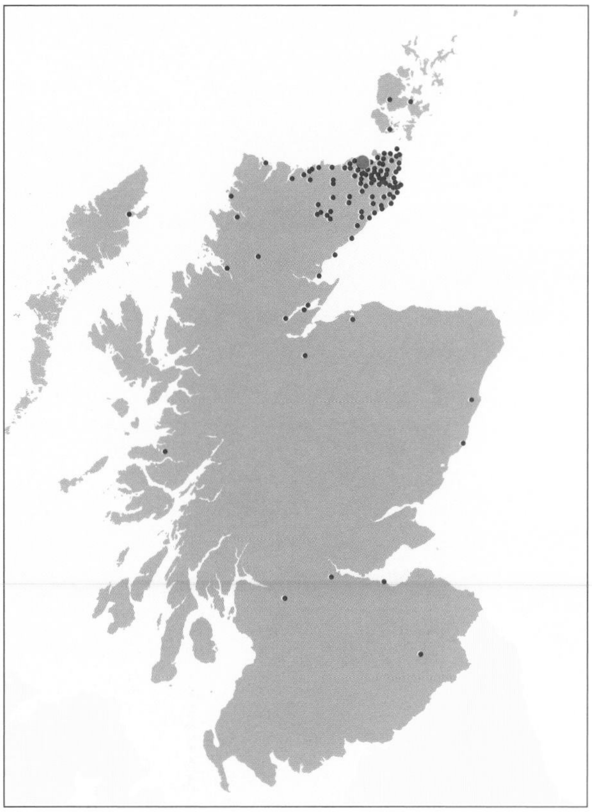

Sinclair Macdonald & Son

Provenance
The Sinclair Macdonald & Son Collection (Accession No. 2001/40) was presented to RCAHMS by Mr James Campbell in 1996 following survey by the SSAP. The Collection had been stored in the roof space of 18 Princes Street, Thurso. Drawings were stored in numbered rolls wrapped in brown paper, with each roll containing a large variety of projects. It is thought that this numbering took place in either the 1940s or 1950s. A typed list of roll numbers and the projects contained within each roll was included with the Collection.

The Collection is held at the North Highland Archive, Wick Library, Sinclair Terrace, Wick under a Charge and Superintendence Agreement.

History
The practice was founded by Barbaretus Sinclair Macdonald (1864-1936), a native of Brora, Sutherland. Trained in Aberdeen and later in Inverness under the tutelage of Alexander Ross (1834-1925), Macdonald opened an office at 14 Olrig Street, Thurso *c.*1889. A few years later, the office moved to 18 Princes Street, Thurso. Later, secondary offices in Wick and Kirkwall were established. Among those who worked for the practice were James C Leed, FRIBA, who joined for a time in the 1930s; Archibald James Baxter, RIBA, a partner in the firm from 1935 to the 1940s; and C I Edmonstone who served as an architectural assistant in the practice from 1939-42. Sinclair Macdonald's son Hugh Macdonald (1903-1979) became a partner in 1931, and was a constant presence in the company, except for a six-year period of service in the forces during the Second World War.

In 1960, James Campbell (apprenticed with the firm 1948-51 before attending Edinburgh College of Art), and John Barnie (ret.1990), an architectural draughtsman apprentice in the Wick office from 1938-39, were assumed as partners with Hugh Macdonald. This arrangement continued until the late 1970s at which time there were five partners – including Alastair (b.1943), Hugh's son – and offices in Thurso, Kirkwall and Edinburgh. In 1995, Sinclair Macdonald & Son amalgamated with Stockan & Sloan Surveyors of Kirkwall to form a multi-disciplinary firm. James Campbell was principal of Sinclair Macdonald & Son from the mid-1980s until 1995 when he became a partner in Stockan Sloan & Sinclair Macdonald, architects and surveyors. He retired in 1999.

Scope and Content
The Collection consists of 7,689 drawings and 319 manuscripts comprising job files, specifications, budgets, correspondence, drawings and some photographs relating to buildings in Caithness and Sutherland. It demonstrates the practice's position as the main architect in the North Highlands during the 1890-1940 period and thus reflects the general living conditions in Scotland's two most northern mainland towns and their rural hinterland.

Projects from the first three decades of the practice include designs of church and manse buildings for both the United Free Church and the Church of Scotland,

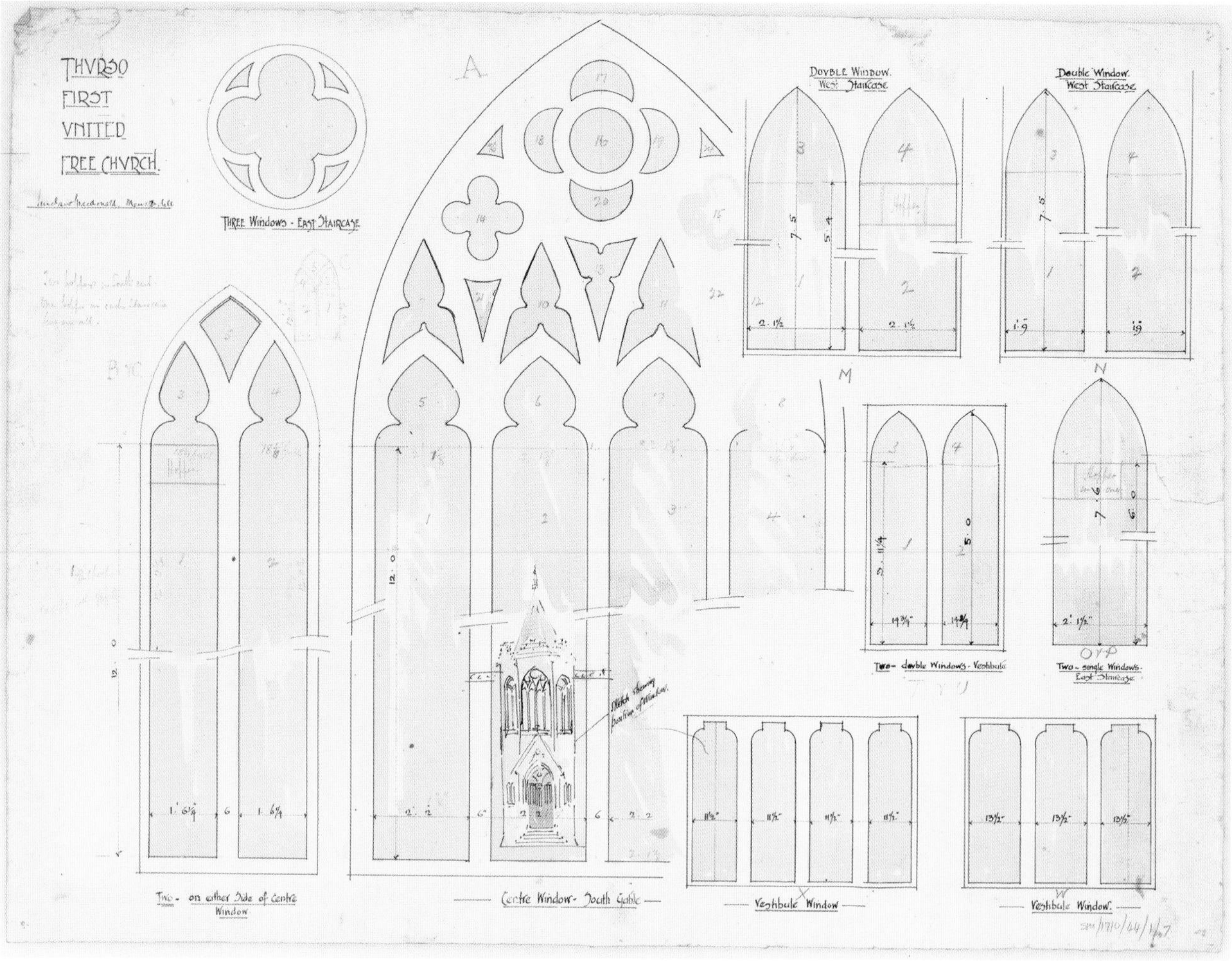

Details of windows for the First United Free Church, Olrig Street, Thurso by Sinclair Macdonald, 1910, from the Sinclair Macdonald & Son Collection. [SC879300]

such as Invergordon (1895), Brora (*c.*1900, manse 1902), Lybster (*c.*1908, manse *c.*1900), Keiss Manse (1909-22), and Olrig Parish Church in Castletown (1913, manse 1916). The Collection includes designs for the Ross Institute village hall in Halkirk (1909) and drawings of the Northern Gate House, originally named Dwarwick House, at Dunnet (*c.*1910, later alterations 1948-51), for [Admiral Sir] Alexander Sinclair of Dunbeath Castle.

The practice's provision and improvement of education buildings throughout the North Highlands is evident in the Collection, with small schools such as Kirtomy (1892), Brawlbin (1892), Banniskirk (1893), Thurso (*c.*1899-1913), Forss (*c.*1900-39), Brora (*c.*1901) and Brabster (1903), along with later work including alterations and additions to Miller's Institution, Davidson's Lane, Thurso (1934-35); Lybster Primary School (1934-37); and Wick North Primary School (1937).

Well documented in the Collection is the substantial amount of reconditioning work that the practice undertook on workers' housing between the late 1920s and the 1950s. These improvements, such as re-roofing, the introduction of sanitary arrangements, and the subdivision of living space, came about as a result of the Association for the Preservation of Rural Scotland's call in 1926 for an improvement to croft dwellings throughout the country. Later in the same year, the 'Housing (Rural Workers) Act' initiated an assistance scheme for the improvement of agricultural housing and Sinclair Macdonald won the Caithness county contract.

Other commissions received in the 1920s and 1930s and featured in the Collection include alterations and additions to Thurso Castle (1918-26, 1946-52); designs for Town Halls at Wick (*c.*1920-31) and at Thurso (*c.*1931-47); the Station Hotel, Bridge Street, Wick (1925-37), in collaboration with Alan Reaich (1910-1992); the restoration of Strathmore Lodge (1928-33); and the offices and power house for the Thurso & District Electric Supply Co Ltd in Wick (1937-47).

During and after the Second World War, the practice continued to receive commissions for a variety of building types, such as hospitals, hotels, commercial, industrial, civic and military buildings. Major projects contained in the Collection include Bignold Hospital, Wick (*c.*1921-50); Dunbar Hospital, Thurso (*c.*1923-50); Garvault Hotel (*c.*1949-50); and the Territorial Army headquarters in Thurso (*c.*1938-40).

The practice executed work for other architects and it is through this role that acquired material can be found in the Collection, such as drawings by Leadbetter & Fairley for the Carnegie Library, Sinclair Terrace, Wick, (1895); by Ninian MacWhannel for Miller's Institution, Davidson's Lane, Thurso (1891-94); and by Greig Fairbairn & McNiven, whose winning standard design for Highland United Free Churches was executed at Bruan (1909-12). In the 1950s and 1960s the practice was commissioned to restore the Castle of Mey for HM

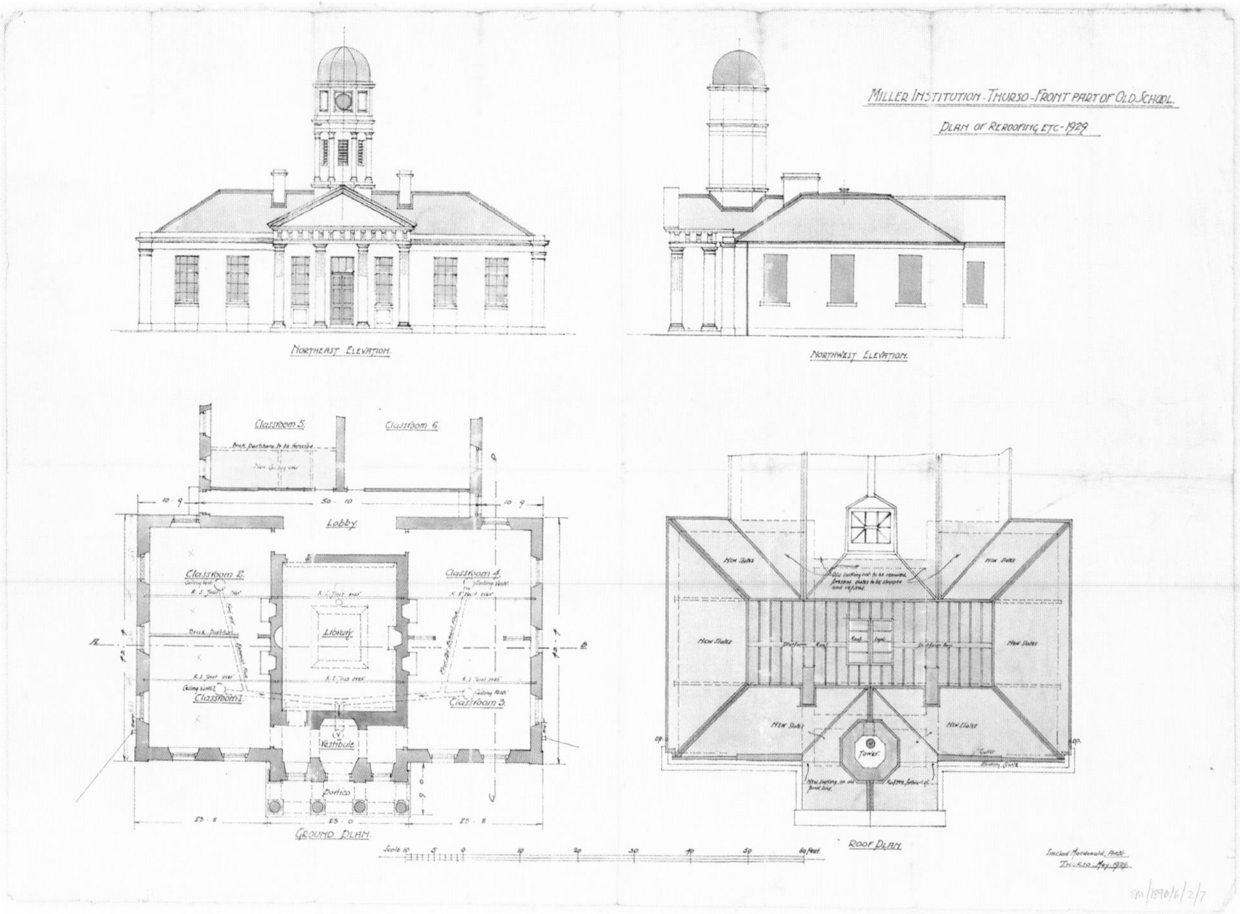

Plans and elevations of the Miller Institution, Davidson's Lane, Thurso by Sinclair Macdonald, 1929, from the Sinclair Macdonald & Son Collection. [SC879302]

Perspective view of shop frontage for Messrs Fred Shearer Ltd at 12 Rotterdam Street, Thurso by A Edmonds & Co Ltd, 1935, from the Sinclair Macdonald & Son Collection. [SC677609]

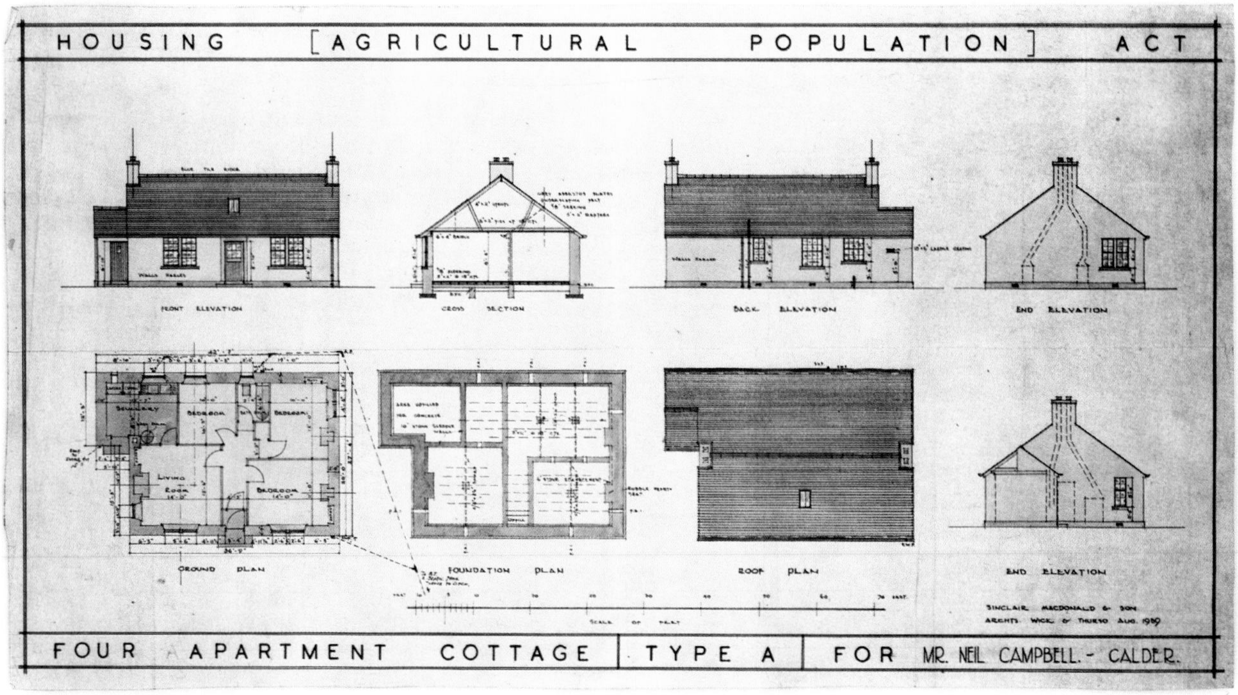

Plans, section and elevations showing reconstruction work on a four apartment cottage at Old Calder, Caithness by Sinclair Macdonald & Son, 1939, from the Sinclair Macdonald & Son Collection. [SC773891]

the Queen Mother and as a result acquired drawings by William Burn (1789-1870) showing his 1819 alterations and additions to the original 16th century fortification.

The practice's work of the 1950s is only partly represented, and no new projects from the 1960s and 1970s are contained within the Collection. Omissions thus include Dounreay power station workers' housing (*c*.1954); Papdale housing; St Anne's Roman Catholic Church, Thurso (1960); and Tollemache House, Thurso (1963).

References

Local Authority of the County of Caithness 1937 *Housing (Rural Workers) Act, 1926*. Wick.

Anon. 1936 'Mr Sinclair Macdonald', *Caithness Courier*, 17 January 1936.

Aldred, N 2003 'From filling the kist to fitted kitchen: 100 years of rural housing in Scotland', *Architect Heritage XIV*, 8-21. Edinburgh: Edinburgh Univ Press.

Aldred, N and Gregory, N 2002 'Scottish Architects' Papers from Rural Practices in the Highlands and the North East' *Vernacular Buildings Working Group J*, 15-9.

Gregory, N 2001 'Scottish Architects' Papers Preservation Project: Local Collections', *Architect Heritage Soc Scot Mag*, 13 (Winter 2001), 28.

Houston, L 2004 'Sinclair Macdonald & Son: A Century in Practice', *Architect Heritage Soc Scot Mag*, no. 16/17 (Spring 2004), 52-3.

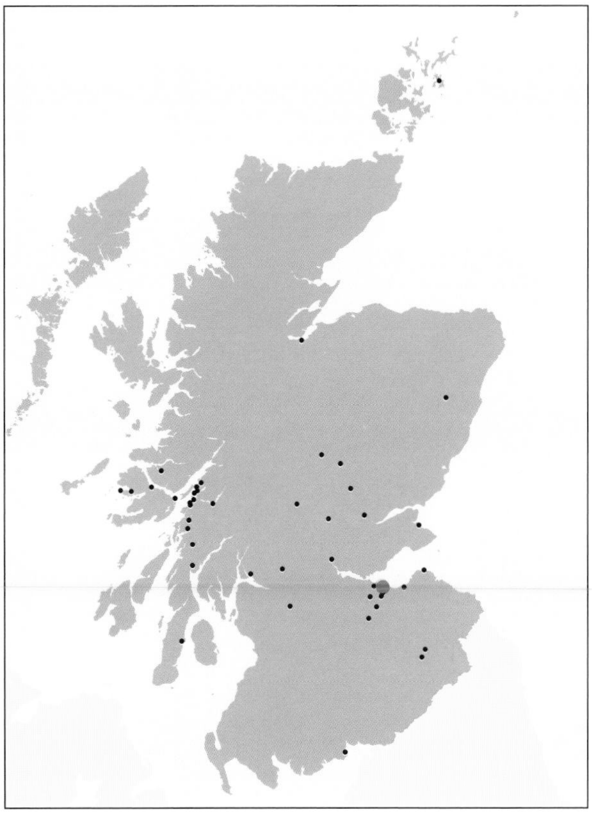

Leslie Grahame Thomson (later MacDougall)

Provenance
The majority of the Leslie Grahame Thomson (MacDougall) Collection was deposited with RCAHMS by his wife, Madame MacDougall, in 1983 (Accession No. 2000/95). During the same year, RCAHMS purchased an album of press cuttings compiled by the architect at the sale of MacDougall's library (MS 275). In 1994, RCAHMS bought additional drawings comprising student work and presentation perspectives.

History
Leslie Grahame MacDougall (1896-1974) was born Leslie Grahame Thomson but renamed himself MacDougall after his second wife, Collean Helen Elizabeth MacDougall, became the Chief of Clan MacDougall in 1953.

After attending Merchiston Castle School, Edinburgh in 1920, he started his architectural training at Edinburgh College of Art under the direction of Sir George Washington Browne PRSA (1853-1939), followed by John Begg PPRIAS (1866-1937). In the same year, he began serving an apprenticeship with Sir Robert Lorimer (1864-1929), working under Alfred G Lochhead (*c.*1888-1972). In 1924 he was the first to complete the full RIBA 'Recognised' Diploma course awarded by Edinburgh College of Art.

In 1926, Thomson set up in practice at 10 St Colme Street, Edinburgh. His first major commission was the Reid Memorial Church, Edinburgh (1928-33). In 1931, he moved the practice to 6 Ainslie Place, Edinburgh, where he also lived.

From 1936-39 Thomson was joined in partnership by Frank Connell to form Leslie Grahame Thomson & Connell. Thomson was President of the Edinburgh Architectural Association from 1949-1951 and President of the RIAS from 1953-55. He was also Joint Honorary Secretary of the Association for the Preservation of Rural Scotland (APRS) with Sir Frank Mears (1880-1953).

From *c.*1953 he lived at Dunollie House, Oban. In the early 1960s the practice opened a branch office at 2 Shore Road, Oban.

Scope and Content
The Collection consists of 2,060 drawings for over 100 projects undertaken in the Lothians, the Borders and in the city of Edinburgh itself, as well as in Argyll and Bute following the removal of the practice to Oban. The Collection illustrates Leslie Grahame Thomson (MacDougall)'s position as one of Scotland's leading traditionalist architects of the 20th century, and demonstrates his advocacy of local materials. The drawings cover the architect's entire working lifespan, ranging from his student drawings in the early 1920s to work carried out in the last years of his life.

Approximately 20% of the Collection comprises drawings for the Reid Memorial Church, West Savile Terrace, Edinburgh (1928-33), which show the influence of Sir Robert Lorimer on Thomson. Other ecclesiastical commissions form a significant component of the Collection and include Fairmilehead Church, Frogston Road, Edinburgh, for Church of Scotland Home Mission

Perspective view of The Isobel Fraser Home of Rest for The Aged Christian Friend Society of Scotland, Mayfield Road, Inverness by Leslie Grahame Thomson, c.1935, from the Leslie Grahame Thomson MacDougall Collection. [SC691950]

Perspective view of the Reid Memorial Church, West Savile Terrace, Edinburgh by Leslie Grahame Thomson, c.1929, from the Leslie Grahame Thomson MacDougall Collection. [SC691954]

Committee (1936-38); the Moncur Memorial Church, Isle of Stronsay, Orkney (1945-53); Longstone Hall Church, Edinburgh (1951-57); and Christ Church Dunollie, Corran Esplanade, Oban (1954-57).

Almost half the projects contained in the Collection are domestic commissions, including houses at Silverburn, Penicuik (1939-55); flats for the City of Edinburgh Council at Maidencraig Court, Blackhall, Edinburgh (1950-55); and Melfort House, Argyll (1961-62); as well as Srongarbh, The Loan, West Linton (1934-35), which the architect built for himself. Commercial projects include the National Bank of Scotland Head Office, 42 St Andrew Square, Edinburgh, with Arthur Davis as consultant from Mewes & Davis of London (1934-39); and the Caledonian Insurance Company Offices, 12-13 St Andrew Square, Edinburgh (1937, built 1938-40);

Thomson entered many competitions and those represented in the Collection include unsuccessful entries for the new RIBA premises in London (1932), the National Opera House, Sydney, Australia (*c*.1955) and Coventry Cathedral (1950-51). Also included are 117 drawings for an unexecuted Hall of Remembrance at Westminster Abbey, London (1940-45), and an unbuilt scheme for a Hydro Electric Control Centre, Pitlochry, Perthshire (1948).

The Collection contains an album, compiled by Thomson, of press and magazine cuttings of country houses, mostly from *Country Life*, dating from 1909 to 1936. The cuttings contain exterior and interior photographs of country houses, and provided inspiration and reference for his work. Also included is a set of drawings by John Burnet & Son of Duart Castle (1912).

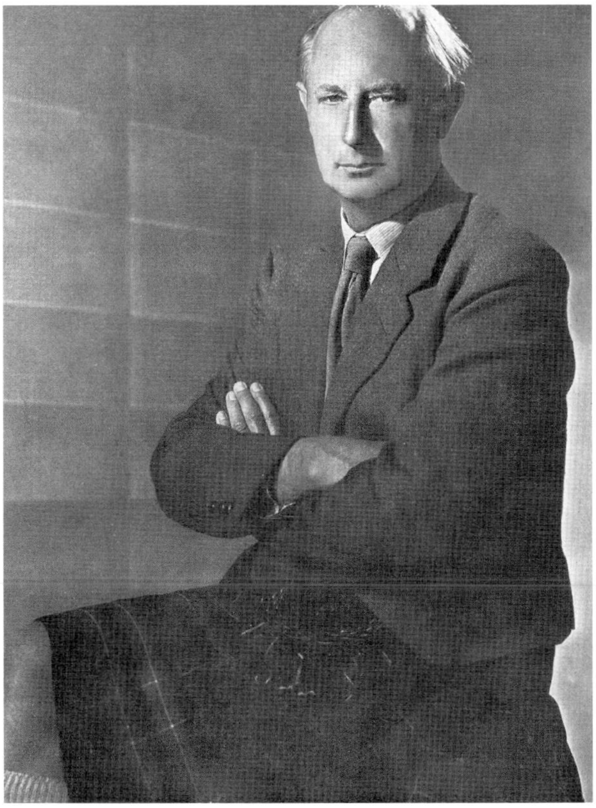

Leslie Grahame Thomson MacDougall (1896-1974), 1956. Image courtesy of RIAS. [SC649536]

Several commissions are not represented in the Collection. These include rural cottage designs Thomson produced with Mears in 1932 for the APRS, and the Pantiles Hotel, West Linton, now destroyed, of which there is only one detail drawing in the Collection dated 1939.

References

NMRS Sources

- 'Inventory and Valuation' of 6 Ainslie Place, Edinburgh taken by Whytock & Reid on behalf of Leslie Grahame Thomson, Architect for insurance purposes in November 1948. The inventory details the furnishings of his 'Drawing Office', 'Private Office' and 'Main Office'. Presented to NMRS by Murdo MacDonald, Argyll and Bute Council in 1997 (Accession No. 1997/40).
- 1983 List of MacDougall's library compiled by Lyon & Turnbull (MS 275).
- **Vass D, 1983** Verbal Reminiscences.

Anon. 1974 'Obituary: Mr Leslie G MacDougall', *The Scotsman*, Wednesday 5 June.
Anon. 1956 'Profile: Leslie Grahame MacDougall', *RIAS Quart*, 105 (Autumn), 16-17.
MacDougall, H 1993 *Christ's Church Dunollie 1901-1957*. Gordon Press.
MacDougall, L G 1955 'Centurial Message', *RIAS Quart*, 99 (February 1955), 4.
Martin-Kaye, H 1947 *Architecture Illustrated* (January 1947).
Thomson, L G 1924 'The Students' Vista', *RIAS Quart*, no. 9, 85.
Thomson, L G 1929 'The Late Sir Robert Lorimer and His Work', *RIAS Quart*, no. 31, 63-79.
Thomson, L G 1932 'Concerning This Heritage', *RIAS Quart*, no. 38, 42-6.
Thomson, L G 1932 'Impressions of the Annual Meeting of the RIAS at Inverness' in *RIAS Quart*, no. 38, 106.
Thomson, L G 1951 'Christian Symbolism', *Trans Scot Eccles Soc*, vol. 14, part 3, 18-30.
Wilkinson, K 2004 'Leslie Graham Thomson MacDougall' in **Postiglione, G ed.** *One Hundred Houses for One Hundred European Architects of the Twentieth Century*, 386-9. Köln: Taschen.

For other Leslie Grahame Thomson MacDougall papers:
Cowie & Seaton Collection
Dick Peddie & McKay Collection

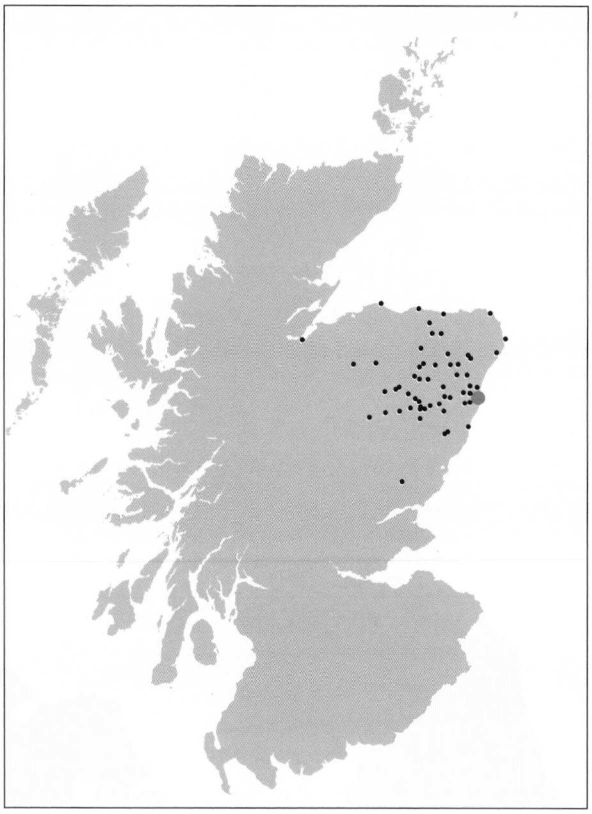

George Bennett Mitchell & Son

Provenance
Robert Alexander and Alan Hamilton, partners of George Bennett Mitchell & Son, presented the George Bennett Mitchell & Son Collection (Accession No. 2001/5) to RCAHMS in 1995 following survey by the SSAP. The drawings were folded and housed in approximately A2-size cardboard packets, the majority of which were stored in the practice's basement. The packets were labelled by project name and numbered. The numbers correlate to a card index but neither the exact meaning of the numbers or the date in which they were added to the packets could be ascertained.

History
George Bennett Mitchell (1865-1941) was educated in Aberdeen and Newburgh. He was articled with architects Pirie & Clyne between 1881 and 1885. From 1885 to 1887, Mitchell continued his training with Jenkins & Marr Architects and Surveyors, after which he became an architect for the Aberdeen firm Davidson & Garden Advocates, working for them until 1904 when he left to run his own practice at 148 Union Street, Aberdeen, the same year that he was elected as a member of the Aberdeen Society of Architects.

Mitchell's son, George Angus (1896-1964), joined his father's practice in 1921 and the following year the practice moved to 1 West Craibstone Street, Aberdeen (from where it operated until its closure in 2004). The practice was renamed George Bennett Mitchell & Son in 1929. In the late 1940s, John Lamb became a partner, followed in the 1950s by Gordon Taylor (d.*c.*1983). Robert Alexander joined the firm in 1971, and Alan Hamilton in 1976.

Mitchell was a well-respected Aberdonian. In 1905 Lord Provost Walker, as Lord-Lieutenant of the County of the City of Aberdeen, made him a Commissioner of the Peace. The following year Mitchell became commander and president of the Aberdeen Battalion of the Boys' Brigade to which he was a dedicated leader for many years, at one point successfully enrolling one in four boys in the city. In 1938, a plaque in his honour was placed at the Boys' Brigade Headquarters at 12-13 Crimon Place, Aberdeen, which had been designed by Mitchell.

Scope and Content
The Collection comprises 15,000 drawings relating to buildings in the North East of Scotland, of which 10,235 have been catalogued as part of the Project. The remainder have been hand-listed. The catalogued material encompasses 215 projects begun between 1904 and 1939 that were identified from the contract books as being the most significant. Additional phases of these projects undertaken by the practice after the Second World War and prior to 1970 were also catalogued. The Collection includes 114 manuscripts, the majority of which are project specifications and contract books, as well as an album of local newspaper cuttings, compiled by G B Mitchell himself, dating from 1904 to 1923.

Although several projects were discarded by the practice through the decades due to lack of storage space, main projects were retained. The Collection is

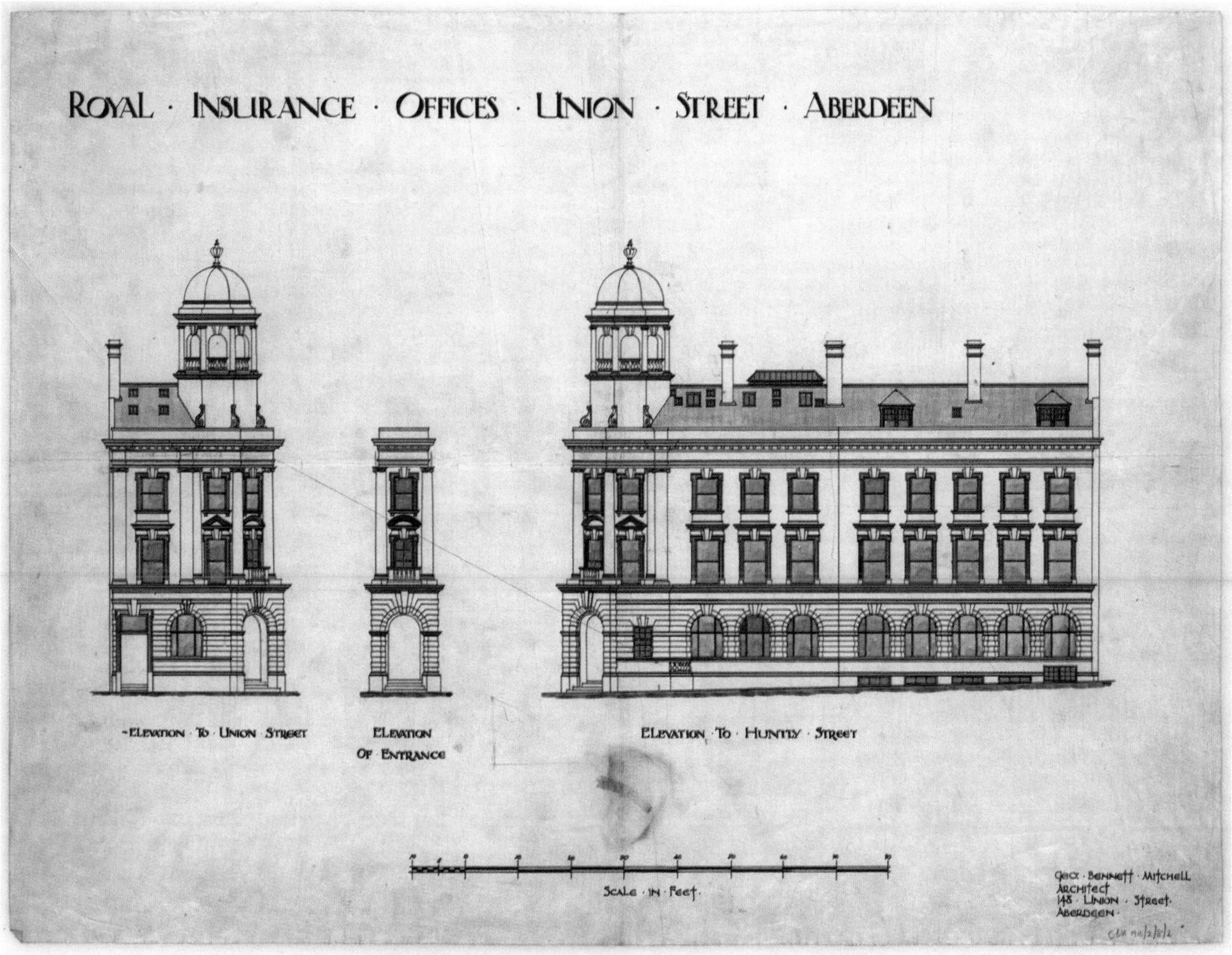

Elevations of the Royal Insurance Company Offices, Union Street, Aberdeen by George Bennett Mitchell, 1910, from the George Bennett Mitchell & Son Collection. [SC634104]

Design for stained glass window at Cluny Castle Chapel, Aberdeenshire by George Bennett Mitchell, c.1927, from the George Bennett Mitchell & Son Collection. [SC675542]

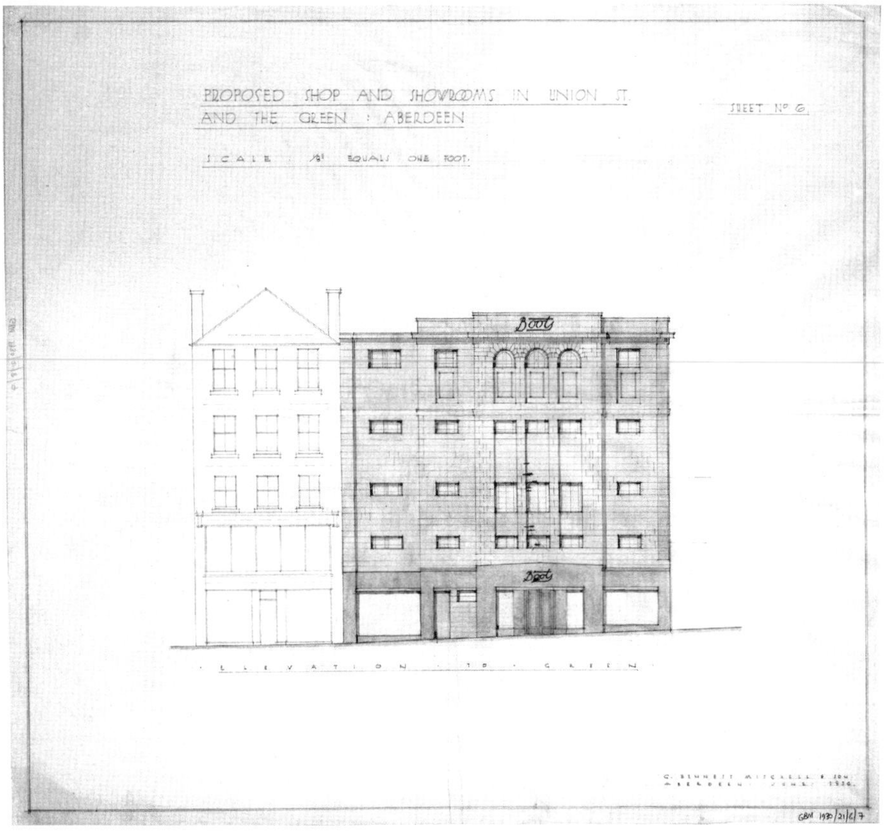

Elevation of Boots the Chemist, 131-139 Union Street/The Green, Aberdeen by George Bennett Mitchell & Son, c.1936, from the George Bennett Mitchell & Son Collection. [SC879092]

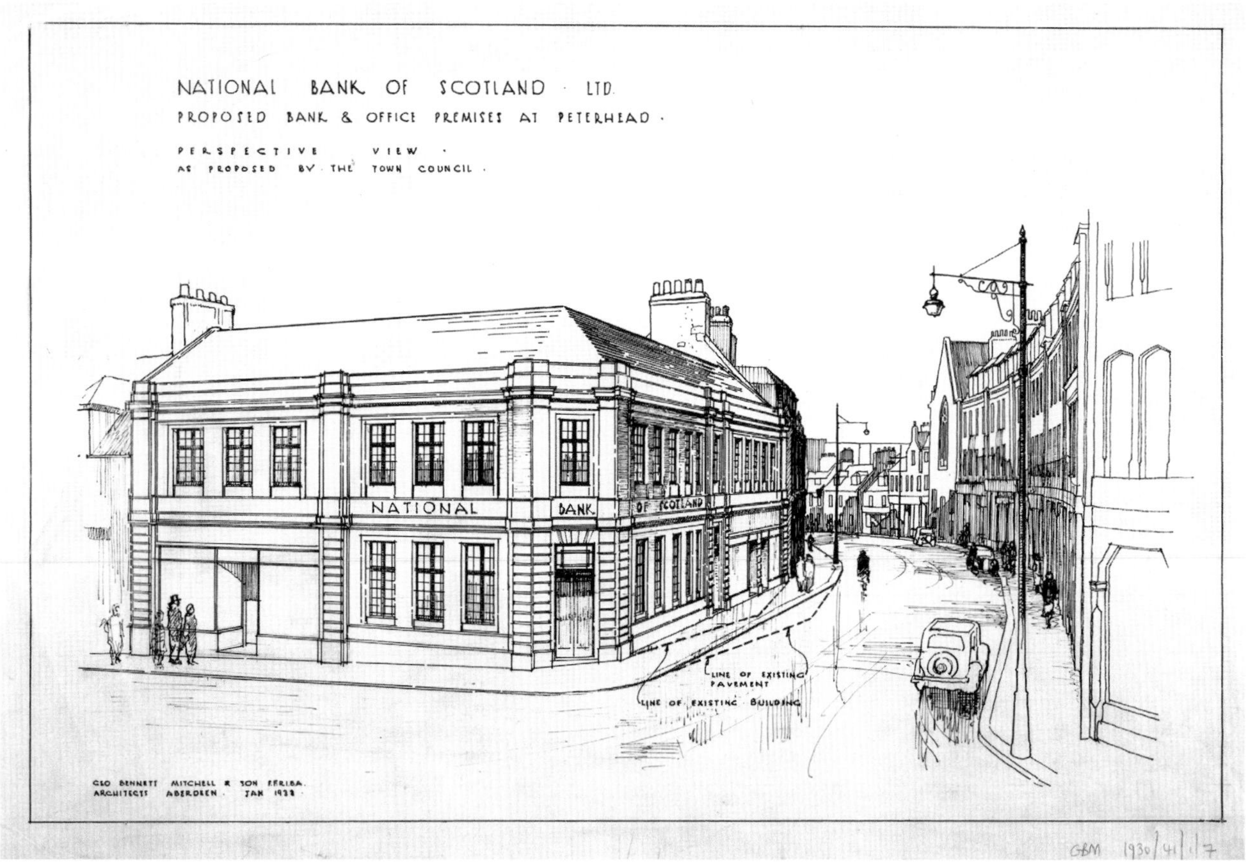

Perspective view of premises for the Bank of Scotland Ltd, 73-75 Broad Street, Peterhead, Aberdeenshire by George Bennett Mitchell & Son, c.1937, from the George Bennett Mitchell & Son Collection. [SC671818]

therefore an almost complete reflection of the work of George Bennett Mitchell & Son between 1904 and 1939. Projects begun during the first decade of the 20th century are mostly cottages and restoration work on country estates, a type of work that continued throughout Mitchell's career. Early work featured in the Collection also includes several houses and villas in the village of Aboyne that were built by the summer of 1907 to accommodate the influx of tourists who were attracted by the golf course, which re-located to the shores of the Loch of Aboyne in 1905, and for which Mitchell provided a new clubhouse.

There are over 500 drawings for Mitchell's 1910 Royal Insurance Company offices, 208-210 Union Street, Aberdeen, the design for which was based on the company's Liverpool headquarters by J Francis Doyle. The building, dressed in Kemnay white granite, was described in a contemporary newspaper as 'one of the finest suite of offices in Aberdeen'.

Reflected in the Collection are projects that demonstrate the firm's involvement with developing industry in the North East during the 1910s and 1920s. The practice designed a number of premises for the motorcar industry, including showrooms in Aberdeen at Holburn Street (1910-15). The practice also substantially extended and altered a number of premises around Aberdeen Harbour, notably a margarine factory on North Esplanade West (*c.*1910-25) for local businessman George Mellis; a sawmill on Provost Blaikie's Quay (1910-37); and a fish curing works for Allan Hanbury Ltd (1922-30). Drawings for these three projects show the accommodation that was required by

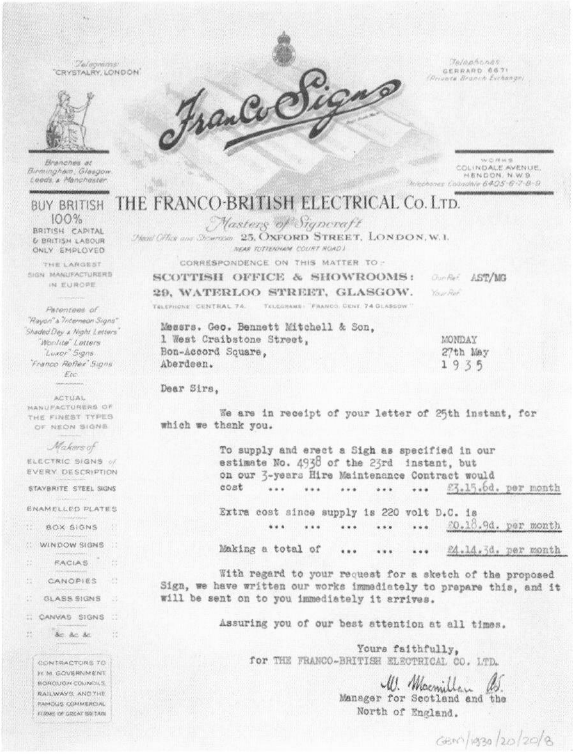
Telegrams: "CRYSTALRY, LONDON"

Telephones GERRARD 6671 (Private Branch Exchange)

FrancoSign

Branches at Birmingham, Glasgow, Leeds & Manchester

WORKS COLINDALE AVENUE, HENDON, N.W.9 Telephones Colindale 6405-6-7-8-9

BUY BRITISH 100% BRITISH CAPITAL & BRITISH LABOUR ONLY EMPLOYED

THE LARGEST SIGN MANUFACTURERS IN EUROPE

Patentees of "Rayon" & "Interneon Signs" "Shaded Day & Night Letters" "Wonlite" Letters "Luxor" Signs "Franco Reflex" Signs Etc

ACTUAL MANUFACTURERS OF THE FINEST TYPES OF NEON SIGNS

Makers of ELECTRIC SIGNS of EVERY DESCRIPTION

STAYBRITE STEEL SIGNS

ENAMELLED PLATES

BOX SIGNS

WINDOW SIGNS

FACIAS

CANOPIES

GLASS SIGNS

CANVAS SIGNS

&c. &c. &c.

CONTRACTORS TO H.M. GOVERNMENT BOROUGH COUNCILS RAILWAYS AND THE FAMOUS COMMERCIAL FIRMS OF GREAT BRITAIN

THE FRANCO-BRITISH ELECTRICAL Co. LTD.

Masters of Signcraft

Head Office and Showrooms 25, OXFORD STREET, LONDON, W.1.
(NEAR TOTTENHAM COURT ROAD)

CORRESPONDENCE ON THIS MATTER TO:-
SCOTTISH OFFICE & SHOWROOMS:
29, WATERLOO STREET, GLASGOW.
TELEPHONE CENTRAL 74. TELEGRAMS: "FRANCO, CENT. 74 GLASGOW"

Our Ref. AST/MG
Your Ref.

Messrs. Geo. Bennett Mitchell & Son,
1 West Craibstone Street,
Bon-Accord Square,
Aberdeen.

MONDAY
27th May
1935

Dear Sirs,

We are in receipt of your letter of 25th instant, for which we thank you.

To supply and erect a Sigh as specified in our estimate No. 4938 of the 23rd instant, but on our 3-years Hire Maintenance Contract would cost ... ... £3.15.6d. per month

Extra cost since supply is 220 volt D.C. is ... ... £0.18.9d. per month

Making a total of ... ... £4.14.3d. per month

With regard to your request for a sketch of the proposed Sign, we have written our works immediately to prepare this, and it will be sent on to you immediately it arrives.

Assuring you of our best attention at all times.

Yours faithfully,
for THE FRANCO-BRITISH ELECTRICAL CO. LTD.

W. Macmillan

Manager for Scotland and the North of England.

GBM/1930/20/20/8

Correspondence and itemised quotation for neon lighting from Franco Signs, The Franco-British Electrical Co Ltd in reference to Menzies & Sons Ltd, 44-46 George Street, Aberdeen, 27 May 1935, from the George Bennett Mitchell & Son Collection. [SC675546]

George Bennett Mitchell (1865-1941) by John M Aiken, 1932.
Image courtesy of George Bennett Mitchell & Son. [SC891719]

the technologically advancing companies related to the fishing industry of the period.

The Collection includes Mitchell's conversion of William Adam's Duff House (1739-45) in Banff from a hotel into a private hospital for people with nutrition-related diseases (1913). Equipped with chemical laboratories and radioactive equipment, it was the only institution of its kind in the UK. Projects following George Angus Mitchell's assumption into the practice include the restoration of Cluny Castle Chapel (1927-32) and Haddo House (1930-31) both following fire damage. There are also several new, or extended, schools for the Aberdeenshire Education Authority, as well as St Margaret's School at Albyn Place Aberdeen (*c.*1920-57).

Commercial commissions include the demolished Menzies & Sons Ltd outfitters shop at George Street, Aberdeen on a site now occupied by the Bon Accord Centre (*c.*1935-36); and Boots the Chemist on The Green, Aberdeen (*c.*1932-38). Spanning between Union Street and The Green on a lower ground level, this project included a complete redevelopment of the area.

All catalogued projects are held at Aberdeen City Archives under a Charge and Superintendence Agreement. Some un-annotated mechanical copies of catalogued material and drawings for smaller projects dating before 1939 are housed at RCAHMS. This material is handlisted only. Post-1939 projects were gifted by the practice to Aberdeen City Archives.

References

Gregory, N 2001 'Scottish Architects' Papers Preservation Project: Local Collections', *Architect Heritage Soc Scot Mag*, no. 13 (Winter 2001), 28.

Gregory, N 2001, 'George Bennett Mitchell and Son: A Very Aberdonian Practice', *Leopard Magazine*, November 2001, 32-4.

For other George Bennett Mitchell & Son papers:
Schomberg Scott Collection

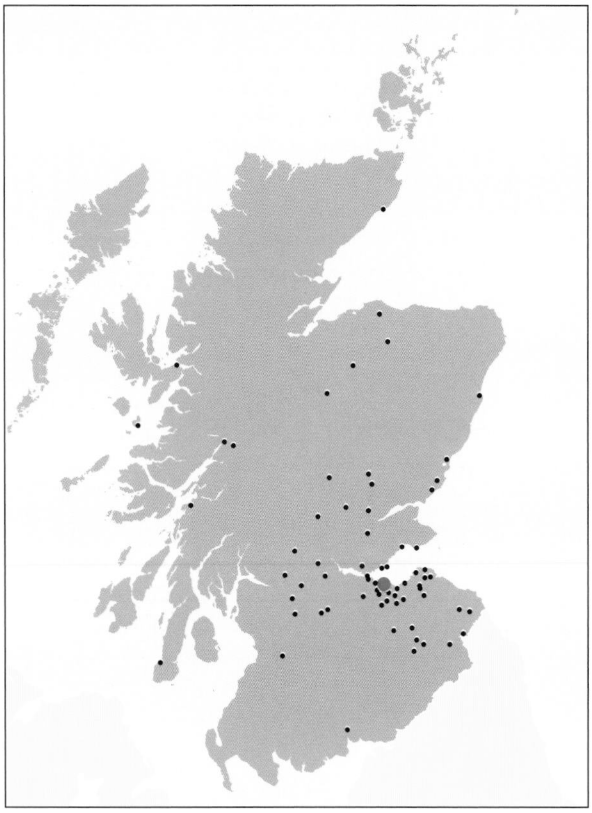

Sydney Mitchell & Wilson

Provenance

The Sydney Mitchell & Wilson Collection (Accession No. 1997/209) was deposited in RCAHMS following the SSAP in 1995 by Mike Henderson, senior partner of Dick Peddie & McKay. The drawings had been stored as part of the Dick Peddie & McKay office archive from *c.*1936, when G Lindsay Auldjo Jamieson joined the practice. Jamieson had inherited the drawings through his father's practice, Jamieson & Arnott, which had taken over the practice of Sydney Mitchell & Wilson in 1911.

The drawings had been stored along with the Dick Peddie & McKay Collection in the system devised in the late 19th century that related to the use of numbered bins in a wine cellar. Drawings of each project were wrapped in brown paper, tied-up with string; later, clear plastic bags were used. A hand-written label accompanied each roll and included the name and address of the project, the number of its original bin location and its bag number. This information has been recorded.

History

Arthur George Sydney Mitchell (1856-1930) was born at Larbert where his father, Sir Arthur Mitchell, was a physician specialising in mental disorders. He attended Edinburgh University and later spent five years as a pupil in the offices of Sir Robert Rowand Anderson (1834-1921). After taking a study tour of Europe he set up his practice in 1882, working initially from his home at 34 Drummond Place, Edinburgh before moving to 122 George Street the following year.

Like Mitchell, George Wilson (1844-1912) had travelled to France and Belgium. He entered the office of David Bryce (1803-1876) in 1864 on completion of his architectural apprenticeship with the firm of Leadbetter & Smith, Architects and Valuators of Edinburgh. Upon Bryce's death he found employment with Rowand Anderson and rose to the position of chief assistant within the practice. He joined Mitchell's practice in 1883 and became a partner in 1887 when it became known as Sydney Mitchell & Wilson. In 1886 the practice moved to 13 Young Street where they were to remain for the duration of the practice's history.

The practice continued after Mitchell's retirement in 1911 under the auspices of Ernest Arthur Auldjo Jamieson (*c.*1880-1937) and his partner James Alexander Arnott (1871-1950). Jamieson opened his own practice at 1 Melville Street in *c.*1909. Late in 1910 or early in 1911 he bought Sydney Mitchell's practice and invited Arnott to join him in partnership. Arnott was articled to John Russell Walker (d.1891) in 1886. In 1888 he transferred to Kinnear & Peddie and remained with them until 1898 when Dunn & Findlay recruited him to help design their North Bridge development in Edinburgh. In 1904 he moved again to the office of Hippolyte Jean Blanc (1844-1917), and in 1907 together with John Wilson (1877-1959), a friend from Peddie's office, he published a folio on the Petit Trianon at Versailles that was to become a key source for architects working in the Louis XV style. In 1908 Arnott commenced independent practice at 21 York Place, sharing an office with a former colleague at Dunn & Findlay's, James Inch Morrison (d.1944),

Arthur George Sydney Mitchell (1856-1930). [SC891730]

George Wilson (1844-1912). [SC891734]

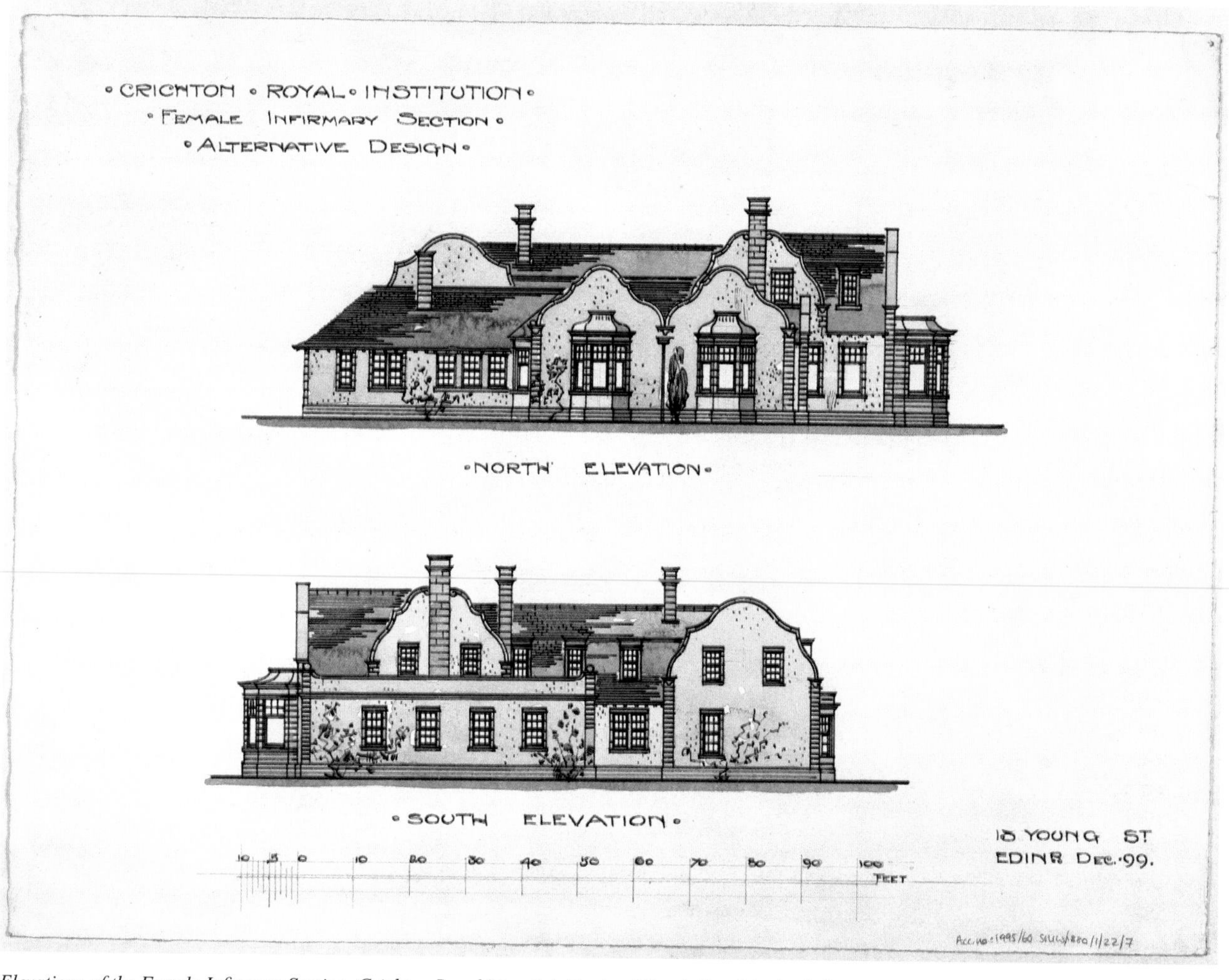

Elevations of the Female Infirmary Section, Crichton Royal Hospital, Bankend Road, Dumfries by Sydney Mitchell & Wilson, 1899, from the Sydney Mitchell & Wilson Collection. [SC582319]

Perspective sketch of Well Court, Damside, Edinburgh by Sydney Mitchell, 1883-84, from the Sydney Mitchell & Wilson Collection. [SC684932]

but this tentative partnership ended when he went into partnership with Jamieson.

Ill-health forced Jamieson to retire in 1936. The firm then dwindled: Jamieson's son George Lindsay Auldjo Jamieson (1904-*c*.1960) joined W J Walker Todd (1884-1944) and David Chisholm (1885-1949) in the Dick Peddie & Walker partnership. Arnott continued the practice alone for a few years, but gradually implemented the partnership with James Inch Morrison - which had been planned 30 years earlier - as Arnott & Inch Morrision in 1940. Their assistant J D (Ian) Carnegie continued the practice after their deaths.

Scope and Content

The Sydney Mitchell & Wilson Collection consists of 6,700 drawings with a small number of related papers, and encompasses around 170 projects that span the main years of the practice's history from the 1880s to the 1930s.

Significant buildings featured in the Collection include Well Court, Edinburgh (1883-85) for *The Scotsman* owner J R Findlay; Ben Nevis Observatory for the Scottish Meteorological Society (1883-89); and the Church of Scotland Offices, 117-121 George Street, Edinburgh (1908-51).

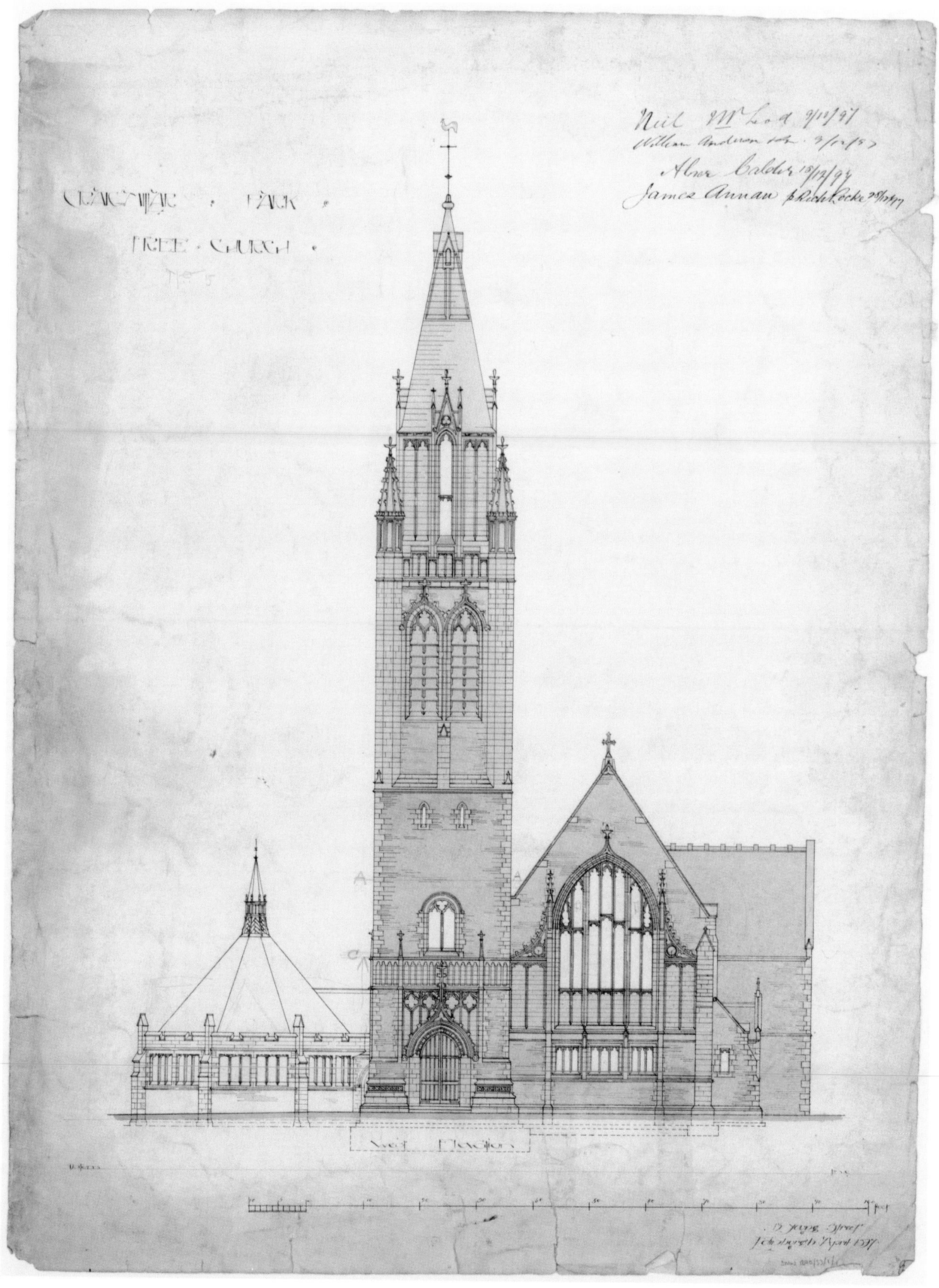

Elevation of Craigmillar Parish Church, East Suffolk Road, Edinburgh by Sydney Mitchell & Wilson, 1897, from the Sydney Mitchell & Wilson Collection. [SC879320]

A dominant feature of the Collection is the range of hospital work tackled by the practice which offers a unique perspective on changes taking place in asylum design and the treatment of patients at the end of the 19th century. The Collection includes papers for Montrose Asylum (1887-88); the Thomas Clouston Clinic, Craighouse, Edinburgh (1889-95); Crichton Royal Hospital, Dumfries (1889-1912); the Valkenberg Asylum, Cape Town, South Africa (1892); Dingleton Hospital, Melrose (1895); and Southfield Sanatorium, Edinburgh (1902-48). Jamieson & Arnott continued the tradition of working on hospital projects and this is reflected in papers for Hairmyres Hospital, East Kilbride (1913-22); Royal Hospital for Sick Children, Edinburgh (1920-26); and Astley Ainsley Hospital, Edinburgh (1928-46).

The practice's many commissions for the Commercial Bank of Scotland are well documented within the Collection and include Mitchell's enlargement of the Bank's head office at 2-8 Gordon Street and 113-115 Buchanan Street, Glasgow (1885-88), along with a number of original drawings of the building by its architect David Rhind (1808-1883). The Collection includes the Commercial Bank's head office in Aberdeen (1887-88), possibly the practice's most controversial building (it was designed with a Gothic façade not perceived as a correct style for a commercial building as in Aberdeen this was to be reserved for religious buildings). Further branches were built throughout Scotland including Oban (1888-89), Comrie (1889), and Kyle of Lochalsh (1895-96), all of which are represented in the Collection.

Sydney Mitchell & Wilson's work on many prominent country houses in Scotland is also reflected in the Collection, including Aberlour House, Banffshire (1885-86), Catrine House, Ayrshire (1888-89) and Lennoxlove, Haddington (1902-34). The mansion house built around the original 14th century keep known as Duntreath Castle, for which the practice designed an arched opening entrance flanked by turrets and a series of lavishly detailed reception rooms (1890-92), now only exist on paper as the mansion house was partially demolished in the 1950s.

There are some notable projects that are not represented in the Collection. These include the work carried out at Ramsay Gardens (*c.*1885) for Patrick Geddes; the practice's winning entry for the Scottish International Exhibition of Industry, Science and Art (1885); and Mitchell's own house, the Pleasance, Duncur Road, Gullane (1902). There is also only one drawing in the Collection showing the work carried out at 3-4 Rothesay Terrace (1883) for J R Findlay.

Details of the Commercial Bank, 78 Union Street, Aberdeen by Sydney Mitchell & Wilson, 1887, from the Sydney Mitchell & Wilson Collection. [SC879322]

References

NMRS Sources

- 187 drawings by Peddie & Kinnear and Sydney Mitchell & Wilson purchased by RCAHMS in 1968 (Accession No. 1968/5).
- Approximately 90 drawings of Colinton Parish Church, Edinburgh, (*c.*1906-08) (Accession No. 2000/38).
- Set of drawings by Sydney Mitchell of Leithen Lodge (Accession No. 1999/225).
- **Mitchell A G S 1886** *The Book of Old Edinburgh* presented to James Gowans (Accession No. 1997/209).
- **Weir, J D** George Wilson and Sydney Mitchell.

Anon. 1912 'Obituary: George Wilson', *The Builder*, CII, 20 September 1912, 342.

Anon. 1912 'Obituary: George Wilson', *The Building News*, vol.103, 20 September 1912, 397.

Anon. 1931 'Obituary: A G Sydney Mitchell', *The Builder*, CXL, 6 March 1931, 463.

Anon. 1944 'Obituary: Morrison', *The Scotsman*, 26 September 1944.

Arnott, A A and Wilson, J 1907-8 *The Petite Trianon Versailles: illustrated by a series of measured drawings and photographs of the entire building, exterior and interior*. Edinburgh: George Waterston & Sons.

Macrae, E J 1951 'Obituary: Arnott', *RIAS Quart, No.38 (Spring)*.

McDowell, D C 2003 'Scottish Assets: the Commercial Architecture of A G Sydney Mitchell', *Architect Heritage XIV*, 45-66. Edinburgh: Edinburgh Univ Press.

Related practices/personnel:
Dick Peddie & McKay Collection
Dunn & Findlay Collection

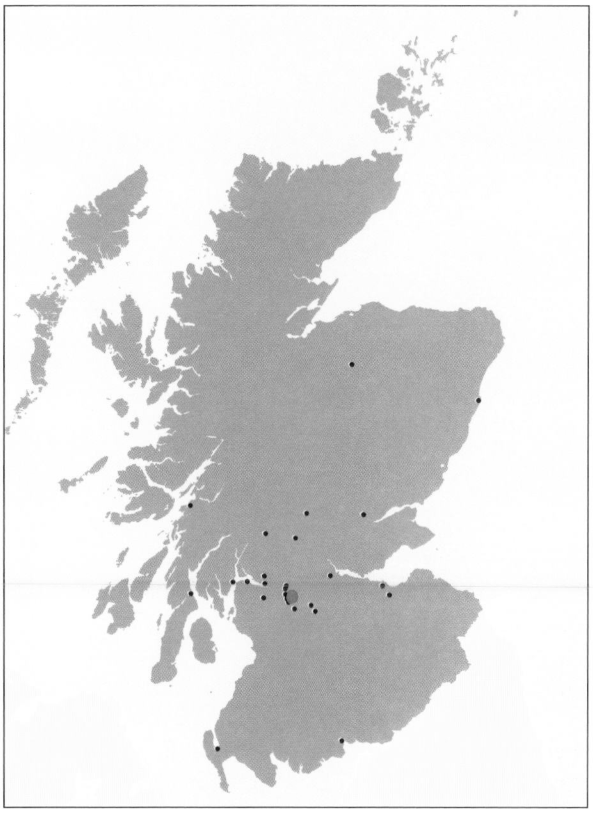

Monro & Partners

Provenance
The Monro & Partners Collection (Accession No. 2000/100) was gifted to RCAHMS in May 2000 by William Monro, son of the architect Geoffrey Monro. Prior to this date it had been stored at a private address in the West End of Glasgow for at least six years.

Within the practice office in Glasgow the papers had been mostly kept flat in a pre-war wooden plan chest. When Gillean Petrie Small joined the practice in 1965, he moved them to plan chest accommodation in the basement print room of the Glasgow premises. He then began to make an inventory of the drawings to allow retrieval. It is thought that the best drawings were framed and kept at Geoffrey Monro's St Fillans and Watford houses.

History
James Milne Monro (1840-1921) was articled to John Henderson (1804-1862) in Edinburgh around 1855. Either just before or at Henderson's death he became an assistant in the office of Brown & Wardrop. In the mid-1860s he moved to Glasgow as assistant to William Spence (1806-1833) at 52 Renfield Street. This experience enabled him to set up his own practice at 33 Bath Street, Glasgow in 1870, which moved to 28 Bath Street in 1874.

Monro's son Charles Ernest (1876-1945) was apprenticed to the firm at some point between 1882 and 1887, becoming an assistant in 1888 and a partner in 1893. In December 1902 he passed the RIBA qualifying exam. In 1912 the practice moved further down Bath Street to number 134 and it was around this time that Charles took over the firm following James's retirement. By this time the practice had become known as James M Monro & Son but after James' death in 1921 C Ernest Monro began operating from the same address. It was possibly during the late 1920s that Charles' son Geoffrey Monro (1907-1985) joined his father's practice.

In 1936 the practice moved to 307 West George Street. Between this date and 1942 they were listed in the *Post Office Directories* under the names C Ernest Monro and James M Monro & Son. The sole name of C Ernest Monro was listed from 1942-1948, after which the firm was entered in the directories as James M Monro & Son until 1955.

During the 1930s and 1940s the practice received commissions from the aircraft industry and the Glasgow-based Macfarlane Lang biscuit company for premises in England. This resulted in Geoffrey Monro purchasing a house at Clarendon Road, Watford, which was later to become the firm's second office. In 1947 a third office was opened in London.

In 1955 the Glasgow office moved to 25 Woodside Place. Two years later Geoffrey Monro introduced the first non-family partners to the new firm of Monro & Partners, Architects and Engineers, to cope with the post-war building boom. This intake included John Forbes who ran the Glasgow office until his death in 1970. In 1966 Ian Cruickshank, who had worked in the Buchanan Campbell practice in the early 1950s, and David Samson (ret.1970) were assumed into

Perspective view of the Grand Hotel, Gillespie Terrace, St Andrews by James M Monro & Son, 1893, from the Monro & Partners Collection. [SC582324]

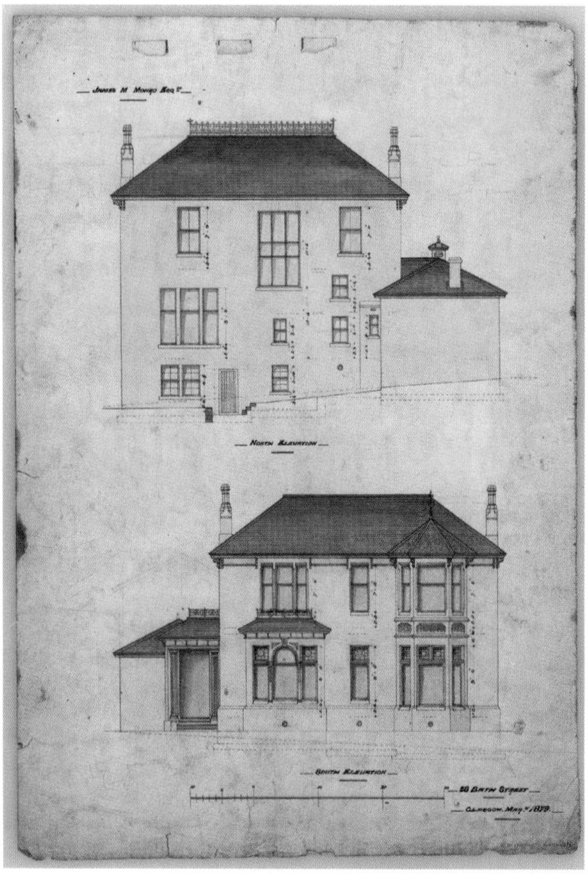

Staff of James M Monro & Son at the site of the De Havilland Aircraft Company, Hatfield Estate, Hertfordshire, c.1935, including Charles Ernest Monro (third from left) and Geoffrey Monro (centre). Image courtesy of Gillean Petrie Small. [SC896706]

North and South elevations of Saxonholme, Manse Road, Bearsden by James M Monro, 1879, from the Monro & Partners Collection. The architect designed the house for himself. [SC651363]

Sketch design of Comet Flight Shed, De Havilland Aircraft Company, Hatfield Estate, Hertfordshire by James M Monro & Son, 1952, from the Monro & Partners Collection. [SC600872]

partnership, followed in 1972 by Alistair Anderson Taylor and in 1983 by Gillean Petrie Small (ret.1991) and George Walter Waterston (left 1991).

In 1991, Monro & Partners merged with Tibbalds Colbourne Karski Williams to become Tibbalds Colbourne Karski Williams Monro, known as Tibbalds Monro. In 1994, the Glasgow office closed.

Scope and Content

The Collection comprises 895 drawings, 397 photographs and 41 manuscript items, most of which are from the period before the Monro & Partners partnership began in 1957. After the merger with Tibbalds Colbourne Karski Williams in 1991, professional indemnity insurers for the merged firm assumed legal responsibility for the work of the Monro & Partners practice. The bulk of drawings and files from the Glasgow and Watford offices went to the Tibbalds head office in London before the Glasgow premises closed in 1994. The Collection, thus, consists of material not taken down to England at this time.

The majority of projects date from between 1890 and 1909 and are largely for commercial commissions in the West of Scotland. Only a few papers, mostly presentation drawings, show work after 1930. Early projects featured in the Collection include tenement blocks and a number of villas in Bearsden, notably Monro's own family home 'Saxonholme' at Manse Road (1878-79). Also included are papers showing renovation and extension work that James M Monro & Son undertook for the Catholic charity The Little Sisters of the Poor at their premises in Greenock, Glasgow and Edinburgh (1880-1907). The Collection contains work on bars in Glasgow and hotels across Scotland, notably the building of The Grand Hotel at St Andrews (1893-99); the rebuilding of the Callander Hydropathic (1896-1907); the Alexandra Hotel, Oban (1898-1904); and an extension to the Grant Arms Hotel, Grantown-on-Spey (1900-02).

In the 1930s Geoffrey Monro won a competition to design the first building for the de Havilland aircraft company at their new Hatfield estate, now British Aerospace. The bulk of the photographic material in the Collection shows building work in progress at various de Havilland aircraft company sites in the south of England during the 1950s. This includes the Hatfield estate which was developed entirely by the practice with commissions from de Havilland, Hawker Siddley, Rolls Royce Aero Engines, and for an aluminium flight shed for the Comet jet passenger aircraft.

The Monro practice in all its guises either designed or altered a significant number of commercial and industrial buildings in the Strathclyde area, including several shoe shops for Bayne & Duckett; a factory for the Macfarlane Lang biscuit company at Tollcross (*c.*1925); and additional premises for Templeton's Carpet Factory, Glasgow Green, Glasgow (*c.*1960). However, there are very few drawings in the Collection that reflect this. Similarly, there are only a handful of presentation drawings and photographs that reflect the substantial amount of work for Marks & Spencer, the practice's main client from the late 1920s to the 1980s and for whom 126 stores and warehouses across the United Kingdom were produced.

Unexecuted design of proposed store for Marks & Spencer, 2-12 Argyle Street, Glasgow by Monro & Partners, c.1960-64, from the Monro & Partners Collection. [SC879283]

References

Gregory, N 2001 'Scottish Architects' Papers Preservation Project: Local Collections', *Architect Heritage Soc Scot Mag*, no. 13 (Winter 2001), 28.

Gregory, N 2003 'Monro and Partners: Shopping in Scotland with Marks and Spencer', *Architect Heritage XIV*, 67-85. Edinburgh: Edinburgh Univ Press.

Related practices/personnel:
Buchanan Campbell Collection

For other James Monro & Son papers:
Houston & Dunlop Collection

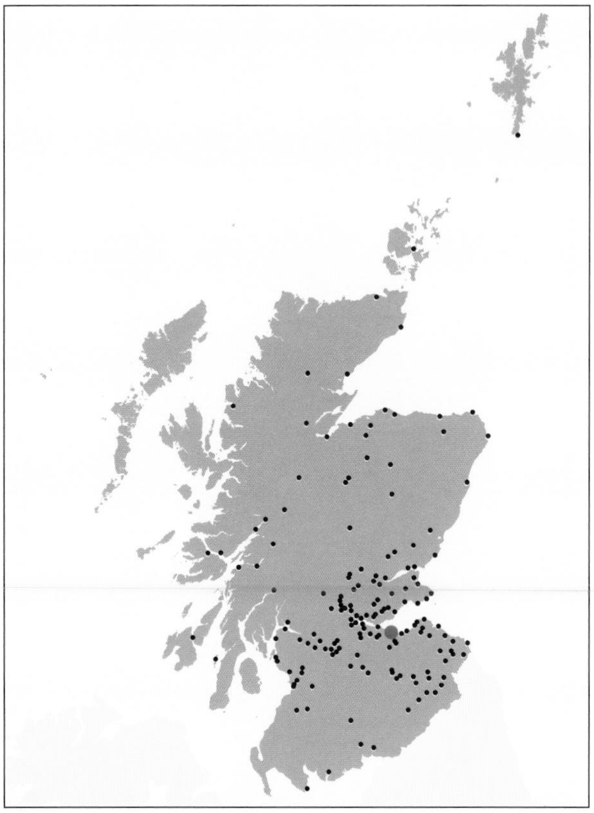

Scott Morton

Provenance
The Scott Morton Collection of designs for architectural woodwork and furniture has been formed from two different accessions to RCAHMS, the first being a donation by Peter Miller to the RIAS in the latter half of the 1980s. This was subsequently presented to RCAHMS as part of the McKean Collection in 1999 (Accession No. 2002/179). The second part of the Collection was presented to RCAHMS by Elspeth Hardie, the granddaughter of William Scott Morton, in 1991 (Accession No.1991/11). The majority of drawings and photographs arrived in brown paper folders labelled either by furniture type or by subject matter (i.e. 'chairs', 'fonts', 'carvings', 'running ornament' etc). This information was retained during cataloguing.

The two accessions were physically amalgamated into one and items were catalogued primarily by the location for which the woodwork was intended. However, many of the drawings and photographs in the collection were not identifiable, as they feature neither location nor date. These were catalogued according to type (i.e. 'chairs', 'tables', 'religious art and design elements'). A thesaurus of terminology was created to inform the cataloguing the collection, this can be consulted in the NMRS library along with a hand-list of the collection.

History
The Lanarkshire-born architect, artist, craftsman and decorator William Scott Morton (1840-1903) began his career in the 1850s. Having attended classes in decorative design in Glasgow, he was apprenticed to the Glasgow architect James Smith (1808-1863) along with William Leiper (1839-1916) and William Forrest Salmon (1843-1911).

Towards the end of the decade Morton moved to London with his family where he contributed to the household finances by selling his designs to carpet and lace warehouses. He also painted architectural backgrounds for some of the leading painters of the day, including William Powell Frith (1819-1909), for whom he drew the structural work for the *Railway Station* (1861-2); Sir Edwin Henry Landseer (1802-1873); and the Scottish painter John 'Spanish' Philip (1817-1867).

During the 1860s Morton was employed by the furnishing house of Johnstone Jeanes and Co, New Bond Street, London. By 1870 he had moved back to Scotland to set up the Morton & Co furniture business of Tynecastle, Edinburgh with his brother John (1842-1904). As well as manufacturing furniture, Morton became involved in other aspects of interior design. His firm began to stock oriental carpets and other upholstery items. He also produced carpet and curtain designs for Templeton's of Glasgow, and ceiling decorations for the company Shrigley & Hunt of Lancaster.

In the 1870s the firm began to manufacture wallpaper, and became renowned for their invention known as Tynecastle Tapestry. This sought to evoke 15th and 16th century Spanish and Italian embossed leather wall hangings, using moulded canvas. The overall result was a product with a repeated pattern, be it Rococo, Tudor, Classical or domestic in style. It could be copied

Sydney Gocke carving a flower design at the workshops of Scott Morton & Company, Murieston Road, Edinburgh, c.1952, from the Scott Morton Collection. [SC879311]

economically and was a lighter, cheaper, yet durable alternative to plasterwork.

The manufacture of Tynecastle Tapestry became a separate business entity from Scott Morton & Company. The two businesses were listed separately in *Post Office Directories* as Scott Morton & Co and Tynecastle Co up to 1920. Thereafter they were sited under a single entry as Scott Morton and Tynecastle Co Ltd until 1958 when the manufacture of wall coverings may have ceased and they were simply known as Scott Morton Ltd.

Three of Scott Morton's four sons – William Stewart (1868-1933), Robert (1870-1905) and Alexander (1877-1965) – were involved in the running of the business. David Ramsay, an apprentice at the start of the century, was a director during the 1930s and 1940s. In 1948 Peter Miller, a former employee of Scott Morton & Company who had left in 1946, returned to take over from David Ramsay as director and designer, a position that he held for the remainder of firm's trading years. Miller had started work at Scott Morton as an apprentice in 1931 at the age of sixteen. A skilled draughtsman, he also provided freelance perspective drawings for architects such as J & F Johnston.

Many of the apprentices from the post-war period went on to become architects, including John Jackson, who was subsequently employed by Dick Peddie & McKay, Ian G Lindsay, and Cairns & Ford; Ernie Weir who worked for J R McKay; and George Hay who became a partner of Ian G Lindsay.

In the early 1950s Miller won a trip to Scandinavia in a Danish furniture design competition. His winning designs were for white sycamore chairs with slender 'chicken bone'-shaped arms, a style employed many times thereafter. Miller also achieved success by

Design for flower carving by Scott Morton & Company, c.1952, from the Scott Morton Collection. [SC800066]

carving the winning model for Basil Spence (1907-1976) in the competition to rebuild Coventry Cathedral.

In 1966 Scott Morton Ltd went into receivership. Peter Miller was subsequently employed until his retirement at Whytock & Reid of 7 Charlotte Square, Edinburgh, another Edinburgh company of woodworkers. Whytock & Reid bought the goodwill of Scott Morton Ltd and used their standard designs, allocating them with new design numbers. Several advertisement brochures after this date acknowledge the incorporation of Scott Morton Ltd into a company that still remains in business [2004], trading from premises at Belford Mews.

Scope and Content

There are 4,680 items in the Collection, including working drawings, presentation drawings, 19 sketchbooks, acquired books, source material, 11 plaster models and approximately 1,300 photographs.

Also included is a press cuttings book that features newspaper cuttings, trade pamphlets, exhibition brochures, transcribed copies of lectures given by

Carved staircase finials for Kinfauns Castle, Perthshire by Scott Morton & Company, c.1912, from the Scott Morton Collection. [SC756771]

Design for an Old Venetian Mirror by Scott Morton & Company, c.1900-20, from the Scott Morton Collection. [SC879306]

William Scott Morton, magazine features on houses and ships furnished by the firm, material related to war work undertaken by women in the company's workshops, and office memorabilia. The press cuttings book includes several projects such as 25 Learmonth Terrace, Edinburgh (1893) and the Queen Mary Cunard-White Star ocean liner (launched 1936).

There are also 11 hard-backed letter books containing copies of correspondence (1881-1924) and a job book for Scott Morton Ltd (1889-1960) listing drawing office staff and clients together with design, order and drawing numbers for each commission. The range of commissions include cabinets, chairs, bookcases, mantelpieces, panelling, pedestals, tables, wardrobes, bedsteads, screens, desks, elder's chairs, kneelers, hymn boards, pulpits, pews, notice boards, memorials, organ cases, and miscellaneous woodwork such as heraldic carving and trophies.

The Collection relates predominantly to the work of the Scott Morton Company rather than Tynecastle Tapestry, although trade catalogues, samples and assorted advertising pamphlets from the latter business are included. The Collection also features some work by the Whytock & Reid firm of woodworkers.

The majority of drawings gifted by Peter Miller are sketches and finalised working drawings for small sections of ornamental carving. These full-size working drawings provide mostly no indication as to the location for which they were intended or the date that they were executed. Some are tinged blue showing traces of the

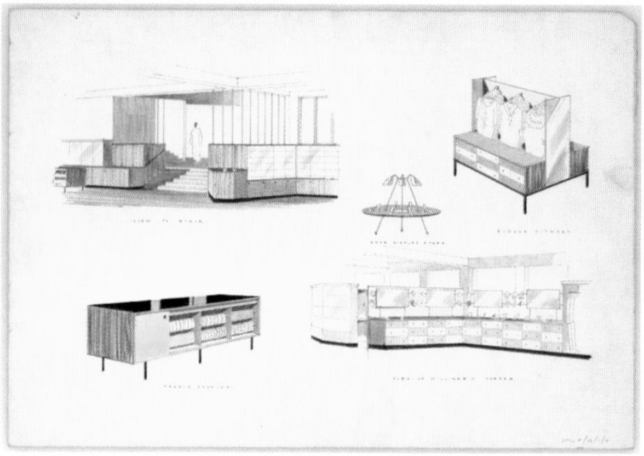

Presentation drawing of designs for a shop interior, possibly Forsyth's, 26-30 Princes Street, Edinburgh by Scott Morton & Company, c.1950-60, from the Scott Morton Collection. [SC778098]

carbon paper that was placed underneath them so that the design could be transferred onto the wood. Others have prick marks which indicate the use of a point by the carver to measure the distance between certain components of the drawing and ensure that the same measurements were executed on the piece of wood. The Collection also contains some presentation drawings for commissions including the Robin Chapel, Edinburgh (1949); county offices, Elgin; and a Commercial Bank manager's office; as well as a set of designs for the Fourteen Stations of the Cross dating post-Second World War. The Scott Morton Collection also contains acquired drawings from the architects' practices for which Scott Morton provided carvings, including Sir Robert Lorimer and Reginald Fairlie & Partners.

The photographs in the Collection include the substantial work that Scott Morton provided for the Reid Memorial Chapel, Edinburgh (*c*.1928-32); the East Lancashire Masonic Lodge, Manchester; Jenners department store, Princes Street, Edinburgh; Reginald Fairlie's National Library of Scotland, Edinburgh (*c*.1955); and the Advocates' Library, Edinburgh.

The Collection features several photographs of the Scott Morton showroom interior at their Murieston Road premises, including views of an exhibition held in conjunction with the 1953 General Assembly of the Church of Scotland, photographs showing the carvers at work, and trade pamphlets advertising the company's wares. Also included are 250 images probably taken by William Scott Morton's son, William Stewart Morton (b.1868). These have an architectural flavour and were taken mainly in France between 1890 and 1930, possibly as useful source material.

There is a wealth of acquired source material in the form of six unbound scrapbooks. Dating approximately 1868 to 1900 these contain cuttings from periodicals such as *L'Art Pour Tous* and *The Building News* as well as design studies, mostly of floral motifs. The collection features a folder of articles collated from architecture journals of the 1930s and 1940s. These show contemporary restaurants and cocktail bars, mostly from England, with several articles featuring the work of Raymond McGrath.

References

- Eight photograph albums documenting the work of Scott Morton & Company can be seen at Edinburgh University Library Special Collections (Phot. Ill. 149).

NMRS Sources

- Two further accessions of Scott Morton material donated by Elspeth Hardie (Accession Nos. 2000/197 and 2000/198), including a list of Sir Robert Lorimer's account with the firm.
- A large collection of glass plate negatives showing furniture made by Whytock & Reid (Accession No.1994/92), and a collection of carpet and tapestry designs from the same firm (Accession No. 1996/13).
- Scott Morton press cuttings book (facsimile copy, H2.MOR).
- A taped interview with Peter Miller held as part of the SAPPP Scott Morton Collection.
- Typescript notes of interviews with John Jackson – apprentice with Scott Morton Ltd from 1946 to 1951 – carried out by Neil Gregory and Daniel Parker 20 May 2002 and 2 July 2002 (MS 926/4/1).
- Typescript notes from conversation with Scott Morton's granddaughter, Elspeth Hardie, on 18 March 1985.
- **Hardie, E** William Scott Morton 1840-1903: Architect, Artist and Craftsman.

Cant, M 1995 *Gorgie and Dalry*. Edinburgh, 124-129.
Hardie, E 1988 'William Scott Morton', *The Antique Collector* (March). London.
Monkhouse, C 1897 'A Northern Home', *Art Journal*. London.
Morton, J 1971 *Three generations in a family textile firm*. London: Routledge, Kegan and Paul.
Morton, W S 1943 *William Stewart Morton 1868-1933*. London: Oliver and Boyd.
Ronaldson, M and McDermott, A 2000 'Tynecastle Tapestry: not all 'Hearts' and Flowers!', *SSCR J*, vol.11, No.3 (August). Edinburgh.
Savage, P 1980 *Lorimer and the Edinburgh Craft Designers*. London.

Related practices/personnel:
Dick Peddie & McKay Collection
J & F Johnston & Partners Collection
Lorimer & Matthew Collection

For other Scott Morton papers:
Lorimer & Matthew Collection

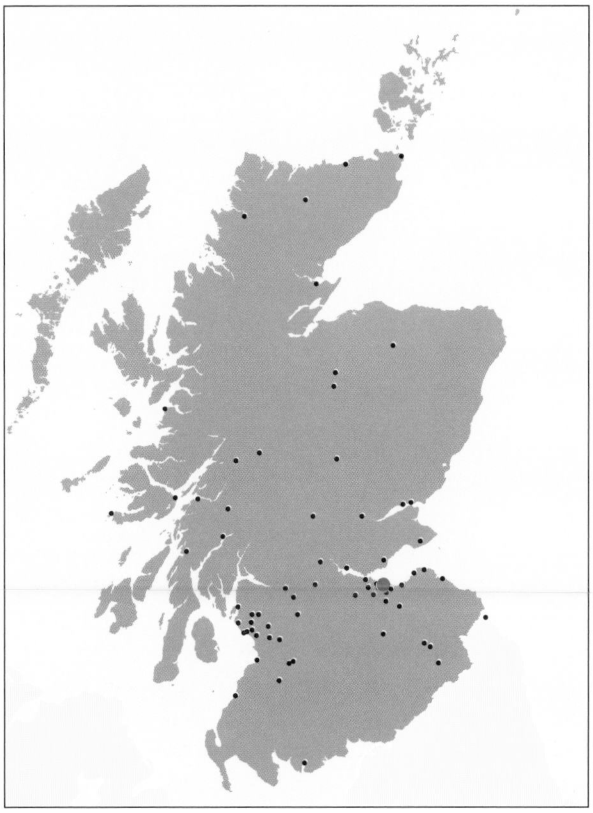

John L Paterson

Provenance

The office papers, drawings, photographs, models, slides and two prototype chairs in the John L Paterson Collection (Accession No. 1991/36) were gifted to RCAHMS in 1991 by the executor of his estate, William Balfour, of the Edinburgh solicitors Balfour & Manson.

History

John Lamb Paterson (1931-1989) was born in Cremorne, New South Wales, Australia. He read architecture at Edinburgh College of Art where he received his diploma in 1957. Around the same time he was apprenticed to Stewart Kaye & Partners. Paterson then turned down a scholarship to the University of Pennsylvania in order to take up a job with Robert Matthew Johnson Marshall & Partners. He returned to Edinburgh College of Art as a lecturer in architecture *c*.1963, becoming director of first year studies in 1970, head of the college's school of design and crafts in 1972, and Principal in 1984. Throughout his teaching career he continued with his own work as an architect, designer, writer, photographer and filmmaker. His written works are always signed 'John L Paterson' but the architectural and exhibition designs tend to be signed 'Paterson and Associates, Architects', the latter produced at Paterson's home addresses in Edinburgh, firstly at 24 Young Street Lane North, and then 10 Wemyss Place. His assistants included Caroline Stephen and Virgil A Anthaney.

Scope and Content

The Collection consists of 2,250 items relating to specific projects, including 610 drawings and exhibition panels; 1,040 photographs and slides; 380 photographic negative strips; 140 folders or files containing manuscripts, correspondence, accounts, trade literature and newspaper cuttings; 36 sketchbooks, notebooks and visitor books; 11 of Paterson's own publications and exhibition catalogues; 22 films and audiotapes; three architectural models; a set of drawing instruments; and two chairs designed by Paterson. In addition to this there are 3,600 topographical photographs and a series of books relating to photography. The drawings span the period from Paterson's student days in the 1950s to his death in 1989 and represent 84 separate projects.

The student material of 1950-58 includes his thesis *A Film Centre* and photography for the 1957-58 Edinburgh College of Art *Prospectus*. His apprenticeship with Stewart Kaye & Partners is represented by the film *We Build Houses* (1953) which shows the unskilled workers of the Dunedin Self Build Housing Association building their own dwellings to the design of Ian Stewart Kaye. Early collaborative work with other architects includes an entry for the international city planning competition, Hauptstadt, Berlin (1958) with Robert Matthew (1906-1975), Michael Laird (1928-1999) and Patrick Nuttgens (1930-2004).

From his years with Robert Matthew Johnson-Marshall & Partners there are photographs documenting the construction of Hutchesontown B, Glasgow (1958) for which Paterson was the job architect.

The Collection contains material covering Paterson's

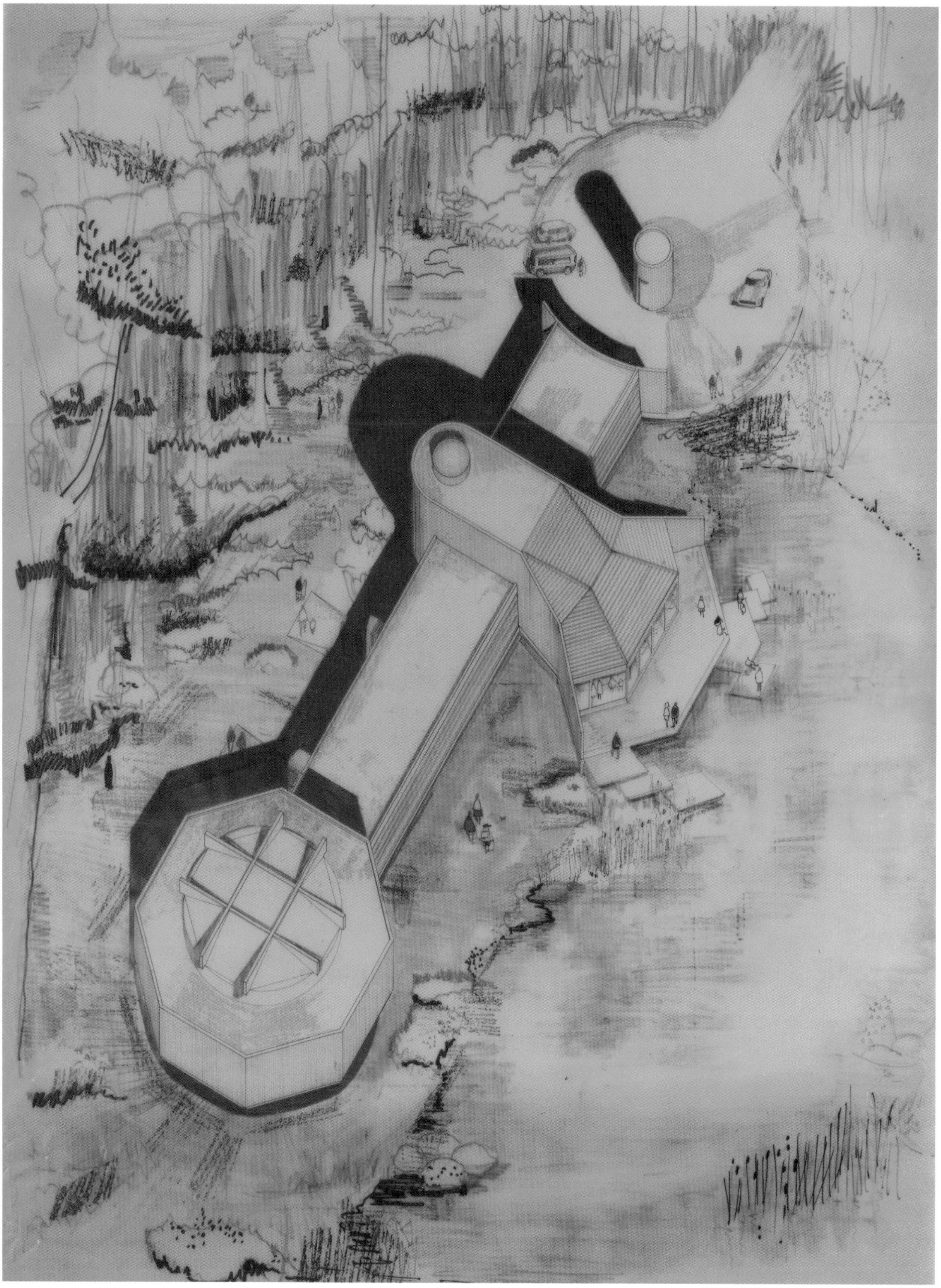

Bird's-eye view of the Landmark Visitor Centre, Carrbridge, Inverness-shire by John L Paterson, c.1969-73, from the John L Paterson Collection. [SC879176]

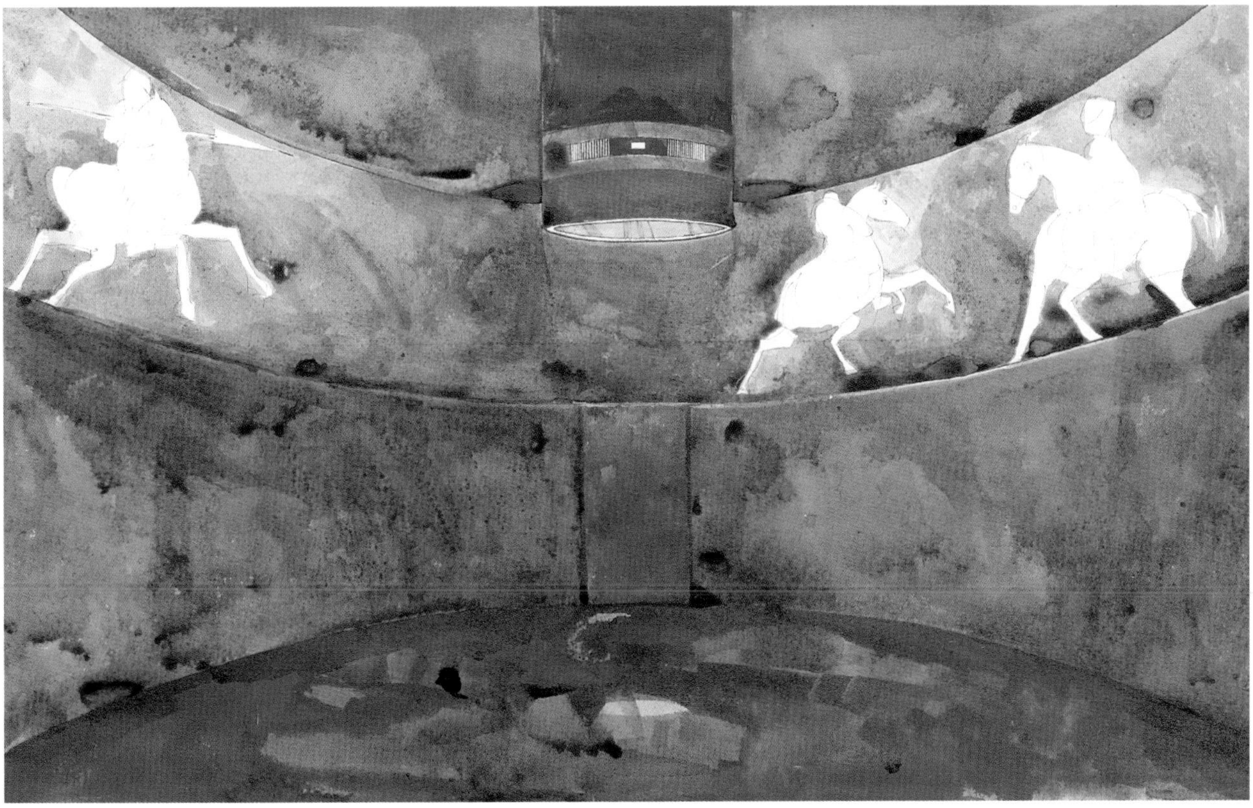

Design for interior of Bannockburn Heritage Centre, Stirlingshire, by John L Paterson, c.1972, from the John L Paterson Collection. [SC800229]

career as an independent architect. These drawings include additions and alterations to domestic buildings around Edinburgh; prefabricated housing (*c*.1963-64); the proposed redevelopment of Newhaven Harbour, Edinburgh (*c*.1960-75); the conversion of 29 Market Street, Edinburgh into offices for the Scottish Arts Council, the New 57 Gallery and the Printmakers Workshop (1974-75); and undated proposals for Bearsden Town Hall, Glasgow and the Goztik Memorial, Libya.

As a designer Paterson formed a reputation for constructing unconventional exhibition spaces, which often incorporated the latest multimedia technology. Designs for permanent exhibition areas or audio-visual installations in arts/visitor centres include Bannockburn Heritage Centre, Stirlingshire (conversion, 1972); *'The Scottish Experience'*, St Thomas Episcopal Church, Edinburgh (conversion, 1980-81); *'The World from a Hill'*, Calton Hill, Edinburgh (installation, 1983-84); and the Tron Heritage Centre, High Street, Edinburgh (conversion, 1984).

Paterson's temporary exhibition designs represented in the Collection include the exhibition for which he is best remembered, *'200 Summers in a City: Edinburgh New Town Bicentenary Celebration'*, Waverley Market, Edinburgh (1967).

Examples of Paterson's written work in the Collection include a number of typescript articles, mostly for *Prospect* (1957-59); catalogues of his own exhibitions; an allegorical book on architecture called *A Design Odyssey* (1976); and an undated notebook of poems. His photography incorporates documentation of his own designs; numerous portraits, landscapes and figure studies; and two published collections: *Imagined City* (1984) and *Iona* (1987).

John Lamb Paterson (1931-1989) at the New Environment Exhibition, 5 Blythswood Square, Glasgow, 1968, from the John L Paterson Collection. [SC800242]

Films in the Collection directed by Paterson are *One Pair of Eyes* (undated); *We Build Houses* (1953); *The Flowering Stone* (1957), which focuses on Le Corbusier's 12-storey apartment block Unite d'Habitation, Marseilles (1946-52); *The Sun Worshippers* (*c*.1963); *New Town Blues* (1966) on the work of architect Peter Daniel for Livingston; *The Iron Rose* (1968), which examines the work of Charles Rennie Mackintosh (1868-1928); and soundtracks for the displays at Bannockburn Heritage Centre (*c*.1972). Several reels of untitled footage show the construction of Sydney Harbour Bridge (*c*.1930-32), on which Paterson's father had worked as an engineer; as well as Paterson's student work (*c*.1950-57); the Festival of Britain (1951); the IUA Conference in Prague (1967); and Expo '67 in Montreal (1967).

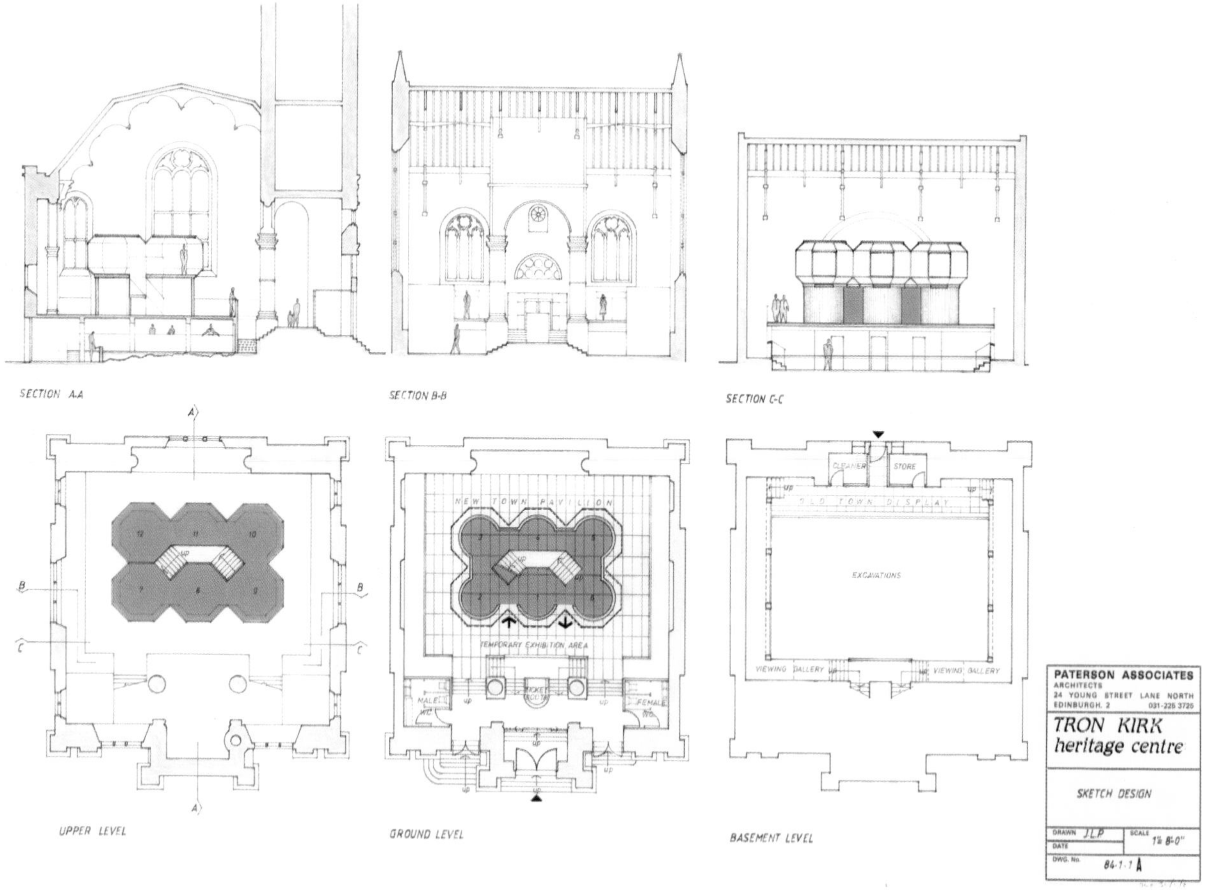

Plans and sections of proposed Tron Kirk Visitor Centre, High Street, Edinburgh by Paterson Associates, c.1984, from the John L Paterson Collection. [SC879174]

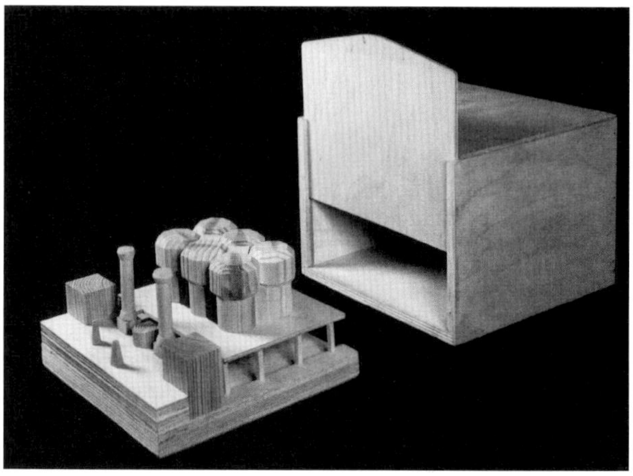

Wooden model of proposed Tron Visitor Centre, High Street, Edinburgh by Paterson Associates, c.1985, from the John L Paterson Collection. [SC879173]

References

NMRS Sources

- Typescript notes of interview with John Knight and Sir James Dunbar-Nasmith – Re: John Lamb Paterson, by Daniel Parker and Siobhan McConnachie, January 2003 (MS 926/5/6).

Anon. 1967 *RIAS Calendar and Annu Rep* (1966-67). Edinburgh.

Anon. 1974 *Year Book*, Edinburgh Architectural Association, 89.

Anon. 1979 *Parade: Dance Costumes of Three Centuries*, Exhibition Leaflet. Edinburgh: Edinburgh College of Art.

Anon. 1982 *Patrick Geddes 1854-1932: On the Side of Life*, Exhibition Catalogue. Edinburgh: Edinburgh College of Art.

Anon. 1989 'Obituary John L Paterson', *Bull Heriot Watt Univ*, Vol.22, No.106 (June), 26.

Daniel, P 1967 *Two Hundred Summers in a City*, Exhibition Catalogue. Edinburgh.

Dunbar-Nasmith, J 1968 'Celebrations for the Bi-Centenary of the New Town', *Edinburgh Architect Ass Year Book*, 12, 97-9.

Dunbar-Nasmith, J 1989 'John L. Paterson – Obituary', *Charles Rennie Mackintosh Soc Newsletter*, no.52 (Winter 1989), 3.

Gerrard, J 1971 'Landmark Visitors' Centre: Appraisal', *Architects J*, no.9, vol. 153, (March 1971), 471-5.

Nimmo, I *Edinburgh: The New Town*. Edinburgh: John Donald Publishers.

Paterson, J L 1957 A Film Centre.

Paterson, J L 1957 'Image for a City', *Prospect*, no. 8, 30-3.

Paterson, J L 1957 'New York', *Prospect*, no.8, 36.

Paterson, J L 1958 'Aspects of Society', *Prospect*, no.10, 21-3.

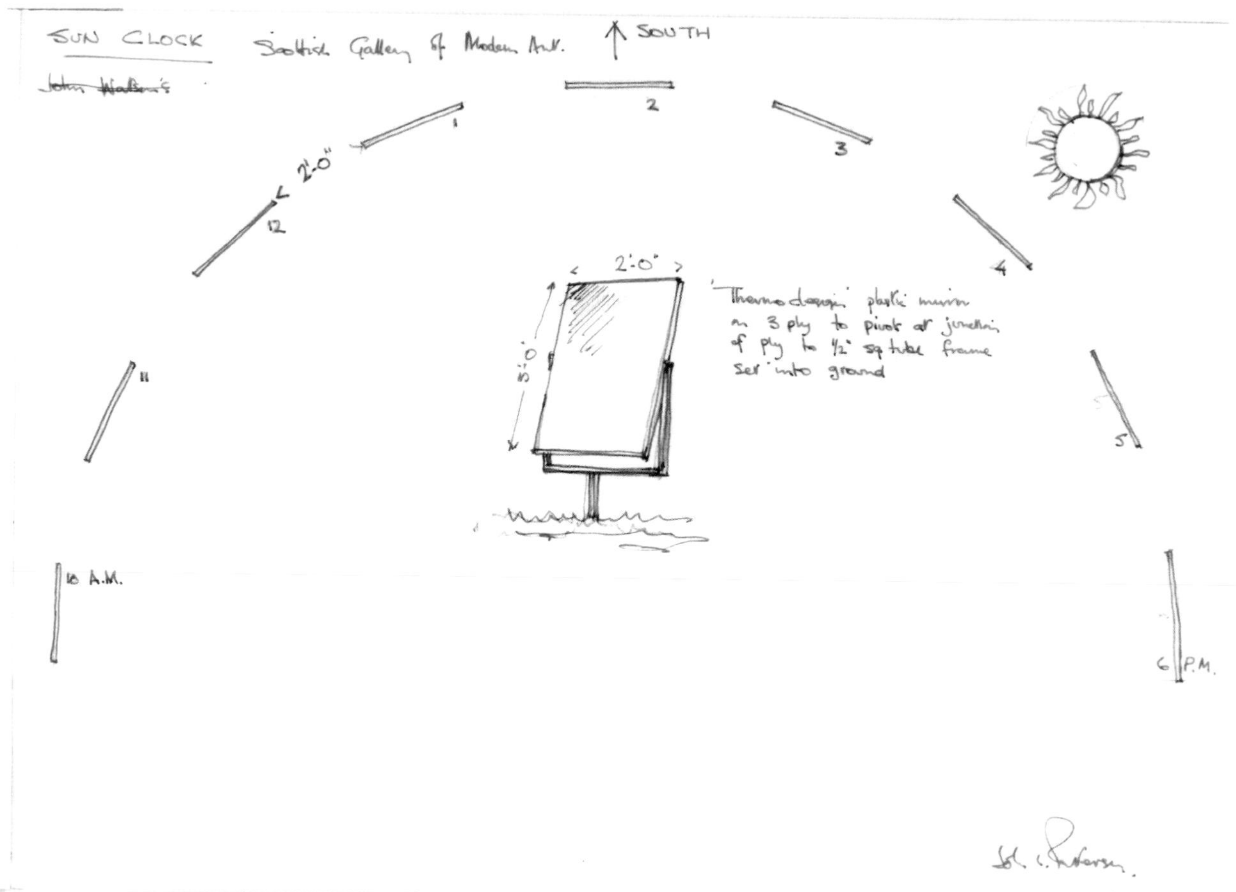

Sketch of a sun clock for the Scottish National Gallery of Modern Art, for installation at the Royal Botanic Garden, Edinburgh by John L Paterson, c.1980-85, from the John L Paterson Collection. [SC879172]

Paterson, J L 1958 'Proposal for a Social Architecture', *Prospect*, no.11, 32-3.

Paterson, J L 1958 'Project: The Edge of the City', *Prospect*, no.12, 38-9.

Paterson, J L 1959 'The Unlit Lamps of Architecture', *Prospect*, no.16, 37-8.

Paterson, J L 1968 'Two Hundred Summers in a City', *Edinburgh Architect Ass Year Book*, 12, 99-102.

Paterson, J L 1968 *New Environment*, Exhibition Catalogue. Edinburgh: Scottish Arts Council.

Paterson, J L 1970 'Recreation in the Countryside: Landmark Visitor Centre', *Official Architect and Plan*, vol. 33 (October), 867-69.

Paterson, J L 1971 'Landmark Visitors Centre', *Architects J*, no. 9, vol. 153 (March), 467-71.

Paterson, J L 1971 *Writer to a Nation*, Exhibition Catalogue. Edinburgh: Edinburgh Corporation.

Paterson, J L 1976 *A Design Odyssey*. Edinburgh: Edinburgh Architectural Association.

Paterson, J L 1984 *Imagined City*. Edinburgh College of Art: The Eagle Press.

Paterson, J L 1985 *Tron Heritage Centre*. Edinburgh: Edinburgh Heritage Trust.

Paterson, J L 1986 *The World from a Hill*. Edinburgh.

Paterson, J L 1987 *Iona*. London: John Murray Publishers.

Paterson, J L 1987 'Designing the Theatre Museum', *Apollo*, No. 125 (April 1987), 290-3.

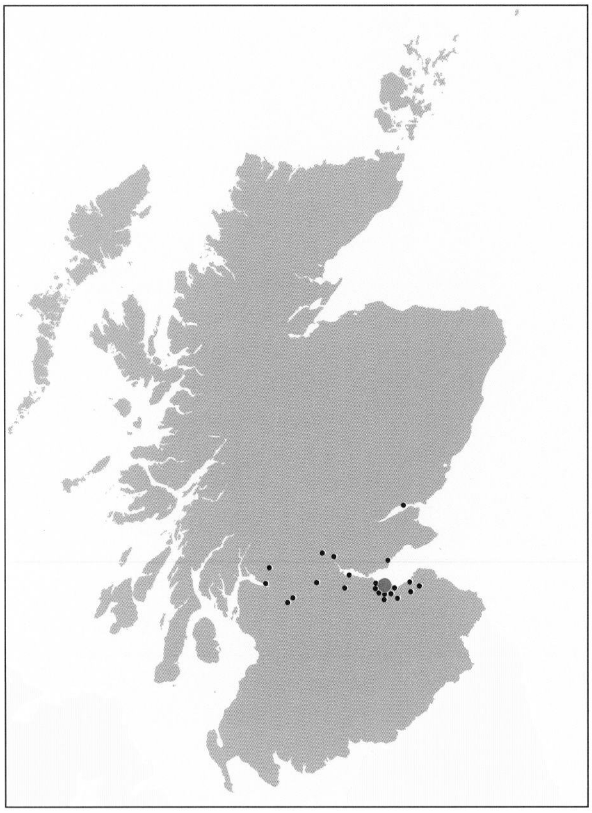

Alan Reiach

Provenance

The Alan Reaich Collection comprises drawings selected by Alan Reiach shortly before his death in 1992 and represents virtually all that survives of his architectural graphic work. Following his death, ownership of the drawings passed to his widow, Mrs Pat Reiach. They were partially sorted and listed at this stage by his partner Stuart Renton. The SSAP surveyed the collection in 1993 and it was subsequently presented to RCAHMS (Accession No. 1993/104).

Already ordered by project, the collection comprised 38 rolls or flat packets. This original order has been maintained and the items arranged chronologically and according to drawing type (i.e. plans, sections, elevations and details) within each project.

History

Alan Reiach was born in London on 2 March 1910. He became an apprentice of Sir Robert Lorimer (1864-1929) in 1928 whilst studying at Edinburgh College of Art. He qualified as an architect in 1934, having won the RIBA Tite Prize, Soane Medallion and the RIBA Silver Medal. The following year he gained a Postgraduate Diploma in Town Planning and embarked on a tour of America, Eastern Europe and Russia with the assistance of a Major Andrew Grant Travelling Scholarship. Whilst travelling in the USA, he met with Frank Lloyd Wright (1869-1959).

In 1933 Reiach started in private practice from his house at 14 Randolph Place, Edinburgh, on small-scale private domestic commissions. In 1936-7 he worked in the London offices of the architects Robert Atkinson & Partners, and Grey Wornum. He returned to Edinburgh College of Art in 1938 as a research and teaching fellow and by 1940 he had joined the Scottish Office as a member of the Clyde Valley Regional Planning Study Team.

In 1946 Reiach set up practice at 7 Albert Terrace, Edinburgh, returning the following year to Edinburgh College Art to take up a senior lectureship which he held until 1957. In 1948 he formed a professional association with Ralph Cowan, the Head of the School of Architecture at Edinburgh College of Art, when they were jointly appointed as architects for the new College of Agriculture at Kings Buildings, Edinburgh. This single project partnership, known as Reiach & Cowan, was based at 30 Melville Street, Edinburgh and moved to 22 Ainslie Place, Edinburgh in 1955 until the project's completion in 1960.

Meanwhile Reiach continued to work under his own name. George McNab (*c.*1927-2003) joined the practice in 1954 after winning the RIBA silver medal in 1952. In 1955 Stuart Renton (b.1929) joined the practice. Renton was born in Edinburgh and educated at the Royal High School and Edinburgh College of Art. Whilst studying, he was apprenticed to Burnet Tait & Lorne, where he worked under the guidance of Francis Lorne (1889-1963). He became a partner in Reiach's practice in 1957.

In 1958 John R Oberlander and Leslie D Mitchell joined the practice. In the same year, McNab was assumed into partnership and the practice became Alan

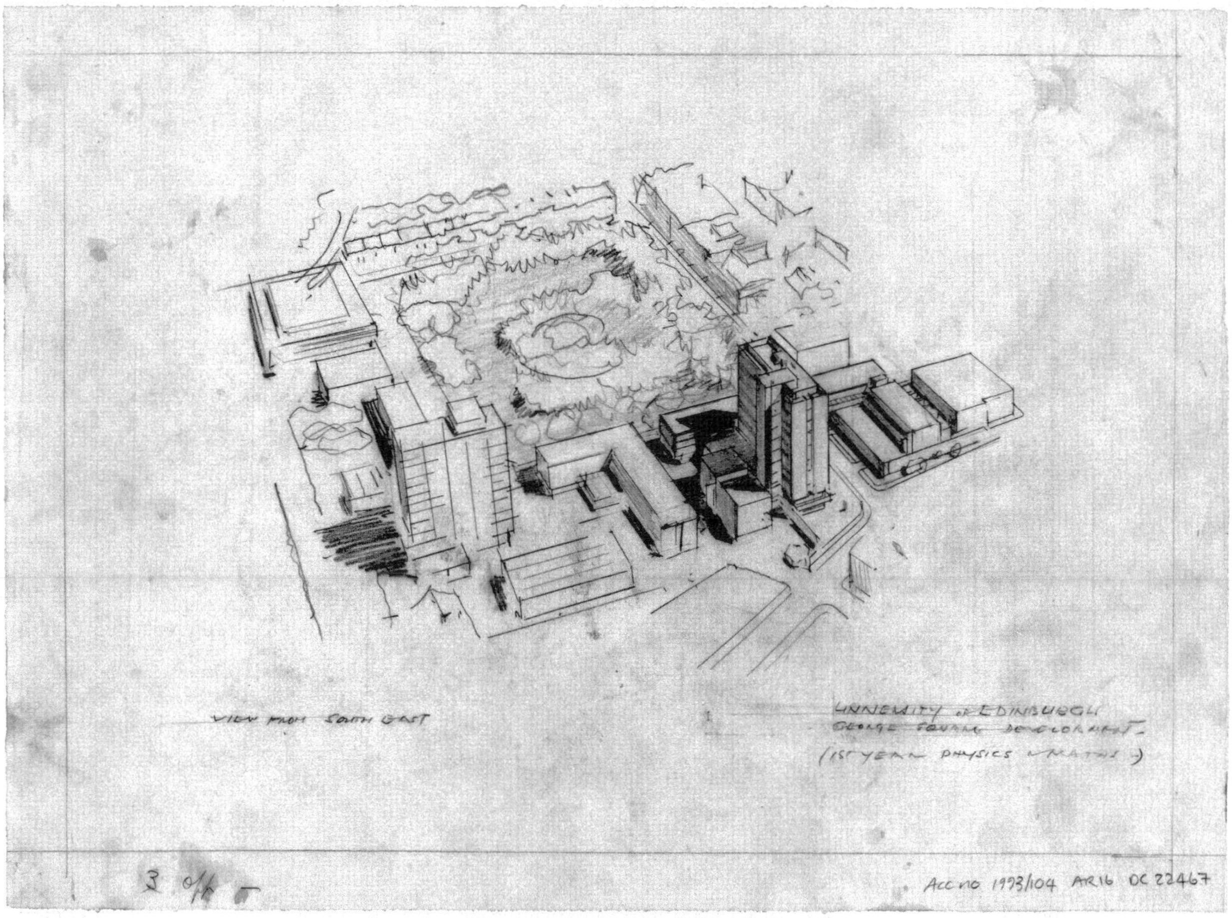

Perspective sketch of the George Square Development (1st Year Physics and Maths) University of Edinburgh, by Alan Reiach, c.1970, from the Alan Reiach Collection. [SC778107]

Alan Reiach (1910-1992) in the drawing room of his home at 14 Randolph Place, Edinburgh, 1938. [SC820555]

Reiach & Partners. In 1965 Alan Reiach & Partners merged with Eric Hall & Partners and the practice was renamed as Alan Reiach Eric Hall & Partners. The new partnership practiced from 16 Moray Place, Edinburgh until 1971 when they moved to 6 Darnaway Street, Edinburgh. In 1967 Mitchell and Oberlander became partners.

In 1975 Reiach retired, remaining as consultant to the practice until 1980. In 1981 the practice changed its name to Reiach & Hall. In his later years, Reiach's talent was recognised through the award of an OBE (1964); and membership of the Royal Fine Art Commission for Scotland (1966-80), the council of the Cockburn Association (1967-76) and the Royal Scottish Academy (Associate Member from 1969, Academician from 1986). He was also President and honorary member of the Scottish Arts Club and the only architect of his time to be elected a member of the Royal Scottish Society of Painters in Watercolour. He died on 23 July 1992.

Scope and Content

The Collection consists of 697 items including 487 drawings, 73 photographic postcards and 134 negatives, spanning from Reiach's student days in 1932 to just after his retirement in 1976. The 93 represented projects reflect Reiach's enthusiasm for a new architecture that was influenced by contemporary continental work while being sympathetic to the Scottish environment. This architectural philosophy is encapsulated in Reiach's seminal publication *Building Scotland: a Cautionary*

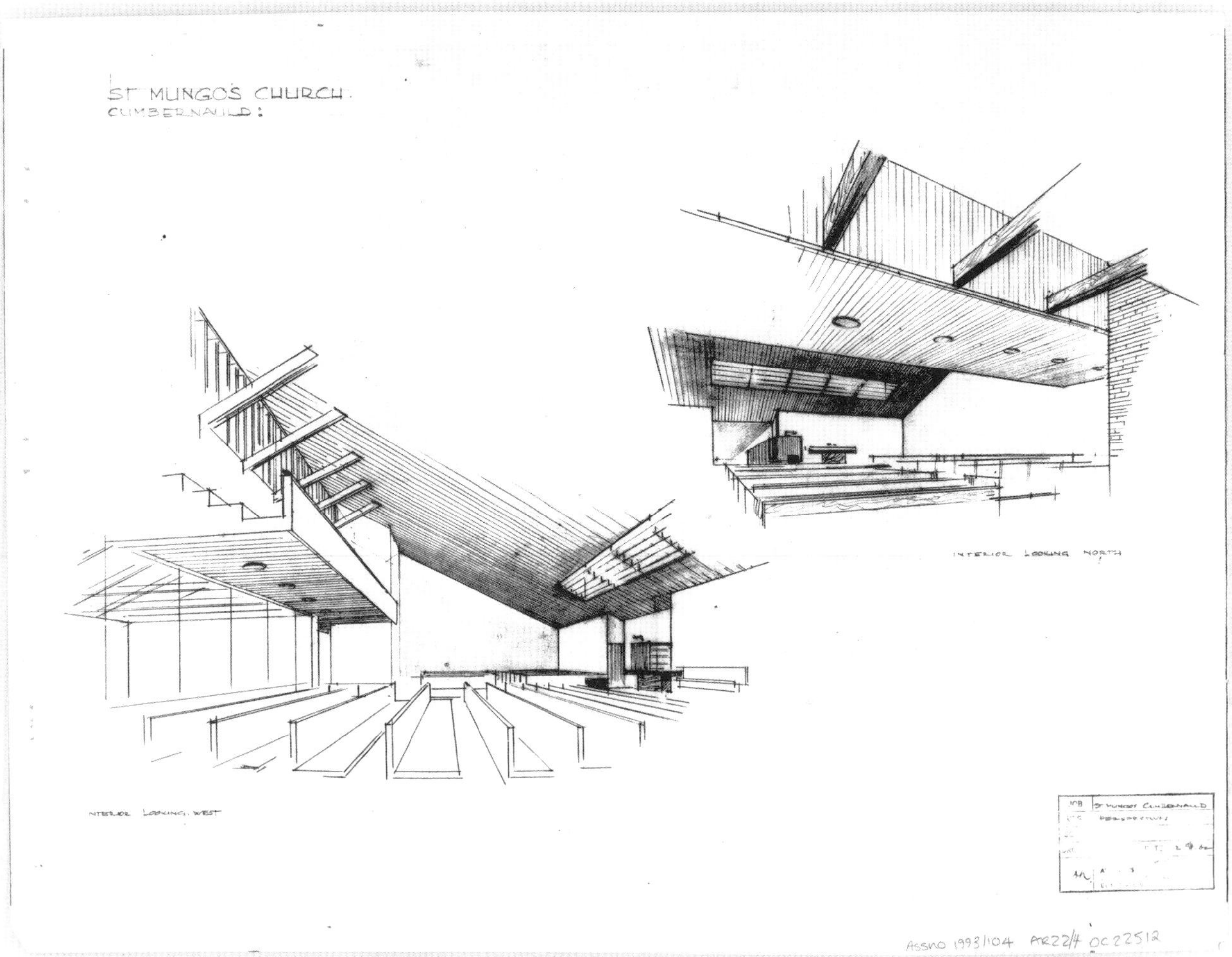

Perspective views of the interior of St Mungo's Church, Cumbernauld by Alan Reiach, 1962, from the Alan Reiach Collection. [SC778103]

Perspective view of the interior of the New Club, 84-87 Princes Street, Edinburgh by Alan Reiach, 1965, from the Alan Reiach Collection. [SC778112]

Guide (1944), written in collaboration with Robert Hurd (1905-1963).

The Collection contains many Edinburgh-based projects and includes the College of Agriculture for the University of Edinburgh (1951); St John's Church, Oxgangs (1956); Reiach's own Danish-inspired house at 3 Winton Loan (1962-79); Appleton Tower, George Square, designed as part of the Comprehensive Development Area for the University of Edinburgh (1962-72); and the new wing of the Royal Victoria Hospital (1964-75). Also included are drawings for the New Club, Princes Street (1967-69), which was designed under the leadership of Renton within the strict guidelines of the Princes Street Panel and involved the demolition of the original building, designed by William Burn (1789-1870) in 1834. A particular need of Edinburgh in the 1970s was for modern office accommodation which is represented in the Collection by a commission from the Scottish Life Assurance Company for Alan Reiach Eric Hall & Partners to design an office in Orchard Brae (1971).

Drawings in the Collection for projects outside Edinburgh include a competition entry for the University of Sheffield (1953); a church at Easthouses, Dalkeith (1953); Knox Academy, Haddington (1956-58); Dumbarton Civic Theatre and Community Centre (1962-66); Stirling University Sports Centre (1969-70); and an unrealised development for George Square, Glasgow (1973). Reiach's contributions to Scotland's New Towns are preserved in the form of designs for Kildrum Parish Church (1955-66) and St Mungo's Church, both in Cumbernauld (1962-64).

Reiach's student and postgraduate work in the Collection features a number of competition entries, including the Rural Workers Housing Competition (1932), the Soane Medallion (1934) and the Rowand Anderson Prize (1934). Collaborative competition entries with Robert Matthew include Ilkestone, Derbyshire (1st place, 1938); Tanfield Primary School, Edinburgh (3rd place, 1939); and the Waverley Market, Edinburgh (1939).

A notable omissions in the Collection is Reiach's first design for a Museum of Modern Art for Scotland, York Buildings site, Queen Street, Edinburgh (1940): the scheme was translated into a model by the then Director of the National Galleries of Scotland, Stanley Cursiter (1887-1976). However, the Collection does include Reiach's designs for the proposed Scottish National Gallery of Modern Art at two of its proposed sites: at East Princes Street Gardens, Edinburgh (1955) and Inverleith House, Royal Botanic Gardens, Edinburgh (1974). Also not contained in the Collection are Reiach's designs for shops and houses at Whitemoss, East Kilbride (1949), which form an early part of the New Town development.

References

In 1994 RCAHMS undertook a photographic survey of 3 Winton Loan, which Reiach built for himself in 1964.

NMRS Sources

- List of over 250 books from Alan Reiach's library made at McNaughton's Bookshop, Edinburgh, 10 January 1994.
- **Cameron, N M 1991** Alan Reiach: Notes of Informal Discussion with Neil Cameron.
- **Thomas, J 1991** Typescript Notes of Conversation with Alan Reiach, 5 March 1991.
- **Thomas, J 1994** Typescript Notes of Conversation with Professor McNab, 18 February 1994.

Anon. 1933 'A Ballroom in the Grounds of an Italian Embassy', *The Builder*, 20 January 1933.
Anon. 1933 'Awards for Edinburgh Students of Architecture', *News Chronicle*, 12 January 1933.
Anon. 1954 'A Conversation with Alan Reiach', *House and Garden* (June), 42-3.
Anon. 1990 'Alan Reiach', *The Scotsman*, 26 January 1990.
Anon. 1992 'Alan Reiach: Obituary', *The Scotsman*, 25 July 1992.
Allen of Hurtwood and Jellicoe, Lady and S 1956 The *New Small Garden*. London: The Architectural Press.
Baxter, J N 1992 'Alan Reiach: a Personal Appreciation', *Edinburgh Architect Ass J*, 31.
Baxter, J N 1992 *Building Design*, 21 August 1992, 28.
Jacques, R 1994 'An Example of the Late Alan Reiach's Contribution to Scottish Architecture', *The Scotsman*, 4 April 1994.
Reiach A *The Lesser Architecture of Scotland* (manuscript held at Edinburgh College of Art).
Reiach, A 1931 'Architectural Jottings', *RIAS Quart*, no.37, 30.
Reiach, A and Hurd, R 1944 *Building Scotland*: a Cautionary Guide (2nd ed.). Edinburgh: Saltire Society.
Reiach, A 1959 'Frank Lloyd Wright', *Architect Prospect* (Autumn), 22-4.
Reiach, A and Hall, E *Architects and Planners: A Client's Guide*. Edinburgh.
Renton, S 1992 *RIAS Newsletter*, no.3, 11 October 1992.
Renton, S 1992 *RIBA J*, November 1992, 56-9.
Scott Morton, R 1990 'Rich Legacy of a Master Craftsman', *The Scotsman*, 26 February 1990.
Scott Morton, R 1989 *Alan Reiach OBE RSA RSW RIBA FRIAS: A Memoir*.

Related practices/personnel:
Lorimer & Matthew Collection

For other Alan Reiach papers:
Schomberg Scott Collection

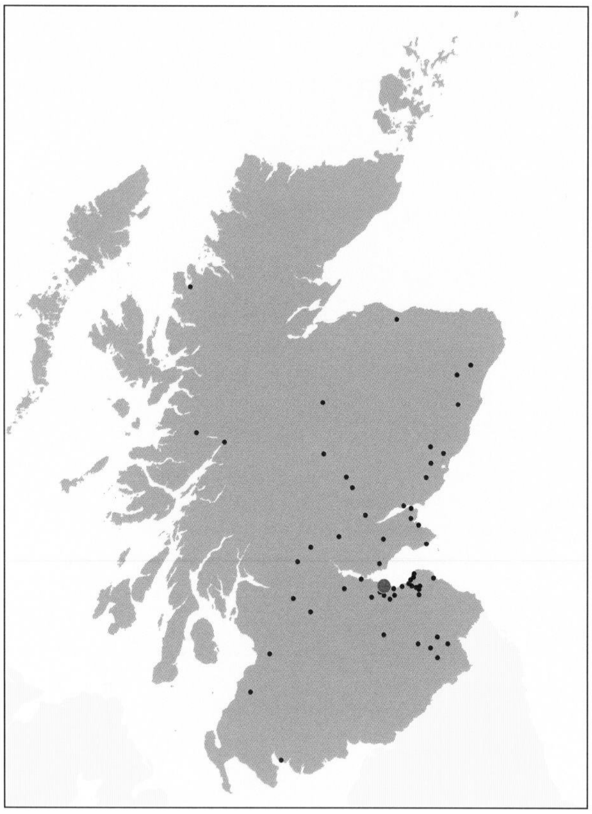

Schomberg Scott

Provenance
The Schomberg Scott Collection of drawings, photographs and manuscripts was presented to RCAHMS in a number of stages, the first by Schomberg Scott himself in 1979 (Accession No. 1979/13). From this initial gift, many drawings relating to work carried out for the National Trust for Scotland were given to them in the same year. Between 1997 and 2003, Anthony Dixon (who had worked in Schomberg Scott's office) made four further gifts of material to RCAHMS on behalf of Schomberg Scott's family (Accession Nos. 1997/39, 1997/99, 1998/67 and 2003/309).

History
Walter Schomberg Hepburn Scott ARIAS RIBA (1910-1998) was born at Monteviot in the Scottish Borders, the son of the Chamberlain of the Duke of Roxburghe at Floors Castle and Lady Isobella Kerr, daughter of the Earl of Ancrum. He was educated at Radleigh College, Oxfordshire and went on to study architecture at Edinburgh College of Art. In the early 1930s he entered the offices of Reginald Fairlie (1883-1952) whom he may have met when Fairlie was adding new lodges at Floors. He then moved to London to work in the offices of Sir Edward Maufe (1883-1974).

During the Second World War he became a Captain in the Royal Engineers, a position that took him to India. In 1946 he joined the Edinburgh-based practice Orphoot Whiting & Lindsay, becoming a partner in the firm when it was renamed Ian G Lindsay & Partners.

Schomberg Scott left Ian G Lindsay & Partners to set up his own practice *c.*1959 at 3 Randolph Cliff, Edinburgh. During 1960 he worked from premises at 22 Ainslie Place before moving his business to 11 Forres Street in the second half of 1961.

In 1967 the ex-footballer Ronald McKinven became a partner, specialising in the design of commercial premises such as shops and nightclubs. In 1974, Anthony Dixon replaced McKinven, and the practice became known as Schomberg Scott & A C S Dixon. The office closed on Schomberg Scott's retirement in August 1979, Dixon joining Stuart Tod's practice.

Schomberg Scott is perhaps best known for his work for the National Trust for Scotland. In 1953 he was appointed to the organisation's Architectural and Artistic Advisory Panel. He initially acted as Advisor on Architecture and Furnishings, then as Architect and Design Consultant, and finally as Consultant for Architecture, Design and Furnishings, a position that took up about three-quarters of his time, leaving the rest for his private commissions. As well as undertaking restoration work on many National Trust houses, he also designed information and visitors' centres for the organisation. He was repeatedly invited to join the staff of the National Trust for Scotland but was unwilling to give up his practice.

Scope and Content
The Collection comprises 1,830 drawings (Accession Nos. 1979/13, 1997/39, 1997/99 and 1998/67) and 840 photographs (Accession Nos. 1997/99 and 1998/67). These reflect the practice's specialism of providing

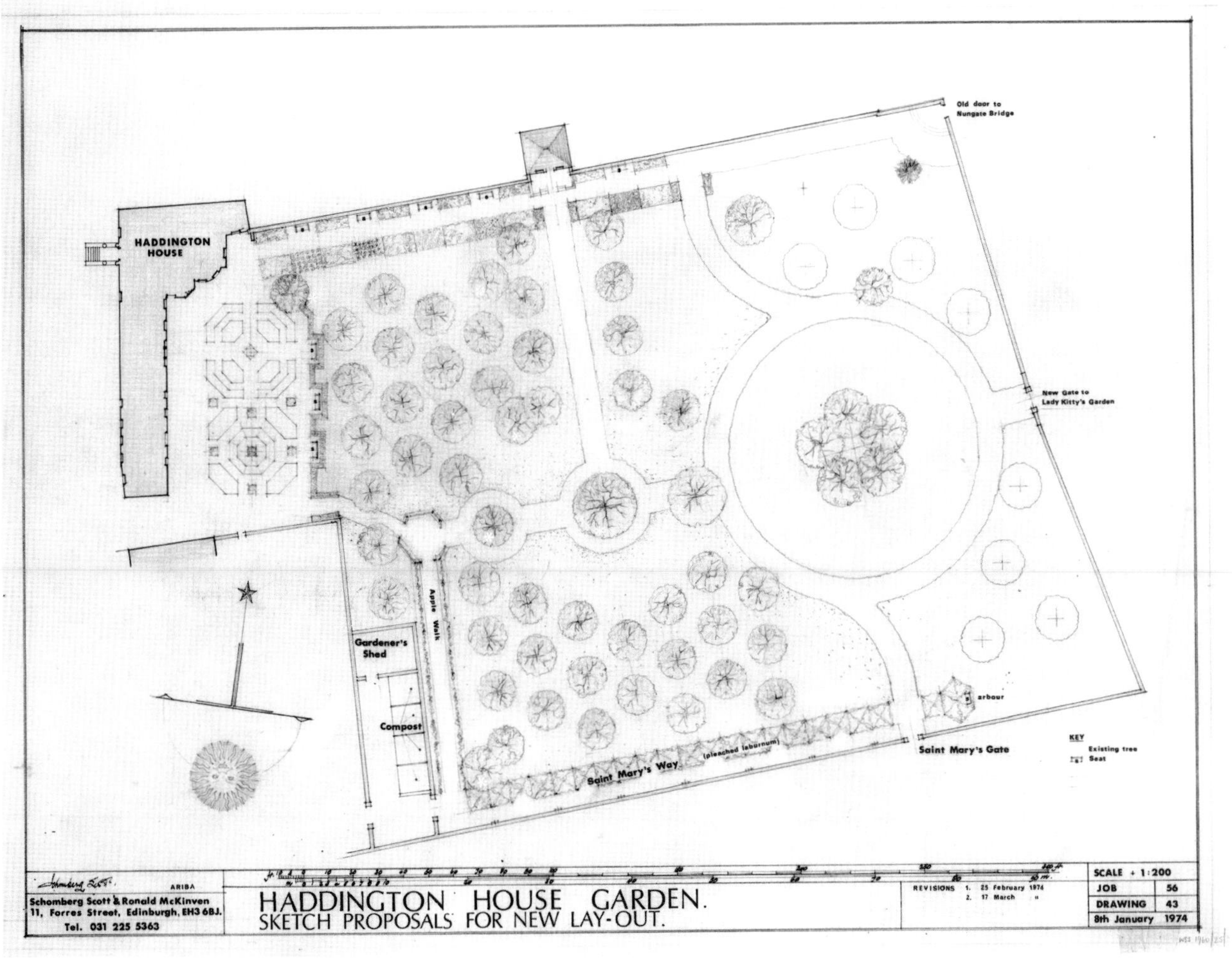

Plan showing garden layout at Haddington House, East Lothian by Schomberg Scott & Ronald McKinven, 1974, from the Schomberg Scott Collection. [SC879331]

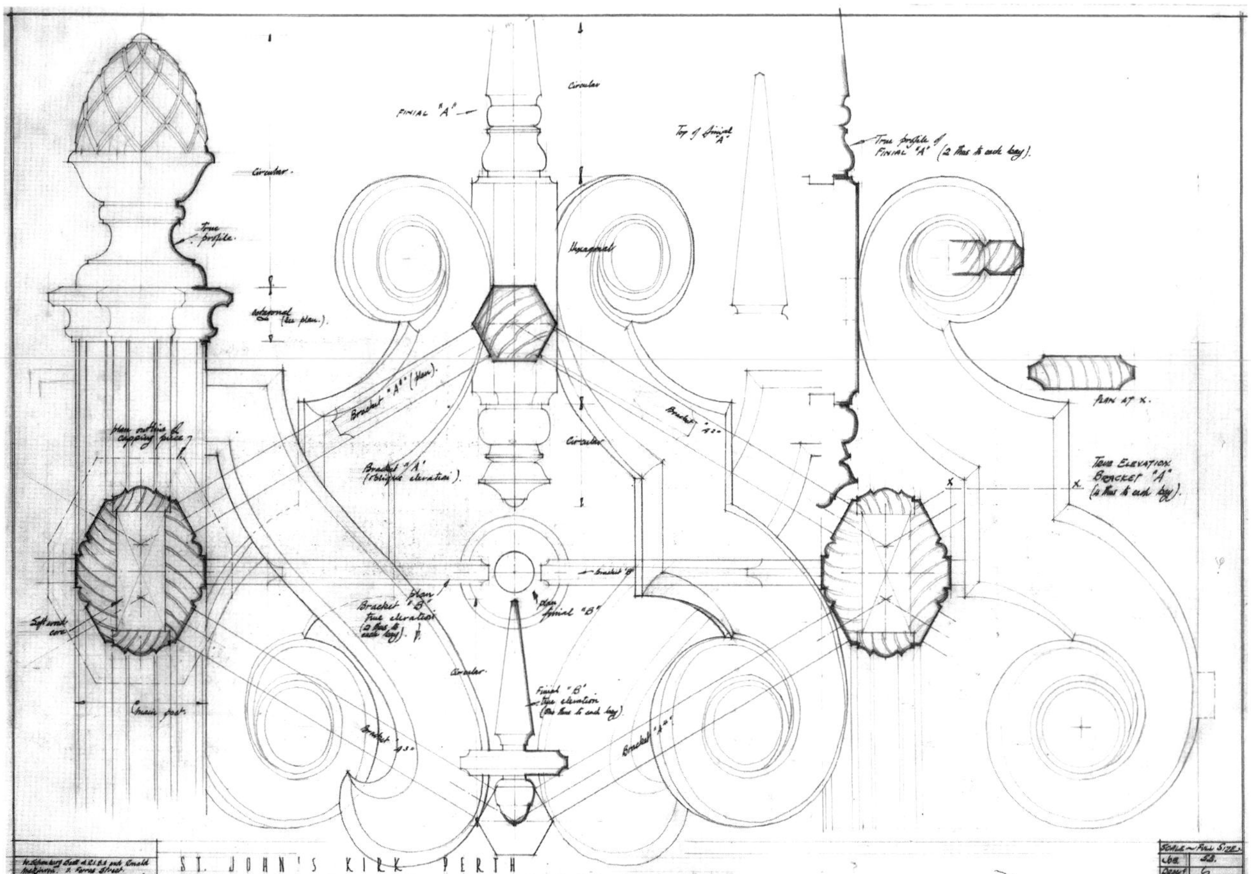

Details of cresting on chapel screen at St John's Church, St John's Place, Perth by Schomberg Scott & Ronald McKinven, 1964, from the Schomberg Scott Collection. [SC879330]

Perspective view showing sculptured gateposts by John Skelton FRSA at Monteviot House, Roxburghshire by Schomberg Scott, 1963, from the Schomberg Scott Collection. [SC879335]

alterations and additions for country houses throughout Scotland, making many of them fit for habitation, sometimes after decades of neglect or wartime use by the military. Such commissions include Abbotsford House, Roxburghshire (1957-58); Dalkeith Palace, Midlothian (1970-73); Mellerstain, Berwickshire (1972-75); Hamilton House, East Lothian (1975-76); Lennoxlove, East Lothian (1974); and Gordon Castle, Aberdeenshire, where the East wing was adapted as a residence after the demolition of the central block (1964-70).

The Collection contains over 200 drawings of Monteviot House and Chapel in Roxburghshire where, between 1957 and 1963, Schomberg Scott reduced the size of the old house, adapted the former servants' hall to form a chapel, and built a separate small house as staff accommodation.

Some of Schomberg Scott's work for the National Trust for Scotland can be seen in the Collection. This includes papers for Falkland Palace (1964-73) and designs for rebuilding the fire-damaged Queen Anne wing of Crathes Castle, Aberdeenshire, as well as 'the house of Crathes' (1972), built in the grounds of Crathes Castle for the Burnett family.

The Collection includes commissions for the subdivision of large houses into flats such as Craster House in Northumberland (*c*.1965-67). Also included are several projects that never made it beyond the drawing board, such as alterations to the kitchen area of Balmanno House, near Marykirk, Aberdeenshire (1976-77); and the conversion of old houses into flats at 7-11 River Street, Brechin (1972-73). The houses were demolished after the scheme was abandoned by the Burgh Council.

Church furnishings at St John's Perth (*c*.1968-73), the Kirk of St Leonards-in-the-Fields, Perth (1970-75), and Glasgow Cathedral (1966-69), are included in the Collection, as are many drawings for gardens and their related features. These include the design of the gardens at Haddington House, East Lothian (1973-76); along with sundials and armillary spheres for the Centre for Clan Donnachaidh, Bruar (1969-70); Monteviot House, Roxburghshire (1963); and Membland, East Lothian (*c*.1955-58). There are a significant number of designs for wrought iron work, including the memorial gates at Pitmedden Garden, Aberdeenshire (1971).

The photographs in the Collection comprise interior and exterior views of Schomberg Scott's buildings, as well as images that he took for Patrick Nuttgen's monograph of Reginald Fairlie (1883-1952). In addition to the drawings and photographs are 1,540 slides and 520 strips of negatives, although these have not been

Schomberg Scott (1910-1998), left, with Nic Allan outside Scott's home, Northfield House, Prestonpans. [SC374139]

catalogued as part of the project. These include many images of buildings that reflect his general interest in Scottish country house and ecclesiastical architecture.

The material catalogued from the Schomberg Scott Collection does not include any items deposited in 2003, including drawings for the restoration of Schomberg Scott's own home, Northfield House, Prestonpans, a 16th century tower house.

The Collection includes many acquired drawings from Ian G Lindsay & Partners, including a survey plan and details of furnishings at Falkland Palace chapel (1956-58) and alterations to Membland House, East Lothian (1954-58). The Collection also includes copies of drawings from the Harold Tarbolton, Reginald Fairlie, and George Bennett Mitchell & Son practices.

References

NMRS Sources

- **Schomberg Scott, W** 1976 Lairds and Ministers and their Country Houses (lecture given at the Annual History Conference, Hawick, November 1976).

McKean, C 1998 'Obituary to Walter Schomberg Scott', *The Independent*, April 1998.
Nuttgens, P 1959 *Reginald Fairlie*. Edinburgh: Oliver & Boyd.
Schomberg Scott, W 1971 *Crathes Castle*. National Trust for Scotland.
Schomberg Scott, W 1975 *Culzean Castle*. National Trust for Scotland.
Schomberg Scott, W 1983 *Let's Look at Castles and Homes*. National Trust for Scotland.

Related practices/personnel:
Ian G Lindsay Collection

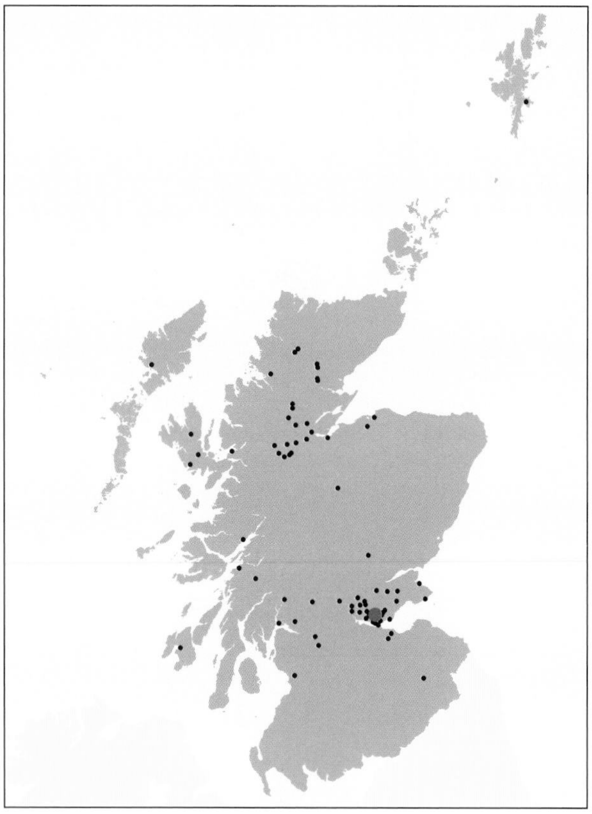

Shearer & Annand

Provenance
The Shearer & Annand Collection (Accession No. 2000/237) was deposited by Marcus Johnston with the RIAS when the practice, based at 11 Maygate, Dunfermline, closed in 1994. The ownership was then passed to RCAHMS in 1999 as part of the McKean Collection.

History
James Grant Shearer, OBE, RSA, FRIBA, FRIAS (1881-1962) was an apprentice to Dunfermline-based architect T Hyslop Ure from 1897 until 1901, before moving to the Glasgow and London offices of J J Burnet (1857-1938) to complete his training. He began his own architectural practice in 1907 in premises at 11 Bonnar Street, Dunfermline, where he remained until *c.*1920. In 1912 he went on a study tour of Germany. Between *c.*1920-31 the practice was based in Queen Anne Street, Dunfermline, before moving to 11 Maygate, Dunfermline.

As well as leading his architectural practice, Shearer held two important town-planning commissions. From 1937 to 1938 he was employed as a part-time planning consultant by Dunfermline Town Council, and from 1944 to 1947 he acted as planning consultant to Clackmannanshire County Council. He is known to have turned down similar roles at Inverness, Forres and Lerwick in 1943, 1946 and 1947 respectively. His major achievement in this field was the Dunfermline Advisory Town Plan of 1946.

In 1949, George Annand (1915-1964), a graduate from Glasgow School of Art, joined the practice and in 1952 was made a partner. The practice became James Shearer & Annand, Architects.

On Annand's death, associate partner James Armstrong, who had joined the practice as an apprentice in 1944, continued as a senior partner until 1967 when he left to take up a post in Edinburgh. The practice then continued with Shearer's son, James D Shearer (1919-1972), who had a practice in London, and Marcus Johnston, another former apprentice, as partners. After the death of J D Shearer, Johnston carried on until the firm closed in 1994.

Scope and Content
The Collection contains over 20,000 drawings and 205 boxes of manuscripts. 14,400 drawings and all manuscripts relating to those drawings have been catalogued. The selection of material catalogued was restricted to the working lifetime of James Shearer (1907-1962); the remainder of the Collection has been hand-listed.

The Collection illustrates the practice's significant contribution to the built fabric of Dunfermline, including designs for many private houses and drawings for one of Shearer's early projects, the Carnegie Birthplace Building, 2-4 Moodie Street, Dunfermline (*c.*1925-54), a commission that led to him becoming consultant architect to the Carnegie United Kingdom Trust. Perhaps one of the practice's most notable

Perspective view of Fasnakyle Power Station, Inverness-shire by James Shearer & Annand, 1954, from the Shearer & Annand Collection. [SC636573]

James Shearer (1881-1962) outside Dunfermline Abbey, c.1955. [SC609992]

Perspective view of the Gatehouse, Mullardoch Dam, Inverness-shire by James Shearer & Annand, c.1947-50, from the Shearer & Annand Collection. [SC609960]

contributions to the town is Dunfermline Fire Station (*c*.1934-36), the largest project represented in the Collection, with over 1,000 drawings.

Other Dunfermline projects contained in the Collection are a war memorial and garden of remembrance at Bee Alley Gardens, Monastery Street (*c*.1947-52); a memorial chapel at Dunfermline Abbey New Parish Kirk (1951-52); the restoration of the Abbot's House, 21 Maygate (1961-4); and a grandstand and terracing at East End Park for Dunfermline Athletic Football Club (1957-69). Shearer's work at Pittencrieff Park in Dunfermline is represented by drawings for the Tower Bridge (*c*.1915), parapet wall (1945) and rabbit house (1951-54), but more significantly by the manuscripts that relate to his role as consultant architect for the later development of the park. During the 1940s, Shearer also acted as consultant architect to the Scottish Youth Hostel Association, although only a few drawings for this work exist in the Collection.

The several thousand drawings that relate to Shearer & Annand's work for the North of Scotland Hydro Electric Board (NSHEB) is arguably the most significant

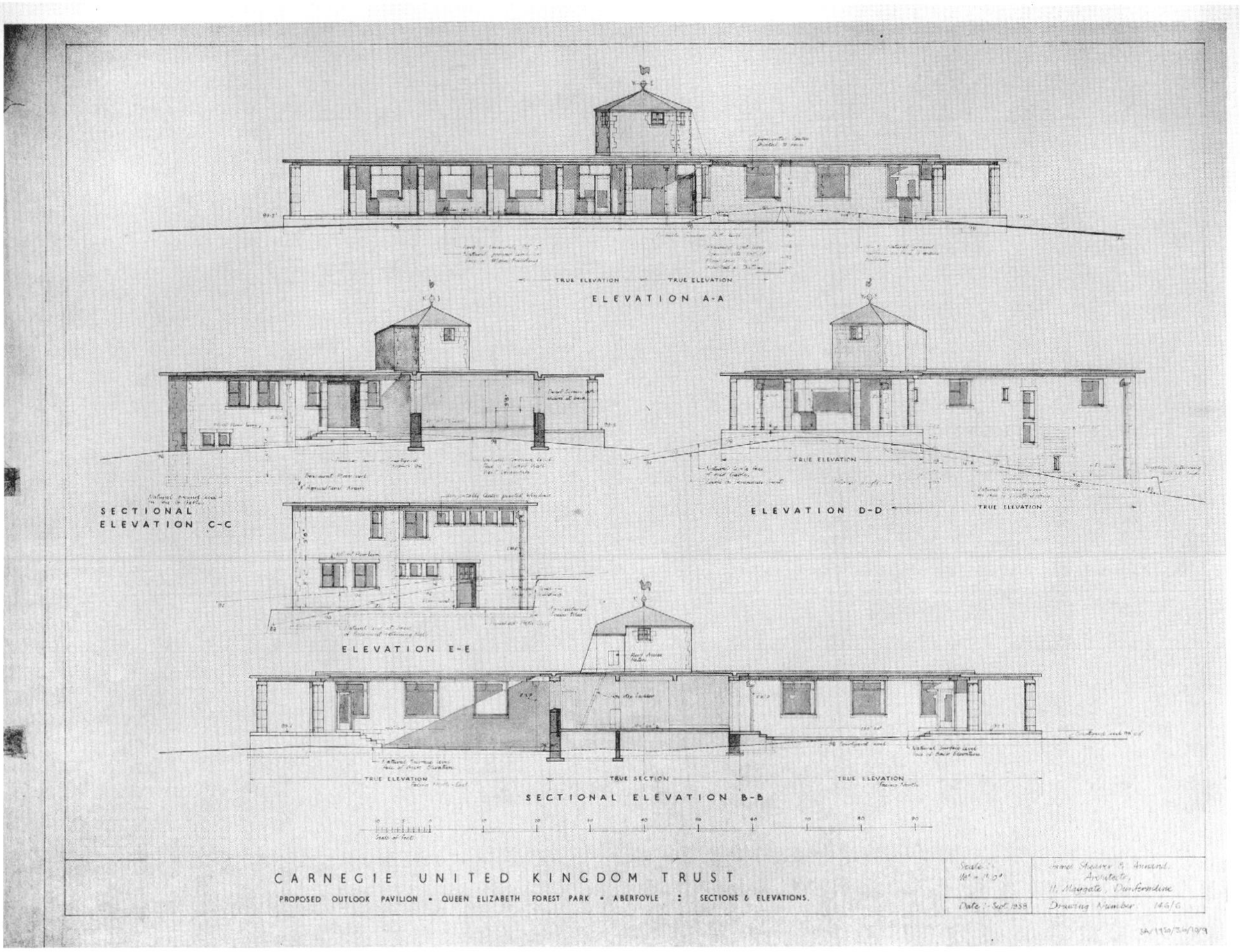

Sections and elevations of the Aberfoyle Outlook Pavilion, known as David Marshal Lodge, Queen Elizabeth Forest Park, Aberfoyle, Perthshire by James Shearer & Annand, 1958, from the Shearer & Annand Collection. [SC609898]

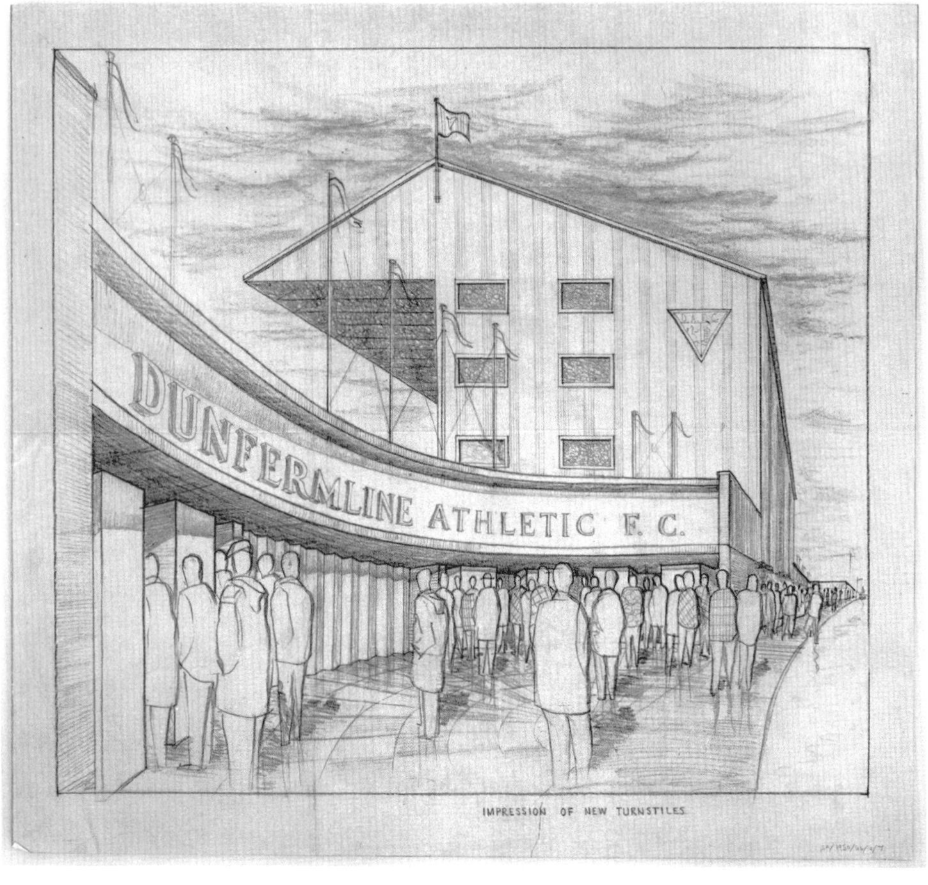

Perspective sketch of Dunfermline Athletic football stadium, East End Park, Halbeath Road, Dunfermline by James Shearer & Annand, c.1957-61, from the Shearer & Annand Collection. [SC609905]

part of the Collection as it offers a detailed insight into the construction of these important schemes. Shearer was appointed as a consultant architect for NSHEB in the 1940s, a role that dominated the work of the practice for the next two decades. From the projects commissioned by the NSHEB, three schemes - Glen Affric (*c*.1946-60), Loch Shin (*c*.1955-60), and Strathfarrar and Kilmorack Power Station and Dam (1959-71) have been catalogued in their entirety. In addition selected buildings have been catalogued from the Conon Valley (1946-60); island schemes such as Loch Dubh (1948-60) and Loch Chliostair (1957-61); and Awe schemes at Loch Nant (1961-65).

Another project well represented in the Collection is the Aberfoyle Outlook Pavilion, also known as the David Marshal Lodge (*c*.1957-61), which was listed category B by the Historic Buildings Branch of Scottish Development on Ian Lindsay's recommendation in 1964, only two years after Shearer's death.

References

NMRS Sources

- A collection of personal papers gifted by the Shearer family (MS/498).
- **Emmerson, R 1985** James Shearer, 1881-1962: Preliminary Outline of His Career and List of Works (MS 498).
- **Owen, C 2001** James Shearer and the Dunfermline Town Plan 1946: An Evaluation of Shearer's Town Planning (Work Placement Report MA Architectural History, presented to Univ of Edinburgh).

Anon. 1923 *The Architect's Journal*, 25 April 1923, 723-30.

McConnachie, S 2003 'James Shearer and the North of Scotland Hydro Electric Board', *Architect Heritage XIV*, 104-18. Edinburgh: Edinburgh Univ Press.

Owen, C 2003 'James Shearer and the Dunfermline Advisory Town Plan, 1946' *Architect Heritage XIV*, 86-103. Edinburgh: Edinburgh Univ Press.

Payne, P L 1988, *The Hydro: a Study of the Development of the Major Hydro-Electric Schemes Undertaken by the North of Scotland Hydro-Electric Board*. Aberdeen: Aberdeen Univ Press.

Shearer, J 1959 'Stonebuilding in Scotland', *Architect Prospect*, vol.13 (Spring 1959), 22-7.

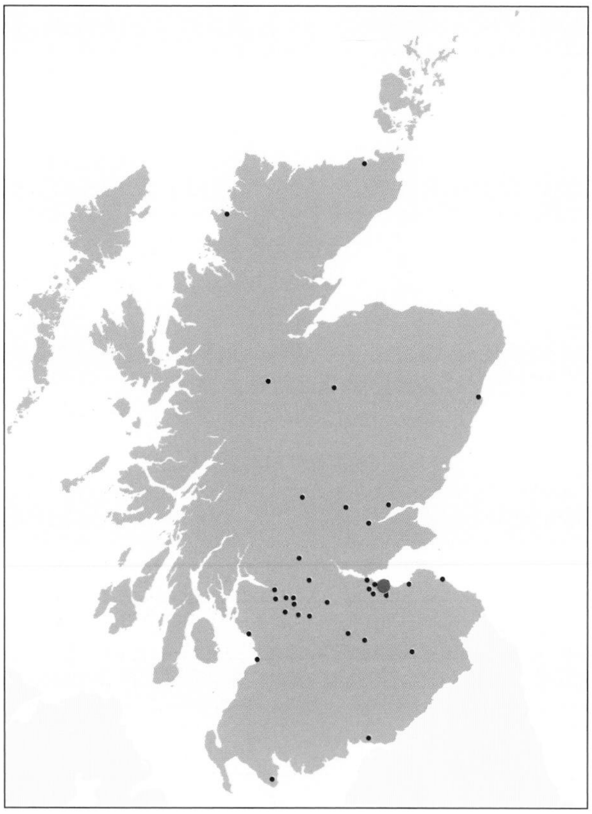

Spence Glover & Ferguson

Provenance
The Spence Glover & Ferguson Collection (Accession No. 1992/53) was gifted to the RIAS by Jim Beveridge, senior partner, when the practice was closed in 1992. The ownership was transferred to RCAHMS in 1999 as part of the McKean Collection.

History
Basil Spence (1907-1976) was born in Bombay, India, and trained at Edinburgh College of Art, initially in painting and sculpture, subsequently in architecture. He was elected to the RIAS Council as a student member in 1927. In 1928 he was awarded the Certificate in Architecture and the following year worked as an assistant in London at the office of Sir Edwin Lutyens (1869-1944). Whilst in London Spence also attended evening classes at the Bartlett School of Architecture and produced perspective drawings for Leslie Grahame Thomson (later MacDougall) (1896-1974).

In June 1931 Spence received his Diploma in Architecture from Edinburgh College of Art as well as a Royal Institute of British Architects Silver Medal for the best architectural student, the Rowand Anderson Silver Medal, and an honorary mention for his sketches and measured drawings of Gothic buildings submitted for the Pugin Studentship Competition. Two years later he was awarded the Pilgrim Studentship.

In October 1931 Spence was employed as an assistant in the practice of Rowand Anderson Balfour Paul, along with his friend William Kininmonth (1905-1988). The pair entered into an informal partnership, designing a number of houses in the Edinburgh area, independently of the practice. Their alliance was to endure beyond their promotion to partnership in the firm in 1934 (renamed Rowand Anderson Paul & Partners).

Spence's skills as a perspective artist were also in demand by other practices such as Williamson & Hubbard of Kirkcaldy, W J Walker Todd and Reginald Fairlie. At this time he was also employed at Edinburgh College of Art on a part-time basis as a studio instructor.

Following a brief return to the Rowand Anderson Paul & Partners practice after the war, Spence left to form his own practice in 1946 with Bruce Robertson. Known as Basil Spence & Partners, the firm was based at 40 Moray Place, Edinburgh. John Hardie Glover (d.1994) was taken on as an assistant in 1947 and was promoted to partner in 1948, the year that Spence was appointed an OBE. Peter Ferguson became a partner, as did Andrew Renton.

In 1951 Spence moved to London, where he was involved in designing exhibition stands for the Festival of Britain. He subsequently moved the main practice office to Canonbury in London, initially operating as Basil Spence & Partners before later dividing the practice under the titles Sir Basil Spence OM RA and Basil Spence Bonnington & Collins. Spence's son-in-law Anthony Blee became a full partner in the former of the two practices.

The Edinburgh office remained at 40 Moray Place under the auspices of Glover and was renamed Basil Spence Glover & Ferguson. Spence maintained links by means of monthly visits, and by retaining overall control

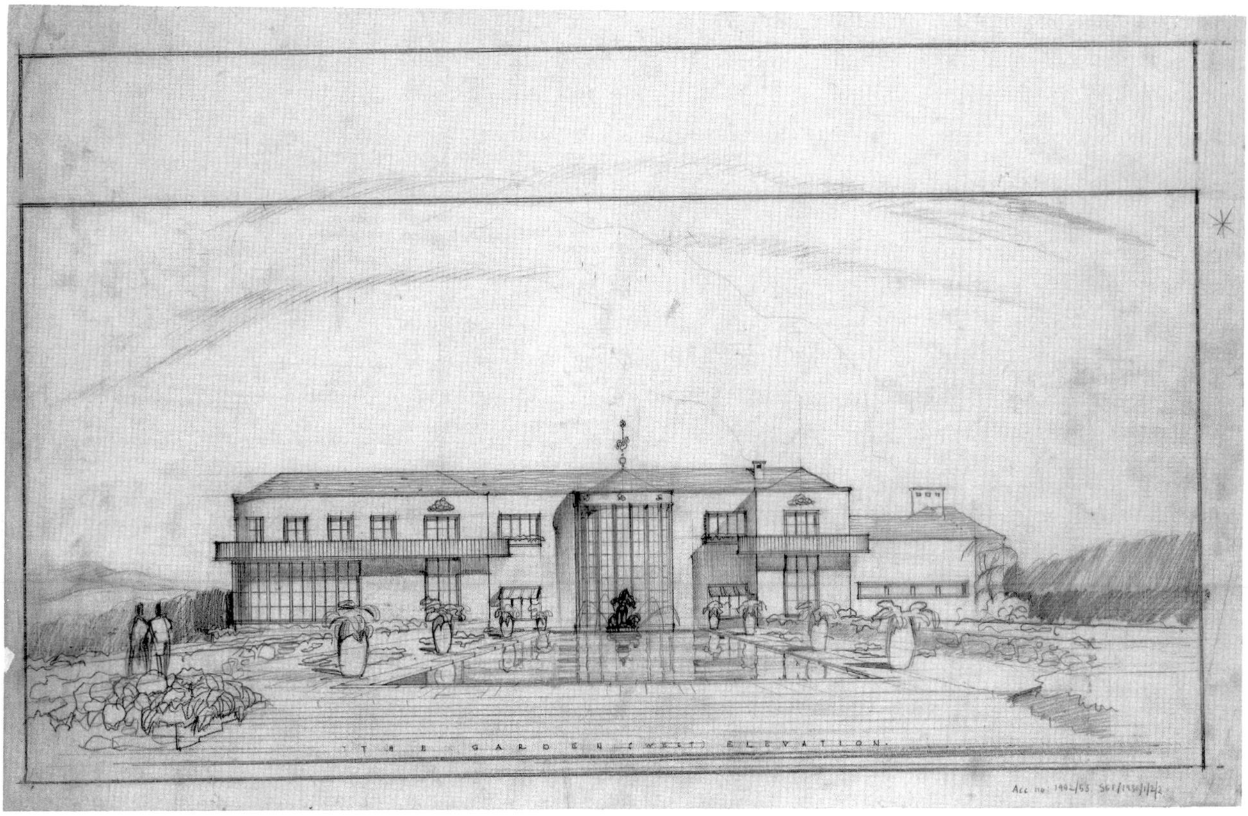

Garden elevation of Gribloch House, Stirlingshire by Basil Spence, 1937-38, from the Spence Glover & Ferguson Collection. [SC582320]

Photograph of model for stand for 1938 Empire Exhibition, Bellahouston Park, Glasgow by Basil Spence, c.1937, from the Spence Glover & Ferguson Collection. [SC806619]

Perspective of Hutchesontown C Development, Gorbals, Glasgow by Basil Spence Glover & Ferguson, 1958, from the Spence Glover & Ferguson Collection. [SC358382]

Sir Basil Spence (1907-1976) at work. Image courtesy of The Herald & Evening Times Picture Archive. [SC888090]

Perspective view of Natural Philosophy Building, Glasgow University, by Basil Spence, 1947, from the Spence Glover & Ferguson Collection. [SC684958]

of design output. Andrew Merrylees became a partner followed by Jim Beveridge in 1968. Ferguson died in 1969 and Hardie Glover retired in 1974. John Legg was consequently promoted to partnership.

Spence was knighted in 1960, awarded the Order of Merit and elected as a Royal Academician. He was also awarded the French Academy Architecture Gold Medal; the Order of St Lucca, Italy; and numerous Honorary Fellowships in the USA, Canada, Rhodesia, South Africa and East Africa. He died in Suffolk on 19 November 1976, after which his London practice name was changed from Sir Basil Spence OM RA to The Sir Basil Spence Partnership, later renamed Blee Ettwein Bridges. Anthony Blee continues in practice under the title Anthony Blee Consultancy at 32 Duncan Terrace, London [2004].

In 1984 Spence Glover & Ferguson's senior partner Andrew Merrylees left the firm to set up his own practice. John Legg and Jim Beveridge continued the business until 1992, when Beveridge retired. The remainder of the practice's work was taken over by John Legg's firm Legg Associates and it was at this time that the practice name Spence Glover & Ferguson finally disappeared.

Scope and Content

Numbering 14,400 items, the Spence Glover & Ferguson Collection consists of drawings, photographs and slides from the Moray Place office. There are approximately 10,000 drawings in the Collection and these consist exclusively of commissions undertaken by the Edinburgh office. The fact that Spence's professional reputation and demand for his work grew considerably after winning the competition to design Coventry Cathedral in 1951 is reflected in the distribution of projects in the Collection: the greatest number of projects date from the 1950s and 1960s.

The Collection includes projects undertaken by

Basil Spence between 1931 and 1946 while he was at the office of Rowand Anderson Balfour Paul, such as early commissions for Gribloch House, Stirlingshire (1937-39); and Quothquhan Lodge, Lanarkshire (1937). Designs for local authority housing schemes include housing at Dunbar, for which he received a Saltire Award (*c.*1945-52); Newhaven Harbour housing (*c.*1961-62); the designs for the Hutchesontown 'C' blocks at the Gorbals in Glasgow (1958-64); and the Canongate flats in Edinburgh (1965).

Spence was sought after as a school and university architect and his work at Kilsyth Academy (1938-53); Thurso High School (1956-62); Ecclesfield Colley Secondary Modern School, South Yorkshire (1950-52); Duncanrig, East Kilbride (1951-56); and Dinnington Secondary Schools, Chelmsford, Essex (1954-55) are all represented in the Collection along with Glasgow University Natural Philosophy Department (1950-57); Durham University Physics Building, Newcastle (1956-61); and Edinburgh University King's Buildings (1968-79).

The photographic component of the Collection includes construction photographs and copies of drawings that are not part of the Collection. Large-scale projects include Glasgow Royal Infirmary (*c.*1966), and the George Square redevelopment and Library for Edinburgh University (*c.*1956-66). Smaller less well-known projects include private houses and Edinburgh-based commercial projects. The photographs in the Collection also illustrate Spence's role as a designer of exhibition stands and furnishings.

In the slide collection, the various stages of building at Glasgow's Abbotsinch Airport (*c.*1965-66) are well documented, and the project includes a set of comparison slides of other major international airports. There are also numerous slides of University College Dublin Library under construction and after completion (*c.*1973-75).

The Collection includes only a very small amount of manuscript material: a single record book relating to the construction of the Animal Behavioural Research Organisation in Edinburgh (*c.*1968), and a number of letters found amongst or attached to the drawings. At the time of the closure of the Edinburgh office the business records and job files for the practice were not preserved.

Drawings for Mortonhall Crematorium, Edinburgh (*c.*1962) exist in slide form, but none of the originals appear in the Collection. Many important non-Scottish projects undertaken by Spence do not feature in this Collection, either in drawing, photographic or slide form.

There is a significant quantity of related material held in other collections both in the NMRS and elsewhere. The William Kininmonth Collection and a number of presentation drawings by Spence are held by the NMRS. Examples of Spence's work can also be found in the RIBA Drawings Collection and at the University of Glasgow Mackintosh School of Architecture.

In February 2003 the Sir Basil Spence Archive was deposited with RCAHMS. Gifted by Gillian and Anthony Blee – Spence's daughter and son-in-law – the Archive contains drawings, photographs and manuscript material mostly relating to English and international projects undertaken from Spence's London offices. There are, however, business records from the Spence Glover & Ferguson practice within the Archive as well as some drawings and photographs of Scottish commissions.

References

There have been many articles written about and by Spence in the press, only a selection of which are cited here.

NMRS Sources

- Notes of interview with Professor Charles Robertson, architect with Basil Spence & Partners, 1957-62, by Dawn McDowell and Siobhan McConnachie on 6 February 2002 (MS 926/3/11).

Anon. 1957 'Hutchesontown-Gorbals, Glasgow', *Architect Rev*, (November).

Anon. 1967 'Mortonhall Crematorium, Edinburgh', *Architect Rev,* (April).

Anon. 1968 'George Square and Edinburgh University Library' *Architect Rev*, (June).

Anon. 1994 'John Hardie Glover: An Appreciation', *Scotsman*, 15 April 1994.

Campbell, L 1996 *Coventry Cathedral: Art and Architecture in Post-War Britain.* Oxford.

Edwards, B 1997 *Basil Spence 1907-1976.* Edinburgh.

Fenton, C 2002 'A Century of Change in George Square, 1876-1976', *The Book of the Old Edinburgh Club*, vol. 5, 35-81. Edinburgh.

Gibberd, F 1977 'Obituary', *Architect Rev*, (April).

Sheppard, R 1977 'Obituary: Basil Spence', *RIBA J*, (January).

Spence, B 1962 *Phoenix at Coventry: The Building of A Cathedral.* London.

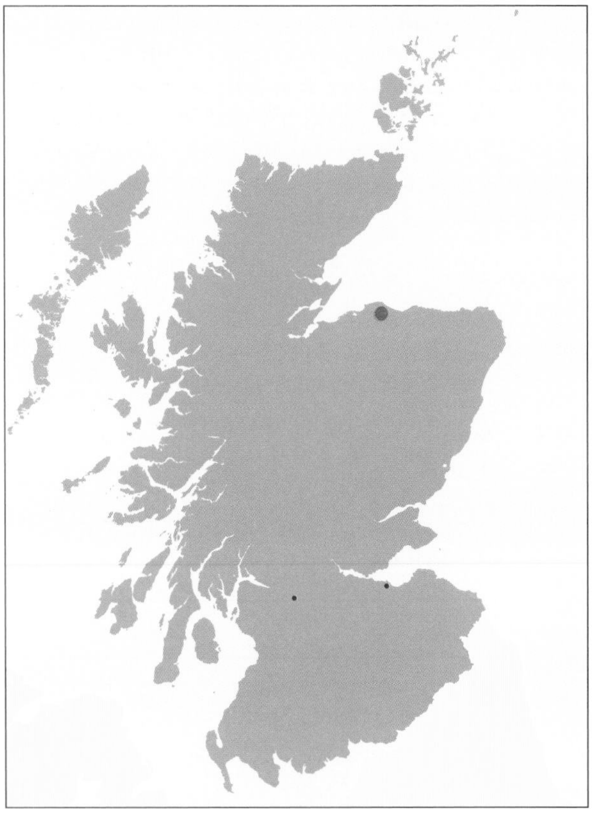

Wittet

Provenance
Stanley Mitchell, a partner in the Wittet practice, gifted the Wittet Collection (Accession No. 1993/175) to RIAS in 1993 on the instructions of the late William Wittet. It was subsequently transferred to RCAHMS in 1999 as part of the McKean Collection. Three volumes of the National Art Survey were gifted directly to RCAHMS.

History
John Wittet (1868-1952) was educated at Bridge of Earn Public School and articled to David Stuart of Perth from 1882 to 1888. He became assistant to Hippolyte Jean Blanc (1844-1917) in Edinburgh until 1892, which enabled him to study at Heriot Watt College, and then briefly to Clarke & Bell in Glasgow. In 1892 he became an assistant to A & W Reid of Elgin, and was taken into partnership by William C Reid (1875-1921) following the death of the senior partner William Reid in 1893. The practice, renamed A & W Reid & Wittet, was based in the Post Office Buildings, Commerce Street, Elgin.

By mutual consent the practice split in September 1903; W C Reid moved to 8 Culbard Street, Elgin and Wittet moved to 81 High Street, Elgin. In the late 1920s, after training at Aberdeen School of Architecture, Wittet's son William (1900-1990) was assumed into partnership and the practice became J & W Wittet. John Wittet went on to become a JP and senior magistrate of Elgin.

The practice became a limited company in 1986 and moved to 26 Hay Street, Elgin in January of that year.

Scope and Content
The Collection contains 44 items, dating *c.*1880 to 1925 and includes student drawings and lecture notebooks. The Collection offers an insight into late 19th century and early 20th century architectural education in Scotland.

The Collection includes two of John Wittet's sketchbooks, one of which dates *c.*1880 and contains figurative and landscape sketches; whilst the other, dating May to September 1890, contains masonry and brass work details, perspective views and survey sketches and was used whilst the architect was studying at Edinburgh. Loose student drawings from this period include details of Holyrood Abbey (*c.*1887); measured details of doors and decorative moldings at Glasgow Cathedral (*c.*1890); and studies of Gothic masonry (*c.*1890).

William Wittet's drawings and notebooks featured in the Collection are from his time as a student in Aberdeen and include drawings for a swimming club house and a customs house (stamped 1921-22). There are nine notebooks in total, three of which are entitled, 'Quantity Surveying', 'Building Construction' and 'Building Materials'.

Within the Collection there is also work by William's brother, J M Wittet (dates unknown) also dating to the early 1920s and also undertaken at Aberdeen School of Architecture. These include designs for a chapel (stamped 1922-23) and construction drawings detailing steel roofs and trusses.

The Collection contains three volumes of the

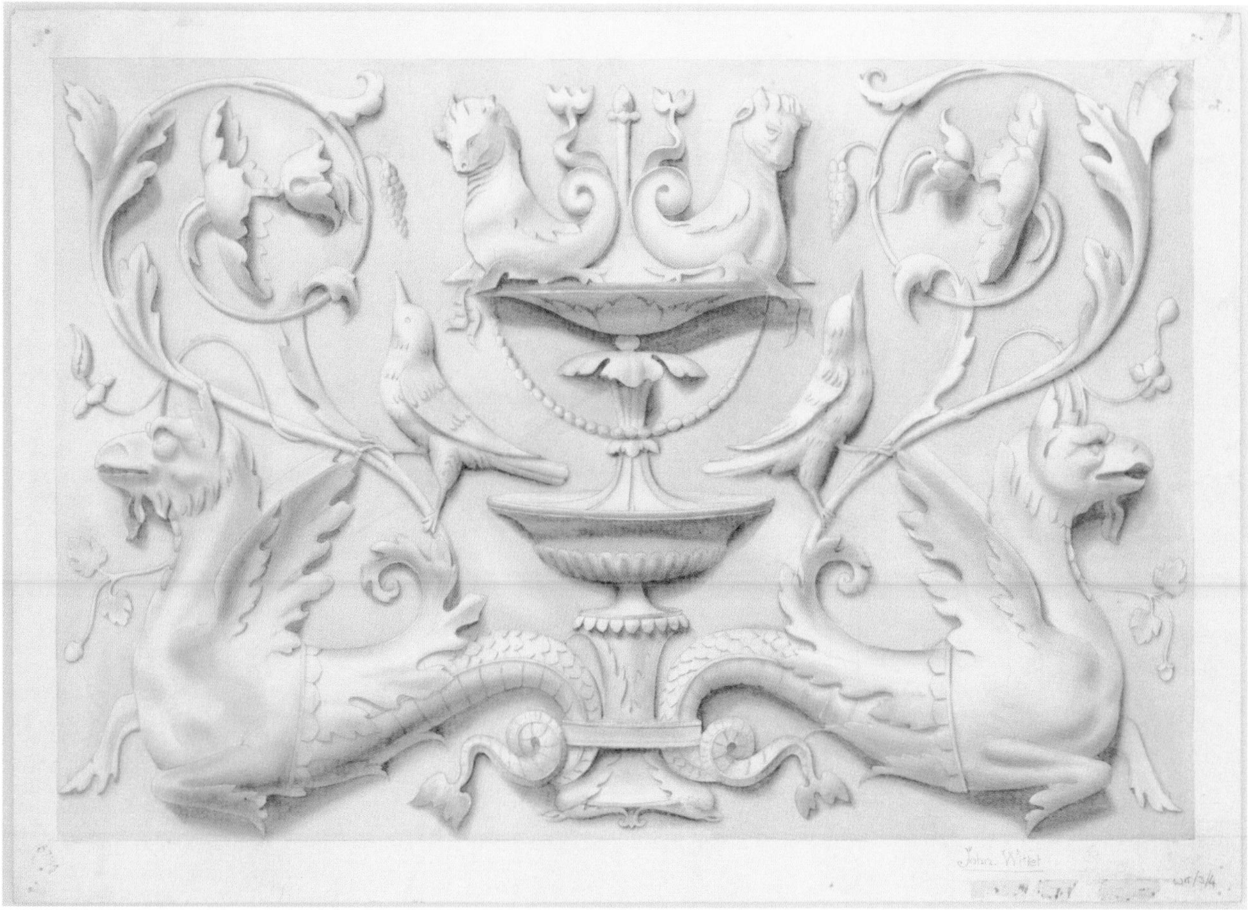

Details of stone carved panel by John Wittet, c.1880, from the Wittet Collection. [SC879327]

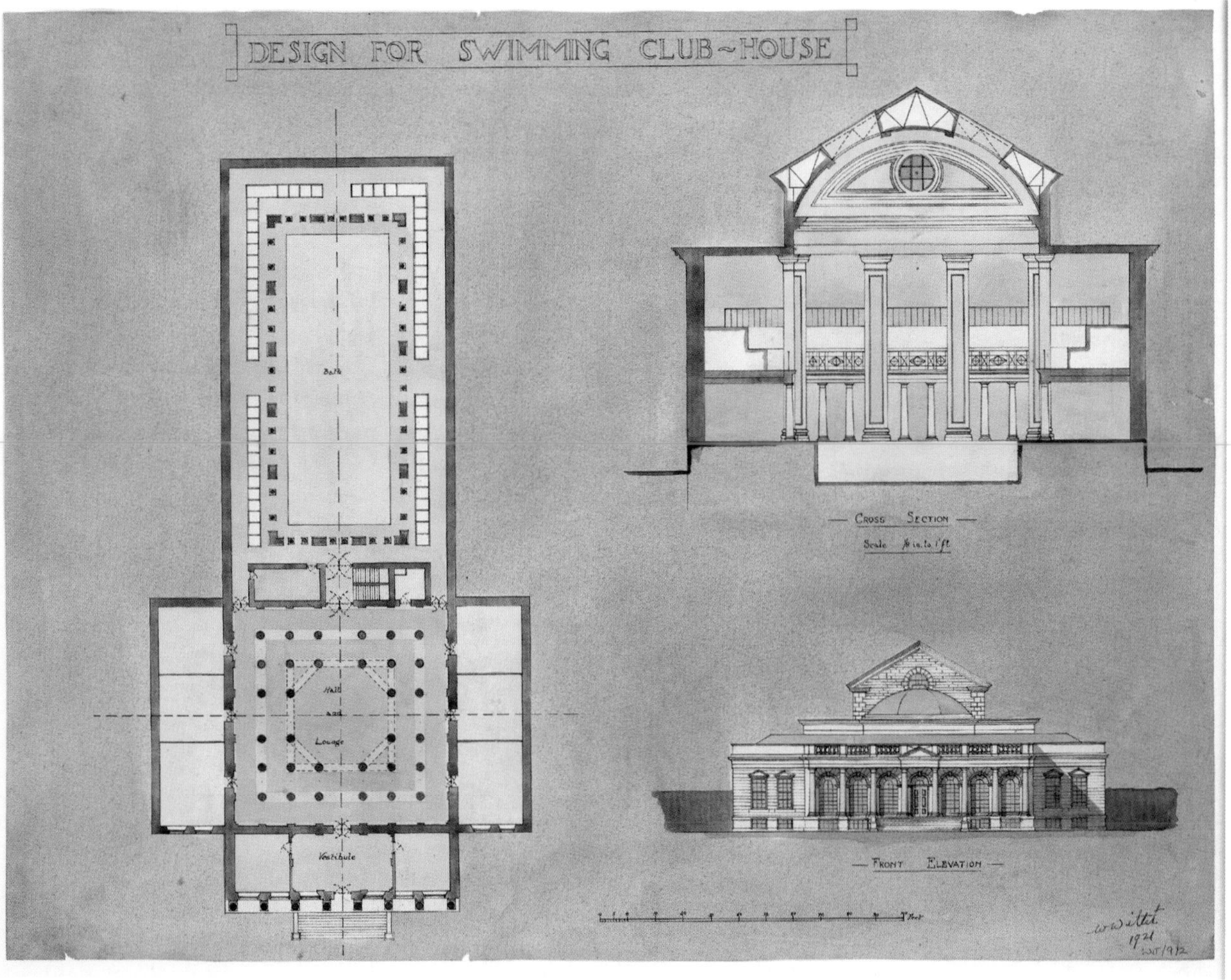

Student design for a swimming club house by William Wittet, 1921, from the Wittet Collection. [DP002358]

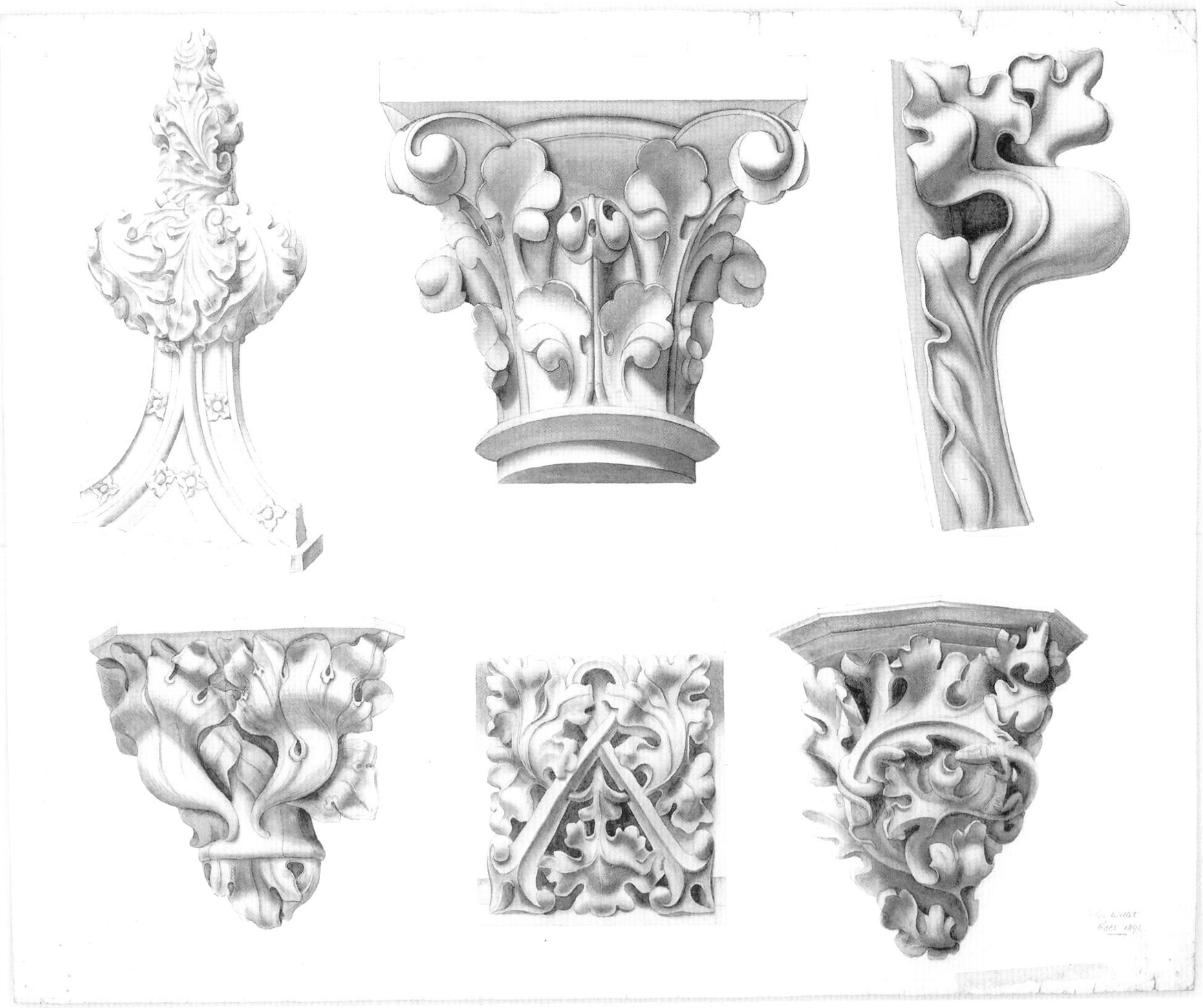

Details of carving by John Wittet, 1891, from the Wittet Collection. [SC800218]

John Wittet (1868-1952). Courtesy of The Northern Scot.

National Art Survey, entitled *Examples of Scottish Architecture from the 12th to the 17th Century* published by a joint committee of the Board of Trustees for the National Galleries of Scotland and the Incorporation of Architects in Scotland by George Waterston and Sons Ltd (dating 1921, 1923 and 1925).

References:

The Grant Lodge Local Heritage Service, Cooper Park, Elgin has a Wittet Collection of 15,000 architectural drawings dating from the early 19th century to the 1960s.

Beaton, E 1984 *William Robertson, 1786 –1841: Architect in Elgin.* Inverness: Architectural Association, Elgin.

Regional divisions in architectural style in Scotland were especially marked during the 19th century. The most dramatic, based on the modern economy and society, was a strong East-West split. Stately, traditional Edinburgh, with its conventional Renaissance classicism and pioneering urban heritage outlook, contrasted with Modern, commercial Glasgow, with its often ferociously eclectic Grecian classicism, exemplified in the work of Alexander Thomson. There were also strong rural or city-and-countryside patterns, notably that of granite, classical Aberdeen and its energetically improving farming hinterland.

By the late 19th century these intense architectural contrasts were beginning to abate. What to some extent replaced them, from around the 1880s, was a wider, pan-British hierarchy of architectural culture, in which many of the most ambitious or intellectually daring young Scottish architects moved temporarily or permanently to London. As a result, in late 19th and early 20th century Scottish architecture, there was a great consistency and equality of everyday building.

The 19th century coverage of the SAPPP collections is particularly strong in relation to the East coast, including a number of key Edinburgh-based practices that typically combined an urban, civic workload in and around Edinburgh with the design of country houses, churches and other building types spread more widely across the country. In one such case, Dick Peddie & McKay, the chronological span is exceptionally wide, stretching from the mid 19th century work of Peddie & Kinnear right through to the late 20th century. Geographical and building-type diversity within that practice is correspondingly great, including classical and Gothic churches (United Presbyterian and Episcopal), Baronial country houses, urban public buildings (notably, the great Aberdeen municipal headquarters of 1867-74), and eclectic hotels and hydropathics, across the whole of Scotland.

The SAPPP collections do not include any other practices working in the mid 19th century (although several start in the 1860s), and therefore do not represent the chief figures of those eclectic years, such as Thomson, Wilson, Bryce, or Playfair. Some of the chief Edinburgh or Glasgow designers of the late 19th century are also not represented in the collections, including the more artistic individualists, such as R R Anderson and C R Mackintosh, or the largest-scale Glasgow practices responsible for major commercial, public or social building programmes, such as Hugh and David Barclay.

Robert Lorimer, the most important Edinburgh traditionalist architect of the turn of the century is represented within SAPPP, both as a sole practitioner and (after 1927) as the partner of John F Matthew. After Lorimer's death in 1929 the traditionalist banner was carried on until the late 1950s by John's younger son, Stuart, who practised in partnership both with his father and with David Carr – both these permutations

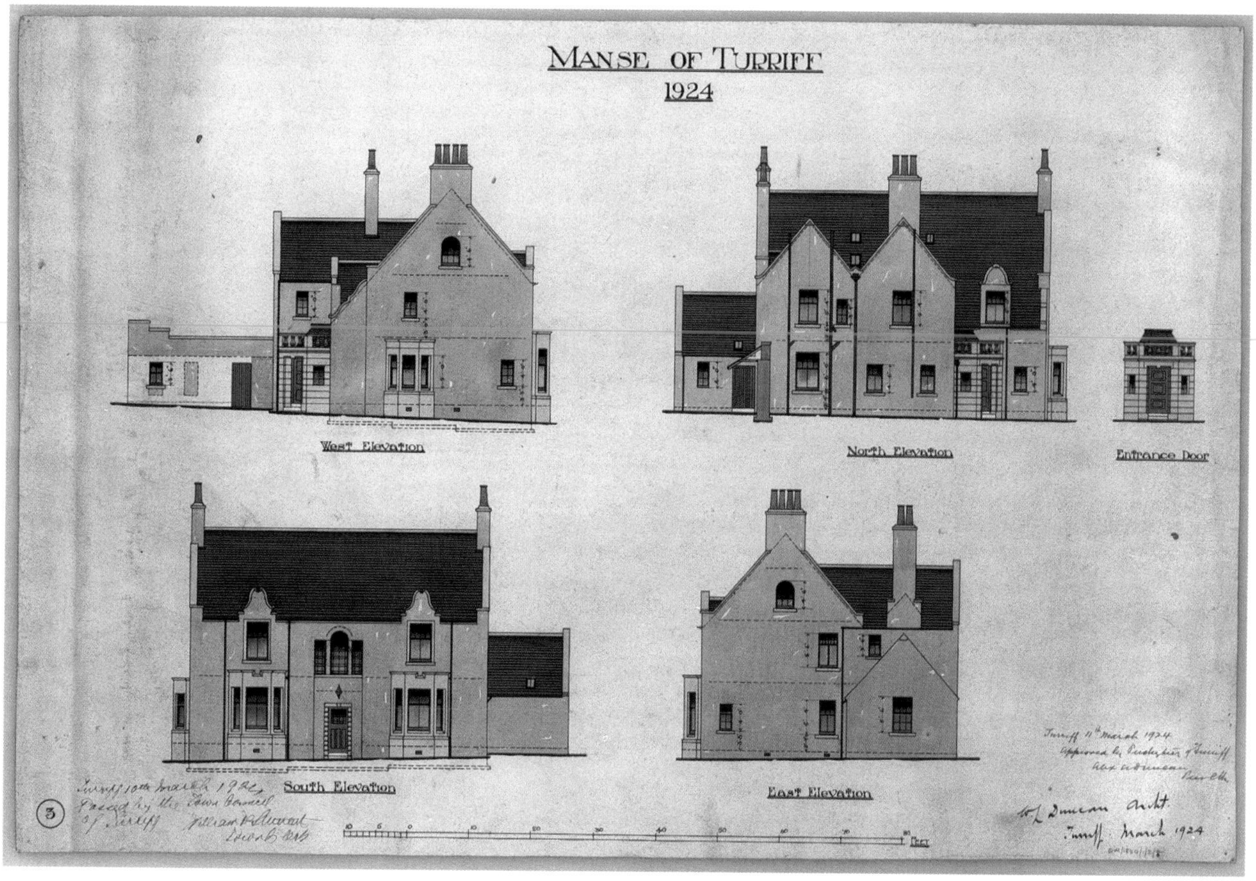

Elevations of Turriff Manse, Aberdeenshire by William Duncan, 1924, from the Duncan & Munro Collection. [SC638702]

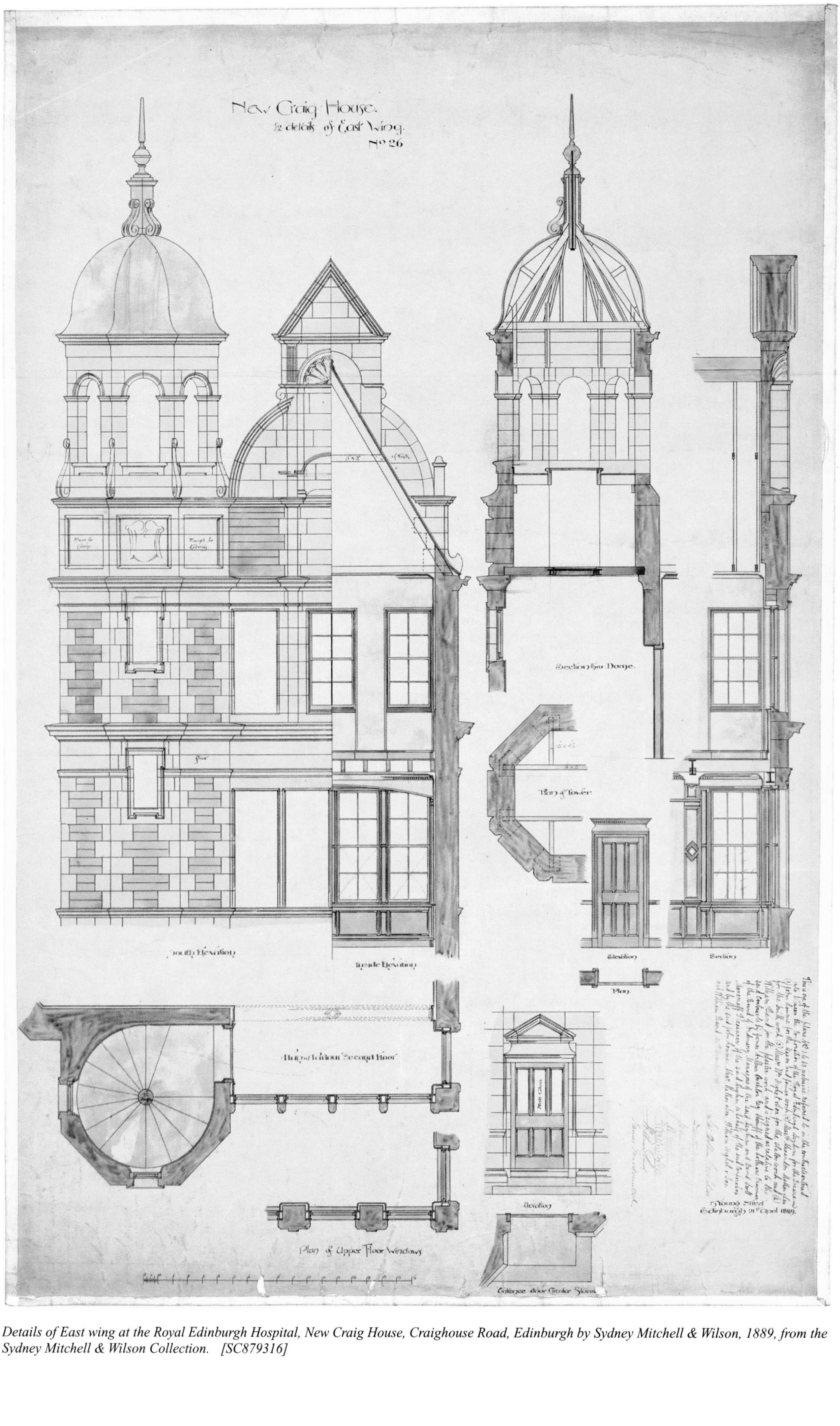

Details of East wing at the Royal Edinburgh Hospital, New Craig House, Craighouse Road, Edinburgh by Sydney Mitchell & Wilson, 1889, from the Sydney Mitchell & Wilson Collection. [SC879316]

View of Abbotsinch Airport, Glasgow by Basil Spence Glover & Ferguson, c.1966, from the Spence Glover & Ferguson Collection. [SC684948]

being represented among the SAPPP collections. Other large SAPPP collections belonging to the same creative sphere as Lorimer, but at a slightly more commercialised level, are Dunn & Findlay, and the prolific asylum, bank and church specialist A G Sydney Mitchell. Complementing the work of traditionalist architects, SAPPP also embraces a rich and largely non site-specific collection of furnishing designs by Scott Morton Ltd, who were collaborators with many Edinburgh architects, most significantly Lorimer.

From the First World War, and even more from the Second World War, the pace of state-financed and controlled social building began to quicken. As a result several polycentric practices with strong connections in London and overseas were established. Most prominent were those of J J Burnet, Basil Spence and Robert Matthew. Burnet's international Beaux-Arts/Modernist practice, with its London principal branch (Burnet Tait & Lorne) and its Glasgow office (Burnet Son & Dick) has left few records, and is not significantly represented in SAPPP, even in the acquired drawings by other architects that occur in many collections. Robert Matthew's architectural world is represented only indirectly in the SAPPP collections, by his father and brother, and by two other satellite Modernist collections, both of diverse, multi-media character. These comprise that of his friend and follower, Alan Reiach, and that of John Paterson, a lively and intellectually provocative ex-student and assistant of Matthew's.

The position is very different in the case of Basil Spence. Although Spence moved permanently to London in the early 1950s and established a design *atelier* at his own Canonbury house, he continued to maintain an office in Edinburgh, which handled the implementation stage of his Scottish and North-East English projects. The archive of the Scottish office – Spence Glover & Ferguson – has been catalogued by the SAPP Project, and provides a partial glimpse into his works in Scotland, including projects such as Abbotsinch Airport, and his more general *modus operandi*.

Arguably, the only unambiguously Modernist practice of national standing not represented in SAPPP is the Glasgow-based church and school specialist Gillespie Kidd & Coia whose collection, held by Glasgow School of Art, includes drawings and files relating to the firm's spatially daring work of the 1960s. Other Modernist architects, of chiefly regional significance, that do feature in the SAPPP collections, include the Glasgow-based A Buchanan Campbell, designer of various Clydeside public buildings and housing schemes, and company architect for private builders Mactaggart & Mickel (many of his drawings are available in the RCAHMS Mactaggart & Mickel Collection). Other

Sketch of interior for Dollan Baths, Brouster Hill, East Kilbride by Alexander Buchanan Campbell, c.1962, from the Buchanan Campbell Collection. [SC883764]

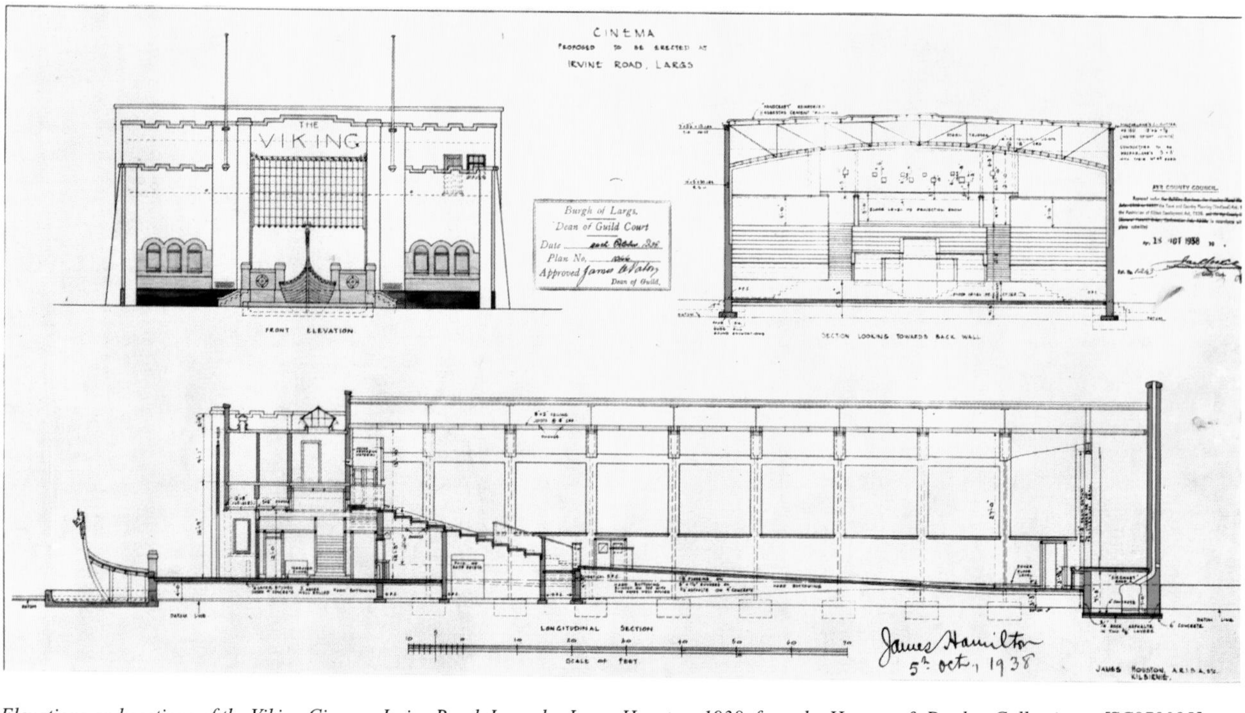

Elevations and sections of the Viking Cinema, Irvine Road, Largs by James Houston, 1938, from the Houston & Dunlop Collection. [SC879095]

slightly less contemporary patterns and styles of early/mid 20th century architecture are represented in the Ayrshire collections of J & J A Carrick and Houston & Dunlop, both featuring Art Deco leisure buildings; in the Edinburgh traditionalist work of Leslie Grahame Thomson (later MacDougall); in the 1940s/50s classical hydro-electric power stations of Shearer & Annand; and in the mainly traditional, low-rise interwar philanthropic or public housing designed by Haxton & Watson and A H Mottram (part of the Dunn & Findlay Collection).

A less obvious type of architectural modernity came from the growing mid 20th century efforts to save the old, irregular, housing groups of Scots burghs, and other historic buildings, from the widespread municipal sanitary redevelopment programmes, a campaign celebrated in the collections of Ian G Lindsay and Schomberg Scott.

The SAPPP collections also include several local practices, spanning the whole of the late 19th and early/mid 20th centuries, and catering for almost all building tasks in their areas. The Monro & Partners collection, for example, focuses on commercial work and public houses predominantly in the West. In the North-East, Duncan & Munro and George Bennett Mitchell & Son,

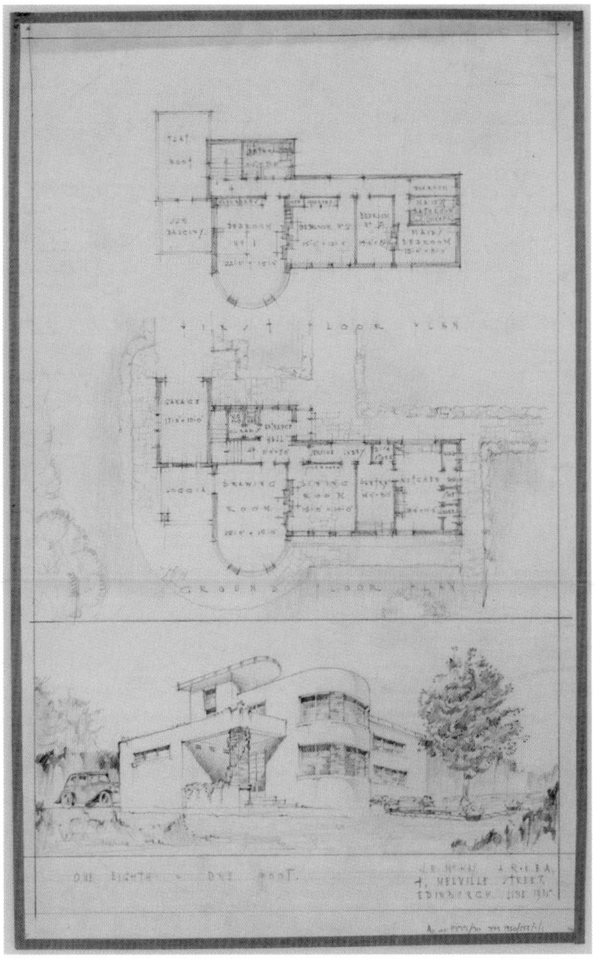

Plans and perspective view of a house for Mr W Allison by J R McKay, 1935, from the Dick Peddie & McKay Collection. [SC879076]

and in the far North-East, Sinclair Macdonald & Son, encompass a vast range of farms, country estates, and small-town commercial and social buildings. For Fife, Haxton & Watson play a roughly equivalent role, while in the Edinburgh area, the A A Foote, Cowie & Seaton and J & F Johnston Collections embrace a wide variety of everyday urban work. Student work features in many of the collections, particularly that of Wittets.

The chief value of the SAPPP collections to the researcher is the sheer quantity and diversity of buildings that they encompass – with humble structures catalogued alongside grand ones – with equal archival care as a point of fundamental principle. This enormous mass of primary data, that spans the entire building stock of the society of the period, helps revive the original aspiration in 1941 of the first Secretary, George Scott-Moncrieff, of the Scottish National Buildings Record (precursor to the NMRS) to record both grand, national monuments and the 'modest homes of the people'. During the 1950s and 1960s, the focus of architectural recording shifted for a time to more elite types, especially to the seemingly almost limitless stock of vanishing country houses, but now, in projects such as SAPPP, the emphasis is returning to a more inclusive approach.

The focus of the SAPP Project towards private practice means that while the late 19th and early 20th century material is reasonably well-balanced, the mid 20th century coverage does not represent the high proportion of buildings of the period where both the production and consumption was dominated by the public sector. This could be seen most notably in the city of Glasgow, with its overpowering municipal ethos, and the five New Towns, dominated by agencies of the central State. There are, however, well-organised public archives specialising in precisely these areas of building – as illustrated by the four examples below from across the country.

The North Lanarkshire archive at Lenziemill, Cumbernauld, contains both the records of the design departments of Cumbernauld New Town, and the regulatory Dean of Guild building-control records of the area's pre-1975 burghs, including Coatbridge, Airdrie, Kilsyth, Motherwell, and Wishaw – records going back in some cases to the beginning of the century. In Glasgow, the City Archives (housed in the Mitchell Library) contain not only comprehensive post-1885 Dean of Guild material for the city but also much design-related material from the city's architecture and planning departments, and more limited county-council building records from the rural areas of Renfrewshire and Lanarkshire. In the North-East, Aberdeen City Archive holds extensive pre-1960 records of both the municipal architecture and planning departments and the Plans Committee regulatory regime (the Aberdeen equivalent of the Dean of Guild). In Shetland, the local-authority archive in Lerwick has collected a wide range of planning, housing and regulatory material relating to the burgh, the rural landward areas (especially including records of agricultural workers' housing) and the late 20th century oil development zones.

Thus the SAPPP collections, from the point of view of researchers, have assumed their significant place in a wider mosaic of primary records, national and local, of the built environment.

Appendix 1 – People on the projects

Advisory Group

Kathleen Dalyell (Chair)	Chairman, RCAHMS
Ian Gow	Curator, National Trust for Scotland
Jill Lever	Retired Curator of RIBA Drawings Collection
George MacKenzie	Keeper, National Archives of Scotland
Michael Moss	Professor of Archival Studies, University of Glasgow
James Simpson	RCAHMS Commissioner
Sebastian Tombs	Secretary, Royal Incorporation of Architects in Scotland
David Walker	Emeritus Professor, Art History, St Andrews University
George Wren/Gordon Davies/Gordon Murray	President, Royal Incorporation of Architects in Scotland
Roger Mercer	Secretary, RCAHMS
Diana Murray	Curator Depute, NMRS, RCAHMS

Management Group

Diana Murray (Chair)	Curator Depute, NMRS, RCAHMS
Peter Anderson	Deputy Keeper, National Archives of Scotland
David Cowling	Collections & Publications, Royal Incorporation of Architects in Scotland
Sebastian Tombs	Secretary, Royal Incorporation of Architects in Scotland
Rebecca Bailey	Education & Development Curator, RCAHMS
Lesley Ferguson	Curator of NMRS Collections and Public Services, RCAHMS
Miles Glendinning	Manager, Threatened Buildings Survey, RCAHMS
Roger Mercer	Secretary, RCAHMS
Jane Thomas	Curator of NMRS Collections, RCAHMS
Dawn Caswell McDowell/ Siobhan McConnachie/ Neil Gregory	SAPPP & DPM Project Managers

Heritage Lottery Fund

Caroline McIntyre	Case officer
Michael Smethurst	Monitor

Architect volunteers

Jim Armstrong
John Barnie
Jim Barton
James Campbell
Marcus Johnston
John Knight OBE
Bill Macdonald
Donald Mackinnes
Iain Rennie
Gillean 'Sam' Small

Other volunteers

Nina Abbot-Barnish
Iain Anderson
Rev. Bernard Blanchard
Louise Boreham
Lucy Davis
Eline Dehullu
Melissa Duffus Wargo
Anthony Ferrie
Rachel Haworth
Dorothy Lawrenson
Cynthia Low
Dragan Masic
Euan Macdonald
Jill MacKenzie
Caroline Owen
Emily Pitts
Hazel Semple
Fiona Stevenson
Fiona Stirling
Joan Taylor

Staff

	1999	2000	2001	2002	2003	2004
Project Managers						
Rebecca M Bailey						
Neil Gregory						
Siobhan McConnachie						
Dawn Caswell McDowell						
Curators						
Norma Aldred						
Darinka Aleksic						
Rohan Banyard						
Susan Casey						
Anne Cassells						
Kathryn Chilcott						
Neil Gregory						
Laura Hourston						
Sarah Jones						
Sandra Martin						
Siobhan McConnachie						
Dawn Caswell McDowell						
Jenny Middleton						
Caroline Owen						
Daniel Parker						
Katherine Prentice						
Hannah Shaw						
Andrew Stevenson						
Kirsteen Wilkinson						
Conservation						
Saho Arakawa						
Victoria 'Kiki' Blum						
Perry Choe						
Stella Ditschkowski						
Victoria Hanley						
Lucy Ingham						
Monica Matthews						
Izabella Park						
Emma St John						
Audrey Wilson						
Digital photographer						
Steven Fairclough						

Appendix 2 – Summary job descriptions

Project Manager
Day-to-day management of the cataloguing, conservation and digitisation programmes, as well as the co-ordination and delivery of promotional activities. Post requires degree qualification in architectural history, history of art (with architecture component) or architecture, good knowledge of Scottish architectural history, understanding of cataloguing and conservation standards, and strong project management and communication skills.

Cataloguers
Sorting, cataloguing, conservation assessment and re-housing of the collections, as well as contributing to the promotion of the project. Post requires degree qualification in architectural history, history of art (with architecture component) or architecture, good knowledge of Scottish architectural history, an accurate and methodical working method, and good communication skills.

Conservators
Preventative conservation treatment and detailed repair, as well as advising on the handling and re-housing of collections. Post requires a post-graduate qualification in conservation of archives or works of art on paper and good communication skills.

Conservation Assistant
Supporting the conservators and the digital photographer through the preparation of materials, organisation of items to be treated and copied, as well as dry cleaning and minor tape removal. Post requires a methodical working approach, experience of working in an archive environment and good communication skills.

Digital Photographer
Creating surrogate digital copies of drawings from the collections. Post requires a recognised professional photographic qualification such as BTEC, SCOTVEC, Diploma in Photography or City & Guilds 744.

Conservation Consultant
Providing advice and support to conservators and project manager on conservation treatments, materials and suppliers. Consultant required to be an accredited paper conservator or have significant professional experience.

Appendix 3 – Cataloguing standards: site record page

This form holds the primary site data for all monuments, sites and buildings recorded in the database. It is also linked to Historic Scotland's Historic Buildings and Scheduled Ancient Monuments databases. Each record within the table is uniquely identified by a numlink (a unique number generated by the computer). This allows each site record to be linked to other associated archive and bibliographic records.

Key to main fields used in the site record
Mapno: Ordnance Survey 1:10,000 map sheet number.
Site: Two fields: Unique number identifying a site on an Ordnance Survey quarter sheet (1:10,000) and Sub-number for a component of Site number (used to identify, where necessary, distinct features or elements associated with or within larger or more complex sites).
1 of: Indicates sites or monuments with sub-numbers.
Numlink: Each site has its own unique idenitification number, which is automatically generated by the database.
Grid Ref, NGR Desc: The British National Grid Reference (NGR) eastings and northings and an additional descriptive field used for e.g. large complex sites to indicate the centre of the site.
NMRS Name, Alt Name: The name given to a site in the NMRS. This is usually the site name or the nearest published place or topographic name on the OS 1:10,000 map sheet. The Name is input from general to specific. The Name applied to a site is the earliest name where appropriate or known, or if that is deemed inappropriate then the name in most common usage. If a building has been demolished and a new building built on the site, each building has its own site entry but may share a grid reference. Other names are placed in the Alt Name field.
Class Group, Class, Sub Class: Three class fields that classify sites by general theme.
Other Status: Indicates any 'additional status' that a site may have, such as legal protection (e.g. Designated Historic Wreck; Guardianship Monument) or protected by the National Trust for Scotland.
Parish, Council, County, District: Administrative areas including the pre-1974 civil parish in which a record (or most of a record) lies; the current administration area in which the site is situated; the former county in which a site is located; and the former district in which a site is located.
Site is: Architectural, Site is: Archaeological: Check box to indicate if a site is archaeological or architectural. Sites can be marked both architectural and archaeological.
HB Num: Link to Historic Scotland's Historic Buildings list database records for sites.
SAM: Link to Historic Scotland's Scheduled Ancient Monuments database records for sites.
Survey: Link to a separate RCAHMS survey database.
HB Status: Two fields indicating the status of a building e.g. A to indicate a category A listed building.

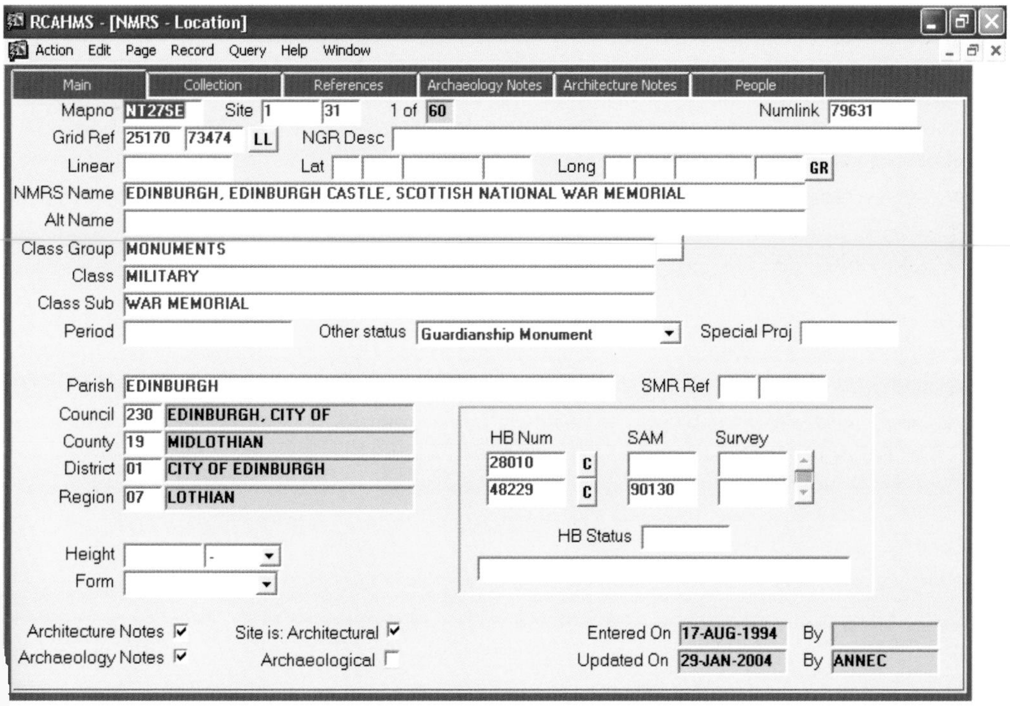

Typical site record page in the RCAHMS database.

Appendix 4 – Cataloguing standards: collections page

Each record is identified by an 'arcnumlink' which links that record to other tables in the database. This enables collection records to be linked to individual sites, and enables many collections records to be linked to many sites. The fields in the collections page identify and describe each collection item and note the location of individual items in the RCAHMS archive, along with storage and conservation instructions.

Key to main fields used in the collections page
Number: Three fields: Prefix, Archnum and Suffix. Prefix is a standardised term that is used to indicate the type, region or collection of an item. Number is the unique number within the prefix for each collection item. Suffix is a standardised term that indicates the type of item e.g. 'CS' for a colour slide.
No. of items: Indicates that there is more than one item associated with the catalogue number. Used to indicate how many items are included in a batch catalogue entry, up to 14 for a batched roll or folder of drawings. Not used for a single item catalogue entry.
Original: There are three fields for the Original Catalogue Number. The equivalent of Prefix, Number and Suffix (see **Number** above) for items that have been copied (e.g. when drawings have been photographed – the number in the Original field relates to the original number of the drawing; when photographs have been scanned). This is linked to the **Number** fields.
Category: Indicates the category of a collection item e.g. 'Prints and Drawings', 'Photographs', 'Digital images' or 'Manuscripts'.
Arcnumlink: Unique identifier automatically generated by the computer.
Location: Indicates whether an item relates to archaeology, architecture or both, and provides guidance to the location of photographs in the library, and slides in the negative room.
Related Sites: This information comes from the site record page and identifies the site or sites related to the collections item.
Description: The description of the collection item. The top line may be used to indicate a site outwith Scotland e.g. , 'Ex-Scotland. England, Buckinghamshire, Rostrum House'. In batch cataloguing, the following lines briefly describe drawings in the following order – site plans, plans, sections, elevations, and details. The client is indicated where available. Different designs for a building or a house are made explicit e.g. 'Alternative designs for iron railings'. In single item cataloguing, information is entered in the same way as a batch catalogue entry but including specific title and inscription details. Descriptions of photographs begin with the phrase 'photographic view of'.
Circa: Tick box to indicate that the date given is approximate.
Date: The date fields DD/MM/YYYY – DD/MM/YYYY are used to indicate the date or date range in which the item was created. Batch catalogue entries indicate the year range only. Single item catalogue entries may be specific to the day. Where a date is not known the circa box is ticked.
Copy Date: Indicates the date when a collection item has been copied.
Notes: Additional information about a collections item considered particularly relevant, distinct from the **Description**. Used for batch catalogue entries to note conservation status of individual items within a batch with phrases such as 'is not available for study due to its poor condition' and 'is stored flat', or to note a sequence of previously numbered drawings eg 'previously numbered as AGD 128/7-12', or to indicate a special location status such as 'THIS COLLECTION IS LOCATED AT ABERDEENSHIRE COUNCIL ARCHIVES'.
Person, Role, Organisation: Three fields containing the names of people, practices or companies who have created the collections item and their role, e.g. Photographer, Draughtsman, Architects, Engineers.
Scale: Indicates the scale of a collection drawing as written on the item. Not used for batch catalogue entries.
Medium: Indicates the support and medium of a collection item. Not used for batch catalogue entries.
Ref.: Indicates a previous or external reference number for a collection item.
Collection: Indicates that an item is part of a specific named collection. This field links to an essay about the collection.
Store: Indicates where a collection item is located when housed away from the normal collections areas.
Copyright: Indicates the Copyright holder.
Acc no.: Unique number given to collection items indicating when the item came into the NMRS, e.g. 2002/43, indicating the 43rd accession in the year 2002.
Permission: Indicates whether permission is required in order to reproduce the item.
SAPPP, DPM: Indicates to which HLF funded project the item belongs.
Flat, Rolled: Indicates how the item is stored.
Archival Wrapping Only: Indicates that drawing is in an archival folder or housed around an archival former and that there has been no conservation undertaken.
Duplicate: Button that automatically duplicates the record.
Survey Link: Button that links to another database.